Val Wright

EVENT MANAGEMENT

FOR TOURISM, CULTURAL, BUSINESS AND SPORTING EVENTS

EVENT MANAGEMENT

FOR TOURISM, CULTURAL, BUSINESS AND SPORTING EVENTS

LYNN VAN DER WAGEN

HOSPITALITY PRESS
MELBOURNE

Hospitality Press Pty Ltd
38 Riddell Parade
PO Box 426
Elsternwick VIC 3185
Australia
Telephone (+61 3) 9528 5021 Fax (+61 3) 9528 2645

Event Management: For Tourism, Cultural, Business and Sporting Events
First published 2001

National Library of Australia
Cataloguing-in-publication data:

Van der Wagen, Lynn.
Event management for tourism, cultural, business and sporting events.

Bibliography.
Includes index.
ISBN 1 86250 507 1.

1. Entertainment events -Management. 2. Entertainment events - Planning. 3. Special events - Management.
4. Special events - Planning. 5. Sports - Management. I. Title.

338.4779

Edited and produced by Bridging the Gap: Publishing & Marketing, Sydney
Design by Bowra+Bowra, Bowral, NSW
Cover and text illustrations by Steven Bray, Sydney
Printed in Australia
Published by Hospitality Press Pty Ltd (ABN 69 935 151 798)

foreword

The event business is characteristically a dynamic one, with 'deliverables' and deadlines constantly driving the process of planning. Event management has a lot in common with project management, and is a popular choice for students planning careers in projects that are diverse, that involve many stakeholders, that are constantly influenced by numerous variables and that carry a high level of risk. Risk management is an essential element of event planning.

TAFE NSW undertook the largest training project in the Southern Hemisphere in training the workforce of the Sydney 2000 Olympic and Paralympic Games, involving in excess of 100,000 paid, volunteer and contractor staff. Lynn Van Der Wagen was a key member of the project team that designed and managed this training. One of her greatest achievements was to successfully conduct a training needs analysis of the workforce, including both volunteer and contractor staff. Lynn effectively designed, developed, implemented and monitored the whole evaluation process for the project, which was in itself the largest single sub-project.

The success of the Games raised Australia's international profile and the profile of the event industry in Australia.

The increase in popularity of studies in event management is a positive development, given the growth in this sector and the pace of change in the industry. For these reasons, the publication of *Event Management* is extremely welcome. This book covers all aspects of event management, ranging from feasibility studies through to operational planning and marketing evaluation. As such, it provides all the business skills necessary for an environment that requires flexibility, commitment and judgement. These were the skills evident during the planning and execution phases of the Sydney 2000 Olympic Games and they have become the benchmarks for a progressive and successful event industry.

DAVID RIORDAN
Olympic and Paralympic Training Unit, TAFE NSW
Director of Business, Sydney Institute

contents

Preface   x

Chapter 1   **Introduction to Event Management**   **1**
             Size of events   4
             Types of events   7
             The event team   12
             Code of ethics   13

Chapter 2   **Concept and Design**   **15**
             Developing the concept   16
             Analysing the concept   22
             Designing the event   23
             Logistics of the concept   26

Chapter 3   **Feasibility**   **28**
             Keys to success   28
             The SWOT analysis   38

Chapter 4   **Legal Compliance**   **41**
             Relevant legislation   42
             Stakeholders and official bodies   49
             Contracts   50

Chapter 5   **Marketing**   **53**
             Nature of event marketing   54
             Process of event marketing   55
             The marketing mix   61
             Sponsorship   62

Chapter 6   **Promotion**   **67**
             Image/branding   69
             Advertising   69
             Publicity   71
             Public relations   75

Chapter 7   **Financial Management**   **79**
             The budget   81
             Break-even point   91
             Cash flow analysis   92
             Profit and loss statement   93
             Balance sheet   94
             Financial control systems   94
             Panic payments   96

Chapter 8   **Risk Management**   **98**

Process of risk management   103
Incident reporting   105
Emergency response plans   107
Standards for risk management   109

Chapter 9   **Planning**   **111**

Develop a mission/purpose statement   112
Establish the aims of the event   113
Establish the objectives   115
Prepare an event proposal   116
Make use of planning tools   116

Chapter 10   **Protocol**   **127**

Order of precedence   128
Titles   129
Styles of address   131
Dress for formal occasions   132
Protocol for speakers   132
Seating plans for formal occasions   132
Religious and cultural protocol   133
Protocol for sporting ceremonies   136
Rules of flag flying   138

Chapter 11   **Staging**   **140**

Choosing the event site   141
Developing the theme   144
Conducting rehearsals   150
Providing services   153
Arranging catering   154
Organising accommodation   155
Managing the environment   156

Chapter 12   **Staffing**   **159**

Developing organisation charts   159
Preparing job descriptions   163
Recruitment and selection   169
Drawing up rosters   169
Training   170
Briefing staff   174
Managing legal requirements   174
Preparing staffing plans   175
Developing recognition strategies   175
Managing volunteers   176

Chapter 13   **Leadership**   **181**

Developing leadership skills   182

Managing temporary and diverse teams   187

Group development   188

Improving communication   190

Time management   191

Planning and managing meetings   191

Chapter 14   **Operations and Logistics**   **193**

Logistics   194

Policies   197

Procedures   198

Performance standards   199

Functional areas   200

Leadership and staff motivation   203

Chapter 15   **Safety and Security**   **207**

Security   209

Occupational health and safety   211

Incident reporting   217

Chapter 16   **Crowd Management and Evacuation**   **221**

The crowd management plan   221

Major risks   223

Crowd management   224

Emergency planning   226

Implementing emergency procedures   229

Chapter 17   **Monitoring, Control and Evaluation**   **233**

Monitoring and control systems   234

Operational monitoring and control   236

Evaluation   239

The broader impact of events   244

Chapter 18   **Careers in a Changing Environment**   **247**

Job opportunities   248

Keeping up to date   254

Appendix 1   **Supplementary Internet Links**   **256**

Appendix 2   **Event Proposal**   **258**

Bibliography   **259**

Index   **260**

preface

My interest in the area of change management developed during my Masters Program at the University of Technology Sydney. At the time I had little idea that this interest would lead to participation in one of the largest training projects ever undertaken — the training orchestrated by TAFE NSW for the Sydney 2000 Olympic and Paralympic Games, one of the largest events held in recent times. This four-year project gave me the opportunity to gain a unique insight into the world of event management and it is to TAFE NSW that I owe a debt of gratitude for my selection on the team and my ongoing involvement in various sub-projects. Like all event management projects, it involved a long lead-time and a very short execution phase. Having spent four years planning and delivering training to management staff at SOCOG and designing and co-ordinating training for the volunteer and contractor workforce, I saw the Sydney 2000 Games flash by me in what seemed like a microsecond!

I thank everyone who worked in the TAFE NSW unit (led by David Riordan and Janet Chester) and all in the Workforce Training Team at SOCOG (led by Claire Houston). In particular, I owe thanks to the many TAFE NSW staff who responded positively to my phone calls and dropped everything to help out every time a request was made. This was a remarkable co-operative effort where everyone went beyond the call of duty.

One of the most successful programs for the Sydney 2000 Games was the Event Leadership course and I acknowledge TAFE NSW for ideas and quotes generated in the process of developing and delivering this program.

My interest in this field led to the implementation of an Event Management course at Northern Beaches TAFE that continues to go from strength to strength. This course was developed by the Community Services, Health, Tourism and Hospitality Division. To my teaching colleagues, students, and the library and support staff, many thanks for your continued enthusiasm and creative ideas.

There are several people who played a direct role in the writing of this book. Warwick Hamilton of Events Unlimited who contributed many ideas and useful information. He is an inspiration. Nerolli Cassidy who provided valuable feedback on several chapters and continues to support the caffeine addiction that fuels many of my mad ideas. And readers Nick Gill, Heather Roberts and Alex Kopra.

Many organisations made invaluable contributions by providing case studies, diagrams and discussion material. They include Australian Blues Music Festival; Australian Bomb Data Centre; Australian Bureau of Statistics; Cairns Convention Centre; Campbelltown Council; Clean Up Australia; Eventscorp WA; Exhibition Hire Service; ICMS; ISES; Maleny Scarecrow Festival; Melbourne Comedy Festival; Mosman Council; Mt Isa Rodeo; New Zealand Festival; New Zealand Royal Easter Show; Panthers Club; Quantum Market Research; Singapore Jazz Festival; Standards Australia; Summernats; *Sun Herald*; Sydney Gay and Lesbian Mardi Gras; *Sydney Morning Herald*; Tourism Training Australia; Tourism Training NSW; Tourism Victoria; Worksafe Western Australia.

Thanks also to Danielle Teutsch, Max Mosley, Jennifer Anson, and the Grand Prix Girls.

Kathryn Lamberton has edited all my books. She has the ability to turn my convoluted sentences into a text that reads exceptionally well — in the most painless way possible. It is a pleasure to work with someone as professional. Designer Natalie Bowra has performed her usual magic with the cover and layout of the book. The marvellous illustrations are by Steven Bray. It really is worth taking a second look at the vignettes at the beginning of each chapter to appreciate his quirky sense of humour. Most importantly, of course, my thanks to David and Jean Cunningham, publishers and winners of the 2001 Tourism Training Australia Chairman's Award for dedication and leadership support to the tourism and hospitality industry.

Finally, I must thank my family for their patience and support while I spent endless hours in the research, writing and re-writing phases of this book. And to my loyal readers, students everywhere, thank you for your feedback. May all your events be successful!

Lynn Van Der Wagen

CHAPTER ONE

introduction
to event management

As the massive storm bore down on the 1998 Sydney to Hobart fleet, the Cruising Yacht Club of Australia 'abdicated its responsibility to manage the race', the State Coroner found yesterday. In a damning indictment of the club, Mr John Abernethy said in his report: 'From what I have read and heard it is clear to me that during this crucial time the race management team played the role of observers rather than managers and that was simply not good enough'.

The roles assigned to individual members of the race management team had been so ill-defined as to be 'practically useless' and the team was organised in a way that made it, in a crisis, 'to all intents and purposes, valueless'.

SYDNEY MORNING HERALD, 13 DECEMBER 2000

On completion of this chapter you will be able to:
- explain the unique characteristics of an event
- classify and describe events according to size
- classify events according to type
- discuss relationships between event managers and other stakeholders
- discuss some of the ethical issues relevant to event management.

The aim of this book it to assist you in your training to become an event manager of the highest calibre. Many of us have observed events, most of us have participated in events, but few of us have managed events. As an event manager, you are there to do far more than just observe. You are there to ensure the smooth running of the event, to minimise the risks and to maximise the enjoyment of the event audience. The demands on an event manager are far greater than one would expect.

Many events carry a significant risk to the safety of participants. The above example focuses on just one of the many safety risks and indicates what can happen when the management team plays the role of 'observers rather than managers'.

Financial risk is also an important concern of the event manager. Events are generally extremely expensive, with high expenditure required over a very short period of time, and there are far higher levels of uncertainty about revenue and profit than there are with the average business.

In the case of voluntary and charitable events, of which there are many in every community, the risk is that the time invested by individuals will be wasted and their objectives will not be achieved.

Finally, one of the most important things about an event is that it is often a highlight of a person's life. This is not to be taken lightly. A significant birthday, a wedding or a christening is so important to the main participants that nothing must go wrong. If something does go wrong, it cannot be easily rectified. A wedding at which the power fails due to overloading of the electrical supply cannot be repeated. The offer to 'come back again at our expense' just doesn't work! To use a phrase much used during the Sydney 2000 Olympic Games, events are often 'a once in a lifetime' experience. The event manager therefore carries enormous responsibility for ensuring that the event, however large or small, is a success as there is often only one chance to get it right.

The Sydney 2000 Paralympic Games were certainly 'a once in a lifetime' experience.

From what we have discussed so far, events are characterised by the following:

- They are often 'once in a lifetime' experiences for the participants.
- They are generally expensive to stage.
- They usually take place over a short time span.
- They require long and careful planning.

- They generally take place once only. (However, many are held annually, usually at the same time every year.)
- They carry a high level of risk, including financial risk and safety risk.
- There is often a lot at stake for those involved, including the event management team.

This last characteristic is crucial, since every performer, whether athlete or entertainer, wants to deliver their best performance. The bride wants the day to be perfect in every way. The marketing manager and the design team want the new product to be seen in the best possible light. Consider for a moment how much easier it is to run a restaurant (where you spread your risk over a number of days and a number of customers) than it is to run a one-off, big-budget product launch — particularly if this launch has 500 key industry players and the media in attendance, and is taking place at a unique location with unusual demands for logistics, lighting, sound and special effects.

Having pointed out the level of demand on the event manger and thus the possible downside of the profession, it is important also to point out that the event industry is one in which people (the event audience) tend to have the time of their lives. Making this possible and sharing this with them is extremely gratifying. The work is demanding, exciting and challenging, requiring a fine-tuned balance between task management and people management. As the newspaper article illustrates, an event manager must bring together a team with clearly defined responsibilities for all aspects of the event, including unexpected crises. The team needs to be both organised and flexible. Events can be unpredictable and do require quick thinking, based on a sound knowledge of procedures and alternatives. Decision-making is one of the most important skills of the event manager, and those with first-class analytical skills are highly sought after by most industries.

Professor Donald Getz (1997), a well-known writer in the field of event management, defines special events from two perspectives, that of the customer and that of the event manager, as follows:

- *A special event is a one-time or infrequently occurring event outside normal programs or activities of the sponsoring or organizing body.*

> • *To the customer or guest, a special event is an opportunity for a leisure, social or cultural experience outside the normal range of choices or beyond everyday experience.*

Another well-known author, Dr J. Goldblatt (1997), defines special events as 'A unique moment in time celebrated with ceremony and ritual to satisfy specific needs'.

In this book, the emphasis is on a wide range of events, including 'special events', as defined above, and more common events such as sporting events, meetings, parties, carnivals and prize-giving ceremonies, which may not meet the definition 'outside the normal range of choices'.

SIZE OF EVENTS

Classification of events can be done on the basis of size or type, as follows.

Mega-events

The largest events are called mega-events and these are generally targeted at international markets. The Olympic Games, World Cup Soccer and Superbowl are good examples. The Superbowl, for which, in 1967, there were 30,000 tickets unsold, now sells out before the tickets have been printed and also accounts for the sale of 30,000 hotel rooms. It is televised to an audience of 800 million and adds $300 million to the local economy.

All such events have a specific yield in terms of increased tourism, media coverage and economic impact. While some cities are continuing to meet a legacy of debt after hosting an Olympic Games, Sydney was fortunate in meeting its budget due to a last-minute surge in ticket and merchandise sales. It was reported after the 2000 Olympic Games that the Sydney Organising Committee for the Olympic Games (SOCOG) had returned $10 million to taxpayers. However, as with all events of this size, it is difficult to calculate the costs accurately with so many stakeholders (mainly government) involved.

While the size of the Olympic Games in terms of expenditure, sponsorship, economic impact and worldwide audience would undoubtedly put it in the category of mega-event, it is worth comparing its size with, for example, that of the Maha Kumbh Mela ('Grand Pitcher Festival'), the largest religious gathering in history.

During 2001, approximately 70 million Hindu pilgrims converged on the Holy River Ganges for a sacred bathing ritual. The gathering takes place every twelve years and the 1989 Maha Kumbh Mela in Allahabad was attended by 15 million devotees. The 2001 festival will no doubt hold the record as the world's largest assembly of people for some time to come.

Hallmark events

Hallmark events are designed to increase the appeal of a specific tourism destination or region. The Tamworth Country Music Festival, the Melbourne Cup and the Adelaide Festival are all examples of tourist destinations achieving market positioning for both domestic and international tourism markets through their annual events. It would be hard to imagine, for example, the Sydney Gay and Lesbian Mardi Gras being held in any other city, since it has been historically based there. This event attracts local and international visitors to Sydney and has a significant positive financial impact on the city. The annual Floriade in Canberra is another good example of a hallmark event.

Major events

These events attract significant local interest and large numbers of participants, as well as generating significant tourism revenue. As an example, Chinese New Year celebrations are held in most capital cities. In Sydney, the three-week festival includes market stalls, food stalls, exhibitions, street entertainment, parades and dragon boat races. Friends and relatives of the Chinese community often visit at this time.

Large meetings, such as the Tech-Ed 2000 conference held in Cairns for 1,300 attendees, also fit into this category. ICMS Australia, an event management organisation, has an outstanding reputation for management of such events, as indicated by the extent of commitment of ICMS and their clients:

9th World Congress of Gastroenterology
7,600 delegates
ICMS Commitment — six years

19th World Congress of Dermatology
6,700 delegates
ICMS Commitment — seven years

20th World Congress of Chemotherapy
4,000 delegates
ICMS Commitment — five years

ICACI 2000
(International Congress of Allergology & Clinical Immunology)
5,000 delegates
ICMS Commitment — seven years

14th World Congress of Cardiology
14,000 delegates
ICMS Commitment — twelve years

It has already been contracted to stage the International Congress of Human Genetics in 2006 for 4,000 delegates, with an expected commitment of eleven years.

The Sydney to Hobart yacht race mentioned at the start of this chapter also falls into this category, as would many other sporting and cultural events. The bi-annual World Solar Challenge is held in October in the Darwin area, while Perth promotes the Hopman Cup and the Whitbread Round the World Race.

Minor events

Most events fall into this last category, and it is here that most event managers gain their experience. Almost every town and city in Australia runs annual events. For example, the Broome area promotes the Pearl Festival, the Battle of Broome and the Mango Festival. A count of special events and festivals meticulously researched for the *Readers Digest Touring Guide of Australia* reveals that nearly 2,000 festival-type annual events are held around Australia. In addition to annual events, there are many one-off events, including historical, cultural, musical and dance performances. At one such event, parents were proudly watching their tap-dancing offspring performing in their expensive, colourful velvet outfits. Their proud expressions turned to dismay when several dancers landed on their rear ends having slipped on the stage. Quick-thinking organisers covered the stage in a mixture of soft drink and cleaning powder — all in a day's work for the event team!

Meetings, parties, celebrations, award ceremonies, sporting finals, and many other community and social events fit into this category.

TYPES OF EVENTS

In terms of type, events may be categorised as follows.

Sporting

Australia recently hosted the world's largest sporting event, with a worldwide audience of approximately 6 billion. At the time, the success of the 2000 Olympic Games was said to have established Sydney as the event capital of the world. Although many might challenge this, *The Times* special correspondent and author Bill Bryson was, like many other overseas correspondents, lavish in his praise: 'I don't wish in my giddiness to overstate matters, but I invite you to suggest a more successful event anywhere in the peacetime history of mankind' (*Sydney Morning Herald*, 5 October 2000).

Sporting events are held in all states and territories and they attract international sports men and women at the highest levels. Tennis, golf, rugby and car racing are just a few examples.

These major events are matched at the local level by sporting competitions for players at all levels. For example, the Pro Am, held annually at most golf courses, allows members to play with professional golfers. This event is usually the highlight of the golfing calendar and requires considerable effort by the team supporting it, including the PGA, the club committee, the club manager, the club professional, ground staff, club administration and catering.

Two very different types of sporting events: race day on Sydney Harbour and the Pacific School Games 2000.

Entertainment, arts and culture

Entertainment events are well known for their ability to attract large audiences. In some cases, the concerts are extremely viable from a financial point of view; in others, financial problems can quickly escalate when ticket sales do not reach targets. Timing and ticket pricing are critical to the financial success of such events. According to a special report by the Australian Bureau of Statistics (1995), popular music concerts were attended by 3,790,700 people in the twelve months ending March 1995. Classical music concerts were attended by 1,081,300 people, opera and musicals attracted 2,722,100, theatre 2,336,300 and other performing arts 2,634,400 during the same period.

All Australian art galleries hold special exhibitions that meet the earlier definition of an event. During the 2000 Olympic Games, the New South Wales Art Gallery featured Australian and indigenous artists in special exhibitions and the number of visitors to the gallery exceeded expectations. At the same time, the Powerhouse Museum exhibited items from the ancient and modern Olympics. These events, both sporting and cultural, were a unique feature of the Games.

A special report showed that, in 1995, 3.9 million Australians visited museums while 3.1 million visited art galleries. Fourteen per cent of all international visitors during 1997 (aged fifteen years and over) visited museums or art galleries (Bureau of Tourism Research, 1998).

Commercial marketing and promotional

Promotional events tend to have high budgets and high profiles. Most frequently they involve product launches, often for computer hardware or software, perfume, alcohol or motor cars. One such marketing activity dazzled attendees with its new launch motorbikes riding overhead on tightropes, with special effect lighting.

The aim of promotional events is generally to differentiate the product from its competitors and to ensure that it is memorable. The audience for a promotional activity might be sales staff, such as travel agents, who would promote the tour to their clients or potential purchasers. The media are usually invited to these events so that both the impact and the risk are high. Success is vital.

Meetings and exhibitions

The meetings and conventions industry is highly competitive. It is governed by an association called MICE (Meetings, Incentives,

Conventions and Exhibitions). Many conventions attract 3,000 or more people, while some meetings include only a handful of high-profile participants. Australia's worldwide popularity as a holiday destination has had a positive effect on its capacity for winning convention bids and attracting delegates. In the year ending July 2000, there were a total of 118,558 visitors to Australia for the purpose of attending a convention or conference, which was an increase of 8.8 per cent on the previous twelve months (Australian Bureau of Statistics, 2000, Source: http://www.atc.net.au/intell/market/mice/profile.htm).

Festivals

Wine and food festivals are increasingly popular, providing a particular region the opportunity to showcase its products. Small towns such as Tumbarumba in New South Wales and Mornington in Victoria attract interest with their food and wine festivals. Many wine regions hold festivals, often in combination with musical events, such as Jazz or Opera in the Vineyard. Religious festivals fall into this category, too, and Australia's multicultural community provides rich opportunities for a wide range of festivals. Chinese New Year and Carols in the Domain are good examples.

About 300 festivals devoted solely, or partly, to cultural activities are staged every year in Australia. Among the biggest are Adelaide's biennial arts festival and the annual arts festivals held in Sydney, Melbourne and Perth. Each lasts several weeks and attracts many visitors.

A balloon artist captivating a child at an Irish Festival.

Family

Weddings, christenings, bar mitzvahs and, these days, divorces and funerals all provide opportunities for families to gather. Funerals are increasingly becoming big events with non-traditional coffins, speeches and even entertainment. It is important for the event manager to keep track of these changing social trends. For example, Asian tourists are a big market for the wedding industry, with many couples having a traditional ceremony at home and a Western wedding overseas. Australia and New Zealand compete with destinations such as Hawaii for this market.

Even a small garden wedding must run smoothly to be a success.

Fundraising

Fetes and fairs are common in most communities, and are frequently run by enthusiastic local committees. The effort and organisation required for these events is often underestimated. As their general aim is raising funds, it is important that children's rides and other such contracted activities contribute to, rather than reduce, revenue. Sometimes the revenue gained from these operations is limited. There is also the risk that attendees will spend all their money on these activities and ignore those which are more profitable to the charitable cause. A number of legal requirements must be met by the charitable fundraiser and these are covered in Chapter 4.

Miscellaneous events

Some events defy categorisation. Potatoes, walnuts, wildflowers, roses, working dogs, horses, teddy bears and ducks all provide the focus for an event somewhere in Australia. The following list of some of the events held in Queensland demonstrates how varied these can be in terms of size and type:

Allora Bush Christmas

Allora Celtic Concert

Almaden Races

Ambiwerra Wine, Food and All That Jazz Festival

American Independence Day

Andrew Fisher Day at Gympie

Anglican Spring Fair

Annual Australian Heritage Festival

Annual Drovers Reunion Festival

Annual Old Station Fly-in and Air Show

Anzac Day Celebrations at Proserpine

Asia Pacific Masters Games

Atherton Tableland Agricultural Show

Australia Day Awards and Citizenship Ceremony at Logan

Australian College of Tropical Agriculture Open Day

Australian Festival of Chamber Music

Australian International Movie Convention

Australian Italian Festival

Australian National Skydiving Championships

Australian Small Winemakers Show

Australian Surf Rowers League Convention

Autumn Gourmet Weekend

Back to the Bush Weekend

Back to the 60s Weekend

Bat out of Hell Raceday

Bayside Art and Craft Spectacular

Big Boys Toys Expo

Birdsville Races

Brass Monkey Season

Bribie Island Apex Mullet Festival

Bundy in Bloom Spring Festival

Burdekin Centenary of Federation Festival

It has to be said that the most common events are community related, and are run on a fairly small scale with voluntary support and sponsorship. These events provide the potential event manager with invaluable experience, as well as the opportunity to contribute to their community. Every event has a purpose and the theme is generally linked to the purpose. Analysis of even the smallest event can provide valuable insight into the general principles that apply to managing all events.

THE EVENT TEAM

An event manager is generally supported by a team which grows enormously as the event draws near. A planning team of twelve that works together for a year can explode into a team of 500 for the short period of the event. This phenomenon has been termed the 'pulsing organization' by A. Toffler, who coined the term to describe organisations that expand and contract in size. This is particularly appropriate for organisations such as the Australian Open Tennis Championships, as they surge in numbers for a short period every year. The second example comes from the 2000 Olympic Games where the head of catering had a small team working with him to negotiate contracts with caterers in the lead-up to the Games, his team expanding to over 200 (including volunteers) in the month before the Games. And there was only one opportunity for the whole group to be together for a training session!

Having just mentioned contractors, it is important to note that the event manager typically works with a number of contractors. These could include any or all of the following:

- venue managers
- stage managers
- lighting, audio and video companies
- decorators and florists
- entertainers
- employment agencies
- rental companies
- public relations and marketing consultants
- security companies
- catering companies
- cleaning companies
- ticketing operations
- printers.

For some events, the manager is also required to liaise with government agencies at a range of levels, from local government through to federal government. Local councils deal with event planning and approval; state governments provide approvals for traffic and policing; and the federal government gives advice on protocol for international dignitaries. These relationships will be explored further when looking in more detail at the planning and staging of an event (Chapters 9 and 11).

CODE OF ETHICS

As with all modern professions, the presence of a code of ethics can enhance the reputations of those involved, and can assist the customer to feel confident in their choice of event manager, supplier or contractor.

The International Special Events Society (ISES) has the following code of ethics:

- *Promote and encourage the highest level of ethics within the profession of the special events industry while maintaining the highest standards of professional conduct.*
- *Strive for excellence in all aspects of our profession by performing consistently at or above acceptable industry standards.*
- *Use only legal and ethical means in all industry negotiations and activities.*
- *Protect the public against fraud and unfair practices and promote all practices which bring credit to the profession.*
- *Maintain adequate and appropriate insurance coverage for all business activities.*
- *Maintain industry standard of safety and sanitation.*
- *Provide truthful and accurate information with respect to the performance of duties. Use a written contract stating all changes, services, products, performance expectations and other essential information.*
- *Commit to increase professional growth and knowledge, to attend educational programs and to personally contribute expertise to meetings and journals.*
- *Strive to co-operate with colleagues, suppliers, employees/ employers and all persons supervised, in order to provide the highest quality service at every level.*
- *Subscribe to the ISES Principles of Professional Conduct and Ethics, and abide by ISES By-laws and Policies.*

Case study

A group of university students decided to hold a rave party in the

●●●●●●●●●●●●●●●●
SUMMARY
In this chapter we have
introduced you to some
of the unique
characteristics of
events, one being that
they are often one-off
or annual occurrences,
thus creating a high
level of risk. This
means that the event
team has only one
opportunity to get
everything right. Most
events take months or
even years to plan,
depending on the type
and size of the event.
And their focus varies,
from the strictly
commercial product
launch to the school
fete which aims to raise
funds with the help of
the local community.
●●●●●●●●●●●●●●●●

mountains in December, and advertised it on the Internet. Three bands attended the three-day party and there was twenty-four-hour music. One young girl described it as living hell, although why she stayed is unfathomable. 'The dance area was in a valley and to get a drink of water you had to climb a steep hill. Even then, the water was dirty and brown. The toilets were so far away that nobody bothered to use them. The music pounded all night and the floor vibrated so you couldn't sleep. My friend was unwell and there was no medical help. The organisers didn't have a clue. They just wanted to make a fast buck.'

- What are some of the things that could go wrong, or have gone wrong, at similar events?
- List three ways in which the organisers were negligent.
- List three ways in which the event could have been improved.
- This event was described to the authorities as a cultural festival. Do you think it belongs in that category?
- The legal compliance issues of such an event will be covered in a later chapter. However, what are some of the ethical issues involved in this and other events?

Activity
Investigate two events (ideally two that are quite different) and describe them in detail. You might like to do your research on the Internet, starting with one of the state or territory tourism web pages such as www.tourism.nsw.gov.au or www.cyberlink.com.au/events/vic-events.htm, or you could visit your local council.

Links
http://www.ises.com (International Special Event Society)
http://www.ises.org.au (International Special Event Society, Australia)
http://www.icmsaust.com.au (ICMS Australia)
http://www.tourism.gov.au (Sport and Tourism Division, Department of Industry, Science and Resources)
http://www.qldevents.com.au/major.cfmm (Queensland events)
http://www.kumbhallahabad.com/ (Maha Kumbh Mela Festival)

CHAPTER TWO

concept
and design

The winner of the 2000 Tourism Awards for Regional Festivals and Special Events was the 4LM Mount Isa Rodeo. The rodeo is one of the biggest rodeos in the world and the population of Mount Isa (a Queensland mining town) almost doubles for its duration.

Steeped in more than 40 years of history, The Mount Isa Rotary Rodeo (as it was first known) was born out of a desire by a young service club to 'think big'. The idea of staging a rodeo was unanimously and enthusiastically adopted, despite the fact that none of the club members had ever been involved in organising one before. Only a couple of members had even seen a rodeo!

With no ground, no stock and no experience, a rodeo organising committee was formed and set about the task of staging the first ever Mount Isa Rotary Rodeo in 1959. Since its inception, the Mount Isa Rotary Rodeo has donated in excess of $2.5 million to charitable, community, cultural, sporting and service organisations. Most of the facilities have been built over the past 40 years by Rotarians. It has long been recognised that the community involvement behind the rodeo is what makes it such a unique festival.

http://www.isarodeo.com.au

On completion of this chapter you will be able to:

- **establish the purpose of an event**
- **develop a theme and décor that is consistent with the purpose**
- **analyse the needs of the event audience**
- **review financial and other resources**
- **identify an appropriate venue to suit the purpose of an event**
- **establish the timing and duration of an event**
- **review the logistical requirements of an event.**

Volunteerism and community support are the backbone of this successful event that injects $7 million into the region's economy. The rodeo is held in August and includes bareback bronc-riding, bull-riding, steer-wrestling and the much-loved rodeo clowns. The support of over 50 sponsors also contributes to the execution of this event and its long-standing success. It is an excellent example of a concept that has worked and continues to work.

Bareback bronc-riding at the rodeo.

© Kenyon Sports

In this chapter we will look at event concept and design — the creative element that inspires many to embark on careers in event management. While it is absolutely essential to be creatively inspired, it is also essential to understand that innovative ideas must also be reasonably practical owing to the limitations of cost, venue and safety. The other limitation on creativity is the taste of the client. In some cases, the client needs to be carefully guided in their choice of venue and theme, and both the event organiser and the client must have a clear idea of the the event's purpose.

Let's look first at the elements of an event that have an impact on the development of the overall concept.

DEVELOPING THE CONCEPT

There are numerous elements which need to be considered in developing an event concept. They include the purpose of the event, the event theme, the venue, the audience, available resources, the timing of the event and the skills of the team. The most important of these is the purpose, although the purpose is strongly linked to the theme and the venue.

Purpose of the event

The purpose of the event should drive all the planning. For example, if you were running a conference for financial planners, there could be two quite different purposes:

1 To facilitate an exchange of information, bringing participants up to date with the latest changes in financial planning software products.

2 To achieve a memorable out-of-body experience for financial planners in order to develop a positive association with a new software product.

To achieve the first purpose would be quite straightforward, as this would require a fairly standard meeting or convention. Fulfilling the second purpose, however, would be more difficult. For this unforgettable experience you would need a unique venue and carefully planned activities that the participants would enjoy. At the same time, the product would need to be reinforced constantly so that attendees would leave with an inescapable association with it. To have the fun without the positive association would defeat the purpose.

The focus of the first of these purposes is **information**, while that of the second is **entertainment**.

While for many events the main purpose is making a **profit**, for many it is not. The mission statement of the Maleny Scarecrow Carnival is an excellent example of an event with a **community** purpose.

Maleny Scarecrow Carnival

Mission Statement

To make this unique event an annual celebration of Maleny's rich cultural and social diversity. To present an opportunity for the community to unite and share creative energy, spirit and pride.

Background

The aim of the celebration is to enrich the social and cultural fabric of our community. Since ancient times, scarecrows have been used by almost every culture in a rural context; in most instances, in the belief that their presence would increase fertility and enrich the harvest.

The Maleny Scarecrow Carnival began in 1998 with the concept of a cultural event that would enhance Maleny's distinctive rural qualities and offer a unique opportunity for the local and wider communities to express their creativity. It is difficult to imagine a more perfect setting for hundreds of artistic and whimsical scarecrows than the rolling emerald green hills of Maleny. The event is based on the creation and display of scarecrows throughout the Sunshine Coast hinterland. It is comprised of four major facets:

- Scarecrow Masquerade
- Scarecrow Contest
- Scarecrow Discovery Trail
- Scarecrow Fiesta.

The Carnival coincides with the September school holidays to maximise the opportunity for families, the local community and visitors to participate in a wide range of activities

The Maleny Scarecrow Carnival provides broad-based regional economic benefits consistent with community values and encourages involvement from all sectors of the community. In doing so, it heightens community awareness of various local groups and services as well as providing the opportunity for entertainers and artisans to showcase their creative skills. Most importantly, the Carnival is based on whole family participation, from toddlers right through to grandparents. Following on from the overwhelming success of the inaugural event in 1998, the organisers are building on the framework already in place. Interactive skill development workshops will add a new dimension and greater opportunities for members of the community to participate.

In 1998 there were 110 scarecrows entered in the competition, with more than 200 on display throughout the region. In 1999 there were 150 scarecrow entries, with more than 300 on display throughout the region.

People involved included community and support groups, hospitals, libraries, Chambers of Commerce, schools, pre-schools and kindergartens, tour groups, garden clubs, retirement villages, businesses, sporting clubs, service groups and, of course, individuals. It is most interesting to note that fourteen towns outside Maleny participated in the Scarecrow Contest; many well beyond the Sunshine Coast hinterland. We even received international involvement, including 30 miniature scarecrows sent by the children of the Australian International School in Singapore.

We have initiated relationships with other Scarecrow festivals throughout the world, including Japan, Canada, USA and Europe and our aim in the future is to seek international participation, with a view to expanding the cross-cultural elements available to the community.

http://www.maleny.net.au/scarecrow

Theme of the event

The theme of the event should be linked to the purpose. It should be completely compatible with guest needs and consistent in all respects. Most events adopt a colour scheme that is repeated on all items produced for the event, such as tickets, programs, uniforms, décor, posters and merchandise. This helps attendees to identify with the theme.

There is an endless number of potential themes, limited only by your imagination and the customer's pocket. Some examples include:

- historical
- geographical and cultural
- sporting
- film, music and entertainment
- artistic
- food
- objects (e.g. scarecrows, CDs, boats).

When coming up with ideas for a theme, it is most important to consider the range of suitable venues available, keeping in mind the constraints of budget and other considerations.

A hall transformed into an underwater world.

© Annabel Moeller

Venue for the event

The event manager needs to carefully consider the planning implications of choosing an unusual venue in preference to a standard venue requiring decoration only to match the theme. Lighting, sound and catering also provide challenges in unusual settings. This will become more evident in the logistics section later in this chapter and in Chapter 3.

The following are examples of unusual venues:

- demolition site
- parking lot
- tunnel
- museum
- research facility
- amusement park
- orchard
- vineyard
- aquarium.

The remaking of the Australian Open is an example of a fully integrated event venue and theme. The Open adopted the theme 'This is Australia' in 2001, the aim being to present Australian culture in an informal way. The 2001 Australian Open poster illustrated the famous Garden Square with all its casualness, friendliness and intimacy. The Australian Open is now the only sporting event in the world boasting two retractable roofs at its venue. When not in use for tennis, retractable seating moves away to reveal a velodrome which is used for cycling events.

A number of Internet links to event venues, including small meeting rooms and large convention centres, are provided at the end of this chapter. Many of these venues provide enormous flexibility and can be readily transformed to meet the requirements of the theme. The range is extremely wide — from hotel banquet rooms to theatres to sporting venues.

When considering the choice of venue, the event organiser needs to look at a number of factors, including:

- potential to fulfil the purpose of the event
- ambience
- location
- access by public transport
- parking

- seating capacity
- built features (such as stages)
- cost of decoration, sound and lighting
- cost of labour
- logistics of setting up
- food and beverage facilities
- safety.

There are many, many factors that need to be taken into account in selecting an event venue, but the overall strategy should be to aim for the best possible fit with the client's and the audience's needs at the lowest possible cost. If all stages, props, carpets, seating, portable kitchens and refrigerators, and so on have to be hired, the cost will be very hard to justify — even if the venue seems perfect in other ways.

Event audience

When organising an event, the needs of **all** participants must be considered before finalising the concept. Just prior to the 2000 Paralympic Games, one of Australia's best known athletes was invited to give a presentation at an event attended by approximately 200 people. The rental agency said that they were unable to provide a ramp to the stage for her wheelchair and wanted to compromise by asking members of the audience to lift her chair onto the stage. This was clearly unacceptable.

In the example of the entertainment-based event held for the financial planners (conservative stereotype!), an organiser would be wise to challenge normal behaviour and encourage participation in unusual activities. However, great care would need to be taken to ensure that such an audience were not pushed beyond its conservative limits. At a similar event, an event co-ordinator found that persuading the audience to wear unusual hats was all that it took to break them out of their normal patterns of interaction. Of course, every audience is different, and the event manager needs to go with the flow and direct the event to meet audience response. This can involve sudden changes in plan.

Financial considerations

The topic of financial management will be covered in detail in Chapter 7. However, it is an important consideration at this early stage of event concept and design. Initial financial estimates can get out of control very easily, and the choice of event concept can certainly contribute to this. Otherwise good ideas should be knocked on the head at an early stage if they do not appear financially viable as it is possible to come up with concepts that are startling in their simplicity and also cost effective. This is where the creative and rational aspects of the event manager's abilities can come into conflict. Very often the creative aspect wins — sometimes at the expense of the company's profit on the event.

Timing of the event

The timing of an event is often linked to the season or weather. For example, a food and wine festival would be better programmed for early autumn than for mid-summer when the heat would be intolerable for both the audience and the stall-holders. And mid-winter is certainly not the time to hold a flower show. While this might seem obvious, it is surprising how often events are programmed to occur at very unsuitable times. The timing of sporting events is, of course, limited by the sporting season and their traditional competitions. Broadcast to international audiences is another consideration. Who could forget the proposal on the ABC show, *The Games*, to run the key athletic events at the Sydney 2000 Olympic Games at 5 am so that they could be seen on prime-time US television?

Evaluation of an event concept must take into account the following four time-related factors:

1 season
2 day of the week
3 time of day
4 duration.

Generally, mid-winter events are poorly attended, while event audiences are faced with an oversupply of events in spring.

Event team, contractors and other stakeholders

The skills of the event team and, just as importantly, the contractors, such as lighting technicians and catering staff, are an important consideration in terms of concept development. Staff working at most events have very limited opportunity for training, making job breakdowns and task sheets essential aspects of planning. In addition, stakeholders such as the waterways police, the Environmental

Protection Agency and the transport authority have all sorts of requirements that could challenge the feasibility of an event, and these must be investigated.

ANALYSING THE CONCEPT

The following elements will be covered only briefly here since they are revisited in a number of later chapters. The aim of introducing them in this chapter is to raise awareness of the problems and pitfalls that can occur if they are not considered at this early stage of concept development. In addition, if not dealt with, they can have a negative impact on the event manager's creativity.

Competition

Prior to involvement in any event, it is essential to conduct an analysis of your competition. This involves looking at the timing and duration of other events, even if they are unrelated. People have limited disposable income and festivals and events tend to be non-essential items in most family and tourist budgets.

Regulations

A wide range of laws and regulations have an impact on the staging of events and these can severely limit creativity. As a simple example, releasing balloons into the atmosphere is considered environmentally unfriendly. Parking, traffic and neighbourhood impact, especially in terms of timing and noise, are all aspects that require the event manager's liaison with local or state government.

Marketing

How to sell an event is a very important part of the initial planning, the timing of your marketing efforts being crucial. Do you advertise months beforehand or the day or week before? Will the audience turn up on the day? How can you encourage them to do so? Should you sell tickets in advance? (Many events actually have no advance ticket sales.) All these questions require the decision-making skills of the event manager or the event management team.

Community impact

The impact of an event on the local or wider community and others is a major consideration of the planning stage. Local traders and other lobby groups can raise hell for the unprepared event organiser so it is absolutely essential that community benefits are explained and other impacts considered as part of the event proposal.

Risk

At this point you must be aware that for most events the weather is the greatest risk to attendance and enjoyment. (You will be reminded of this at several points throughout this book.) Measures to counteract the impact of weather are essential aspects of event feasibility planning. You must also be aware that insurance premiums will be linked to the perceived risk to the safety of participants.

Revenue and expenditure

Finally, losing money is the fastest way to get out of the event business. For this reason, the event concept (and the investment in event design) needs very careful analysis.

DESIGNING THE EVENT

Consistency and links to the purpose of the event are all essential parts of the creative process in designing an event. The following are the main creative elements that must be considered.

Theme

As Goldblatt (1997) points out, the theme should ideally appeal to all senses: tactile, smell, taste, visual and auditory. If the aim of the event is to transport the audience, appeal to all the senses will contribute positively to the outcome. Keep in mind, once again, the needs of the audience when planning, for example, what music will be played. As we all know, taste in music and desirable sound level vary enormously from one audience to another.

Layout

This creative element is so often given far too little consideration. Consider events that you have attended in which you have felt socially uncomfortable. Your discomfort was generally the result of too much open space, too much light or the limited opportunity for people to mix. The worst scenario is being seated at a long, wide table where you are too far away to talk to those opposite and are stuck with people you have little in common with on your left and right. And to add insult to injury the venue is ablaze with light. Worse still is the cocktail party in a huge ballroom where a small circle develops in the centre — not small enough, though, for everyone to talk. The audience needs to comfortably fill the venue to create a positive ambience.

Décor

Fabrics, decorative items, stage props, drapes and table settings can all be hired and it is generally worthwhile investigating these options before settling on the event theme as hiring items can reduce costs enormously. Floral arrangements need to be ordered from florists experienced in larger events. Australian native plants, some of them up to 2 metres high, can produce a stunning effect. In many ballrooms the floral arrangements are elevated above the table, on tall stands, so that guests can talk to each other more easily. The effect is quite dramatic, with the floral arrangements dominating the décor.

The décor has to be carefully considered for a special dinner event.

Suppliers

Good relationships with suppliers of all commodities will ensure that only quality products will be received, including the freshest flowers and the best produce the markets can supply. During most large events, suppliers are pressed for the best quality from all their customers at a time when volumes are much larger than usual. This is when a good long-standing relationship with a supplier is invaluable. It was reported that at Atlanta during the 1996 Olympic Games you could not buy tissues or towels anywhere. The success of the Olympic Games in Australia was due to early planning (especially of menus), allowing farmers and other suppliers to sign contracts well in advance. Consider for a moment that some of the flowers had to be planted years before the event! So, too, some of the fruit and vegetables, which were in good supply despite it being the off-season.

Technical requirements

Few people would have attended an event or meeting where there wasn't a single technical glitch. Speakers put their notes on the laptop and the screen starts changing at a phenomenal rate. Screensavers come on when the speaker goes on too long, the presentation is halted and file names appear on the screen. While none of these problems are caused by technical support, there are ways in which they can be reduced. Technical glitches by the contracted company are unacceptable. Microphones must have back-ups, the power supply must be assured, stages and video screens must be visible to all in the audience. There is no substitute for wide-ranging experience and this is a key attribute that should be sought when choosing technical contractors. New technology, especially anything used to demonstrate new products, needs to be tested thoroughly, through many rehearsals. A back-up system is essential.

There are times when an event concept should remain just that because it is technically impossible.

Entertainment

For some events, entertainment is central; for others, it is peripheral. The most important thing is that the entertainment should suit the purpose of the event, not detract from it. The needs of the event audience must be carefully considered when making this decision.

A clown creating balloon art is something one would consider for a children's party. However, the same idea (with different designs) could also work extremely well at a wedding reception while guests are waiting for the photography session to finish.

Catering

Nothing makes participants at an event more frustrated than delays in service and poor quality food — except, perhaps, lack of toilet facilities! While guests may have patience with other delays, they will become very agitated if hours are spent in queues, especially if these are away from the action. Food quality and selection are notoriously bad, and outrageously expensive, at many events and planning must take this into account. These days an espresso coffee cart can be found every few metres at most events, reflecting changes in the expectations of the audience and event managers' response to this. Creative event planning frequently requires unique or unusual food and beverage products and these can take time to find. They may even need to be imported. Time means money, as does importing, and both can contribute to an escalation in costs.

LOGISTICS OF THE CONCEPT

The following logistical elements must be taken into account when considering an event concept:

- Access to the site (For example, can vehicles come close enough for off-loading or to park?)
- Physical limitations (For example, will the size or shape of the stairs make it impossible to move heavy equipment?)
- Dimensions of site (Is it too high, too low, too narrow?)
- Refrigerated storage (Is it sufficient?)
- Physical space for food preparation (Is it too small?)
- Toilet facilities (Are they fixed or portable?)
- Cleaning (Is it contracted?)
- Catering (Will there be any physical problems with transporting, storing and serving food?)
- Safety (Are patrols, exits, fire procedures, first aid, etc. all in place?)
- Potential damage to the site (Is there a danger of flowerbeds being trampled?)
- Provision of basic services (Are water and electricity laid on?)

This chapter illustrates the careful balance required between the creative and rational aspects of decision-making when considering an event concept. Brainstorming by the planning team will generate ideas but these then need to be considered as to their feasibility in terms of the issues raised in this and subsequent chapters.

Case study

I was asked to plan a woman's 40th birthday party with a difference. The woman's husband was thrilled with the idea of a lunchtime harbour cruise as it would be a good way of surprising his wife. (Holding a party at home is usually impossible to keep secret.) I was to arrange the boat hire and catering, and to decorate the boat on the morning of the party.

As it turned out there were three complications. The first was the weather. It rained, and we could not use the top deck which was wonderful, but only on a sunny day. This meant that the downstairs area became quite crowded. The harbour was also quite choppy and a few people felt seasick because of the small swell.

The thing I really hadn't thought through carefully enough was the needs of the children who accompanied their parents. The older ones were just bored, not difficult to manage. The toddlers were a disaster. Mothers were on the trot all afternoon since they seemed to want nothing more than to climb over the rails (the children, that is). But by the end of the afternoon the mothers were ready to throw themselves over!

Finally, we were out on the water too long — long enough for some of the party to drink too much and long enough for others to get desperate for dry land and peace and quiet.

It was a real lesson for me in planning for the audience (everyone who came), in selecting the venue and in timing. An evening party would have ensured that at least the toddlers would have been left at home.

- What were the three complications?
- How could these problems have been avoided?
- What would you suggest for a family party for a 40th birthday?
- List the types of events affected by weather.
- What are some general suggestions for avoiding weather problems?
- How can you keep young children amused when they are part of an event?
- What would have happened if one of the guests invited to the cruise had been in a wheelchair and there was no access ramp to the boat?

Activity

Start a collection of images that will inspire future event designs. These may come from a range of sources, including magazines, gift wrapping, table napkins, cards and posters. All will give you ideas for themes and colour schemes. You may also like to begin to investigate colours and textures by looking at fabric samples.

Links

http://www.specialevents.com.au/directory/index.html (provides
   links to florists, entertainers, fireworks, furniture, etc.)
http://www.isarodeo.com.au/default.htm (Mt Isa Rodeo)

SUMMARY

In this chapter we have looked in detail at the event concept because it is essential that this be workable right from the start. We have stressed the importance of determining the purpose of the event in conjunction with all stakeholders. Early in the process it is also necessary to identify the potential audience as well as the financial and other resources required to support the event. The event concept can then be further developed to include the theme and the décor, and a suitable venue can be selected. We also pointed out that any logistical requirements of the event must be identified early in the planning process. The purpose, theme, audience and venue need to be compatible elements for the event concept to be successful.

CHAPTER THREE

feasibility

On completion of this chapter you will be able to:

• discuss the feasibility of event concepts

• analyse the factors that contribute to feasibility

• look at infrastructure and other event requirements that have an impact on feasibility

• look at a range of risk factors that could have an impact on feasibility

• identify ways in which risk can be minimised.

> *Fireworks supremo Mr Syd Howard had been dumped from London's New Year's Eve celebrations after London's Lord Mayor cancelled the evening's festivities over transport and security concerns. A dispute erupted between transport organizers, police and the office of the Mayor, which was co-ordinating operations. A director of Howard Fireworks, Mr Garry Suprain, said it had been an 'unfortunate incident'. 'We're philosophical about it but it's a shame for London because they could have had the biggest and the best New Year's Eve [but] they were scared of "could have's" and "mights".'*
>
> SYDNEY MORNING HERALD, 5 DECEMBER 2000

This article clearly illustrates the issues associated with feasibility and risk. There are many events worldwide that are cancelled as a result of risk, not least financial risk. Careful analysis of feasibility and detailed analysis of potential risks are essential when looking at the feasibility of an event. Anticipating risk and planning preventive measures can reduce the liability of the event management company. In the end, however, the event should not go ahead unless there is an unequivocal 'Yes' to the question 'Is this event feasible?'.

KEYS TO SUCCESS

The following keys to success were developed by Ernst and Young, advisers to the Olympic Games, the Emmy Awards and the PGA Tours (adapted from Catherwood and Kirk, 1992):

• Is the event a good idea?

- Do we have the skills required to plan and run the event?
- Is the host community supportive?
- Do we have the infrastructure in the community?
- Can we get a venue at a price we can afford?
- Will the event attract an audience?
- Will it attract media support?
- Is it financially viable?
- Are the success criteria reasonable?

These questions will be used in this chapter to look at the topic of feasibility. In addition to the nine questions listed, we will ask one final question, 'What are the risks?'.

Risk management is one of the most important concerns for the event manager. As mentioned in the first chapter, events can go spectacularly right, but they can also go spectacularly wrong. For an event manager involved in an event that goes wrong, it is not career limiting, it is catastrophic. The opportunity to run another event will not occur and an alternative, vastly different career will need to be considered. This is particularly the case if people are injured or if the event proves to be a financial failure. As mentioned earlier, risk for most business operations is spread more evenly than it is for the event manager or the event management organisation. A bad day's trading for a company that trades all year is not as problematic as a bad day's trading for a one-day event!

In order to consider the questions posed by Ernst and Young, we will focus on two very different examples: the issues that were raised prior to the Sydney 2000 Olympic Games and a proposal for a very small local event, a monthly organic food market.

Is the event a good idea?
While this question appears quite simple, there are many event management teams which ask this question more and more frequently as the event draws near. The measure of public support for the Olympic Games in Sydney was lower than expected until only weeks before the Games when unprecedented interest caused ticketing problems. Booking offices were overwhelmed and distribution channels were challenged. No doubt the organisers had asked the above question many times in the months leading up to the event — and hopefully before they made the bid — only to have their doubts resolved at the last minute when record ticket sales were reported. It

is a major question for any city bidding for the Olympic Games, and one which needs to be extremely well considered at an early stage of the process.

In the case of the organic food market, the organisers must first determine the purpose of the event. To raise the profile of the area and its products? To raise funds for charity? Or is it a straightforward commercial venture? No matter what the answer, the organising committee must then consider carefully if it is a good idea by asking the questions below.

Do we have the skills?

Criticism of the Sydney Committee for the Olympic Games and related stakeholders was well documented in the press in the years leading up to the Games. However, any doubts were quickly resolved when the Games proved to be an outstanding success, demonstrating that the wide range of skills required did exist. Australia's high level of expertise in the field of event management is now internationally recognised.

The skills required to run an organic food market are largely administrative. If, however, the concept were developed as a charitable fundraising event, it would be necessary to carefully consider the on-going time and commitment required by the volunteers to sustain the event on a monthly basis.

The organic food market got it together, but there were a few hiccups along the way.

Is the host community supportive?

Cities tend to feel ambivalent about hosting an Olympic Games. The community as a whole has to commit to significant expenditure and inconvenience, and some businesses and residents undoubtedly experience negative consequences. For example, there were constant complaints about the work being done on pavements and in other parts of the Sydney city centre in the lead-up to the 2000 Olympic Games. There was also the belief amongst many that the funds could have been better spent on schools and hospitals with urgent problems. However, those with an interest in the tourism industry and an understanding of the economic potential of the Games were far more positive. An analysis of community support must take the opinions of all such stakeholders into account.

A monthly organic food market would probably generate little opposition from residents unless stall holders were noisy when setting up early in the morning. However, local food retail stores might be quite antagonistic since the market would not be faced with the same overheads and could thus provide competition through lower pricing. On the other hand, the market could attract visitors from outlying areas and a few tourists which could lead to increased trade for the retail outlets. Most studies show, however, that tourists visiting festivals and markets tend to do so on impulse so it would not make sense to base planning on the tourism potential of such markets.

Do we have the infrastructure in the community?

The infrastructure required for an Olympic Games is enormous, airport facilities being a good example. Although Cape Town in South Africa put in a bid for the 2000 Olympics, most agreed that the infrastructure would never have coped with an event of such size. Bid cities generally have to make a commitment to infrastructure development in order to win the Games and are then faced with the issue of the viability of these venues after the Games have left town.

Transport and parking are generally important considerations. However, in the case of the organic food market, these would not be problems if held in a country town. If the market were held close to a railway station and timing were matched with peak arrivals and departures, this could in fact be advantageous.

Can we get a venue at a price we can afford?

For most event organisers, the cost of venue rental is a key consideration. Many are tempted to save money by hiring marquees and using temporary accommodation, but this can prove a false saving since the cost of décor, lighting, catering and the like is generally more expensive and more risky. The benefits of function rooms include tried and tested facilities, safety plans and insurance, as well as numerous other features. The expertise of venue managers cannot be underestimated and this can contribute to the technical success of an event. With an entertainment event, the location and cost of the venue can have a critical impact on pricing and promotion.

The cost of the venue is also dependent on the time for which it is required. In some cases, the time needed for 'bump in' and 'bump out' (setting up and dismantling) is quite long, necessitating higher than expected rental costs. Motor car and boat shows are good examples, with huge demands on the logistics of setting up. Goldblatt (1997) refers to these as time/space/tempo laws, pointing out that the actual physical space governs the time required. He cites the example of a Superbowl at which 88 pianos had to be moved onto the field during half-time. Loading area access and storage are other considerations. And security is of particular concern because high-priced items can go missing: it was reported that a new model car disappeared from the floor of the 2001 Sydney Motor Show and was taken for a 600 kilometre joyride!

The costs incurred by an organic food market for its venue would be minimal compared with the enormous cost of purpose-built venues suitable for events like the Sydney 2000 Olympic Games. Nevertheless, these costs are just as important a consideration for the market as they are for the organisers of any Olympic Games. Despite the fact that such venues remain a lasting legacy for the host city, their long-term financial viability is always an issue of concern.

Will the event attract an audience?

The location of the event venue or site is crucial for attracting the numbers you require to make the event successful. In the case study at the end of this chapter, you are given a list of potential events and you are asked to rank them in terms of their feasibility. All are located in different towns and cities and a study will have to be made of the local population, as well as domestic and international visitors who may be attracted to the event. Identifying the audience is a key issue for event managers in planning an event.

Sydney was potentially a problematic Games venue as some international visitors had to travel vast distances to attend the event. However, as it turned out, the Olympic Games in Sydney attracted unprecedented numbers of interstate and South East Asian visitors.

Market research into current trends is essential for event feasibility planning. An extensive range of reports is available from tourism authorities, at both state and federal level. For example, findings from a report on the seniors market show that this age group is a tourism market segment with significant potential. These statistics, combined with Australian Bureau of Statistics reports on the changing demographics (including age groups) of the Australian population, clearly point to the size of this market now and its potential in the future. In the next ten years the seniors population will swell from 3 to 4 million, while the 15 to 45 age group will experience zero growth. Seniors from Australia, as well as from international source countries, are living longer than ever before. According to the above research, then, the feasibility of an annual event with seniors as a target market would seem to be far higher than one planned for the zero growth age group.

Returning to the example of the organic food market, this concept could be expanded to include the whole spectrum of health products and so become a highly feasible event targeted specifically at seniors. The location would need to be in an area in which this demographic group was large and continuing to grow, and the venue would need to have facilities that catered for seniors. Most councils and the Australian Bureau of Statistics can provide this type of information.

Figs 3.1, 3.2 and 3.3 illustrate the demographics of Warringah Shire Council in Sydney. As is apparent from Fig. 3.1, Warringah's population is aging in comparison with that of the broader areas of Sydney and New South Wales. It has a higher than average number of people in the age 55 and over demographic. At the other end of the age scale (Figs 3.2 and 3.3), the percentage of people in the 0-11 and 12-24 year demographics in Warringah is lower than those of the Sydney and New South Wales areas.

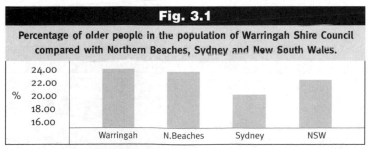

Fig. 3.1

Percentage of older people in the population of Warringah Shire Council compared with Northern Beaches, Sydney and New South Wales.

Reproduced with permission Warringah Shire Council

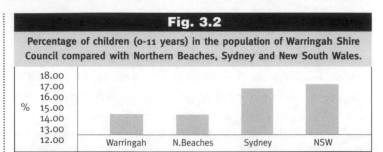

Fig. 3.2

Percentage of children (0-11 years) in the population of Warringah Shire Council compared with Northern Beaches, Sydney and New South Wales.

Reproduced with permission Warringah Shire Council

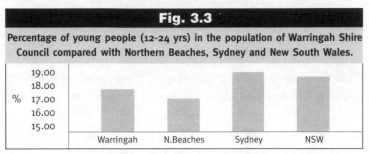

Fig. 3.3

Percentage of young people (12-24 yrs) in the population of Warringah Shire Council compared with Northern Beaches, Sydney and New South Wales.

Reproduced with permission Warringah Shire Council

In view of these statistics, a strategic ten-year plan for an annual event would target the age group showing the highest growth rate in Warringah, in this case people aged 55 and over. Targeting a declining age group would reduce the feasibility of the event in the long term.

Fig. 3.4 shows the population distribution by suburb in the Warringah area and this information could be used effectively to indicate the feasibility of an event designed to attract a local audience. Dee Why and French's Forest are Warringah's most populous suburbs and would thus appear to be the best locations for an event of this nature.

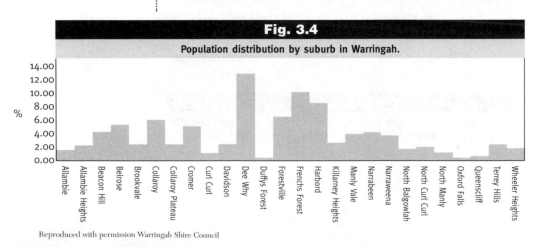

Fig. 3.4

Population distribution by suburb in Warringah.

Reproduced with permission Warringah Shire Council

Will the event attract media support?

Media support is essential. Although this was lacking for much of the planning stage for the Sydney 2000 Olympics, once the show began the media got right behind it and the result was 'the best Games ever'. A smaller event, however, would have been ruined by such negative press leading up to its staging. Media support for a new product launch, for example, is one of the main criteria by which the event is judged successful.

In the case of the organic food market, it would be best to approach local newspapers to seek their support. Stories and images, with a focus on the value to the community and the management of risks, would need to be provided to stimulate both media and community interest in the event. A special feature, including advertisements by exhibitors, would be the type of proposal that would be well received at local level.

Is the event financially viable?

An event that is financially viable and brings benefits to the community can defeat any objections. One that is not viable will have a short life span. The organic food market would be unlikely to make huge profits or generate substantial charitable funds, but it might contribute to community spirit and provide intangible benefits to the local population. For example, it might enhance the reputation of local agricultural products, thus attracting investment in the organic concept. Fees charged to stall holders would need to cover all expenses associated with the event since there would be no charge to visitors.

The Olympic Games held in Montreal in 1976 left a lasting debt for the Canadian people. What began as a glorious vision turned into a financial disaster, and one that took the people of Quebec almost twenty years to pay off. Through planning errors, misjudgements and strikes, and suspected corruption, the estimated cost of $124 million rose to an incredible $1.5 billion. In contrast, the New South Wales taxpayer was free of debt after the Sydney 2000 Olympic Games, which also reaped additional benefits for the people of Australia.

For most events, the decision on the price to be charged to visitors or spectators, and when it is made, is critical. Tickets cannot go on sale the day after an event is over, nor can the merchandise produced for the event. If T-shirts, caps and CDs are not sold this, too, will mean lost revenue. Even the concession outlets that sell food and beverages do not get a second chance at sales. For these reasons, the decision on price — and the timing of this decision — are extremely important in ensuring that the event audience reaches a viable level.

In Chapter 7, on financial management, the concept of a break-even point will be discussed. For the event manager, careful attention to budgeting will provide a reasonably accurate idea of the costs involved in running the event, and this is essential in making a decision as to what to charge for tickets. This judgement is also informed by knowledge of the consumer market and likely perceptions regarding value for money.

However, not all events are ticketed: an exhibition, for example, involves renting stands to exhibitors, and the price charged for exhibiting is based on the cost of staging the exhibition and the likely number of exhibitors. For non-profit events, financial decisions involve keeping within the budget which may be established by another body (for example, the local council). Where a client is paying for the staging of an event, the event management company would develop a budget for the event based on very clear expectations from the client as to the benefits expected from the event. Often the event management company earns a fee and the client is ultimately responsible for the cost of the budgeted items and any variations.

Are the success criteria reasonable?

The criteria on which the success of events are judged vary widely. The Olympic Games is generally judged on feedback from the international audience. While feedback from the athletes on accommodation and sporting facilities is important, the continuing sponsorship of the Games is the result of the response of the world television audience. This is clearly one of the most relevant criteria for the continued success of this four-yearly mega-event.

The organic food market could encourage local growers to develop entrepreneurial skills and to produce and market a differentiated product. This has already been done by many regional wine growers, such as the wine growers from Mudgee, who now hold an annual promotional event at Balmoral Beach in Sydney. Change in consumers' perception of a region's products is difficult to measure, as is the increased confidence of the local producers. These are known as intangible outcomes and seldom form part of the success criteria, which tend to be more tangible results, such as improved

Outstanding service from Sydney 2000 Olympic Games volunteers contributed to the success of the event, while the first-class technical organisation at the 2000 Paralympics marked it for victory.

sales. Increased pride in Australia was one of the intangible outcomes of the Sydney 2000 Olympic Games.

A wedding is an interesting event to analyse in terms of success. Should its success be judged on the criteria of the bride, the groom, the parents or the guests? Were there elements of the wedding (such as lack of compatibility between the bride's and groom's families) that could not be managed? And just about everyone attending has a point of view about the décor and colour scheme.

The criteria for success need to be established before the event takes place, as it is against these that the feasibility of the event is analysed.

What are the risks?

This final question is the most important of all because failure, and even fiasco, are always possible.

Brainstorming, in order to reveal all of the possible risks associated with an event, and then ranking them, is the first step. Risks may include:

- heavy weather, wind and/or rain
- flooding
- fire
- collapse of buildings or temporary structures
- accidents involving workers and/or the event audience
- crowd control
- security of participants and VIPs
- food poisoning
- breakdown in water or power supply.

Contingency planning, in order to deal with potential risks, is the next step. And thirdly, policies and procedures must be put in place to deal with every possible eventuality. In Chapter 8 we will discuss risk management in more detail, with particular focus on priorities and operational plans designed to minimise risk.

The IACC (International Association of Conference Centres) has set international standards for operations, facilities, equipment and management for small- to medium-sized conference centres (20–50 people), and conference venues around Australia are adopting these as a benchmark. This type of accreditation is reassuring for the event organiser and an excellent method of reducing many of the most common risks. Links to this association are listed at the end of the chapter.

To briefly summarise, the aim of the event organiser is to improve feasibility and reduce risk (see Fig. 3.5).

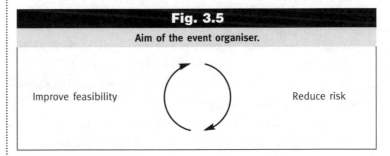

Fig. 3.5

Aim of the event organiser.

Improve feasibility   Reduce risk

THE SWOT ANALYSIS

It is traditional, and important, to do a SWOT analysis for every event. This involves analysing the strengths, weaknesses, opportunities and threats of the event or event concept.

S **Strengths** are the internal strengths of the organisation, for example, the enthusiasm and commitment of volunteers, the specialist knowledge of the lighting engineer or the wide range of products available for planning themes and décor.

W **Weaknesses** are the internal weaknesses of the organisation, for example the skills and knowledge of the management committee or their lack of availability for meetings.

O **Opportunities** are the external favourable things that may occur, such as new sponsorships or unexpected positive publicity.

T **Threats** are also external: competition, poor publicity and poor crowd behaviour would all be classified as threats.

Essentially, the idea of improving the feasibility of an event is to improve the strengths of the organisation (and the concept) and to maximise the opportunities. Likewise, acknowledging potential weaknesses and dealing with them will minimise the risks. Assessing potential threats and introducing contingency plans to circumvent them will also improve the feasibility of the event.

Case study

Use the questions provided in this chapter and any other relevant ideas or information to discuss the feasibility of the following event concepts. Then rank them in order, from most to least feasible.

- Agricultural Show in June in the town of Nerang, Queensland
- Flower Show in Renmark, South Australia, in August
- Wedding on an island in Sydney Harbour in January (with marquee)
- Red Earth Arts Festival in Alice Springs, Northern Territory, in February
- Aboriginal Dance Festival at Cooktown, Queensland, in January
- Marathon in Hobart in July
- Food and Wine Festival in Geelong, Victoria, in June
- Wildflower Show in Albany, Western Australia, over the Easter weekend
- School-leavers Celebration at Merimbula on the New South Wales coast in December.

SUMMARY

In this chapter we have compared two very different types of event and in the process have shown that asking simple questions can help you to determine the feasibility of an event concept. Questions need to be asked about the financial viability of the concept, the demographics of the audience, the infrastructure required to stage the event and, very importantly, the potential risks. We have also discussed the contribution of community and media support to the success of an event. An evaluation of an event's success or otherwise, based on criteria established in the planning stages, should be carried out after the event. Some events are measured by profits, others by the level of community support they attract.

Activity

List the advantages and disadvantages (and thus the feasibility) of the following event durations:

- *one session on one day*
- *multiple days*
- *annual.*

Use an example for each in your discussion, which should be based on some of the concepts in this chapter and Chapter 2.

Links

http://www.families.qld.gov.au/seniors_tourism/facts.htm (Department of Families, Youth and Community)

http://www.iacconline.com (International Association of Conference Centres)

http://www.iaccaustralia.org

http://www.icca.nl/index.htm (larger exhibition centres)

CHAPTER FOUR

legal
compliance

While the press reports would lead one to believe that the party was a disorganised, feral bunch of teenagers running an illegal rave party at which drug dealing was rife, this was not the case. The party had been carefully planned with approvals sought from police and council and had met requirements for liquor licensing, security and amenities. Showers, water and first aid were all provided. The event was supported by a range of sponsors and had taken two years of planning. Recreational drug use is widespread and difficult to control, although it is illegal.

EVENT ORGANISER

This case study clearly illustrates the dilemmas faced by event organisers of dance parties, whether at fixed or open venues. In this case, the organisers had sought all approvals and had the support of the police and St John Ambulance's first aid services. It is easy to see, then, why event organisers must ensure that they comply with the relevant legislation. For example, if you were organising a music event, it would be necessary, amongst other things, to contact the two bodies responsible for music licensing and to pay fees to satisfy copyright agreements with artists.

This chapter will cover all the necessary requirements, such as music licensing, food hygiene plans, the building of temporary structures, entertainment in public places and road closures.

There are three levels of government in Australia — federal, state/territory and local (see Fig. 4.1 over page) — and there are laws and regulations at each of these levels that may require compliance. For example, taxation requirements are covered by federal legislation,

On completion of this chapter you will be able to:

- explain the laws and regulations that may have an impact on event planning
- identify the bodies from whom approval is required, or support is needed, to stage a particular event
- explain the legal compliance requirements of an event
- identify insurance premiums and fees that need to be paid
- describe the contracts required between event organisers and other parties, including subcontractors.

while local council approval would need to be sought for an event to be held in a public space. In fact, local council offices generally give advice on all legal compliance and they will request the event organiser not only to comply with council requirements but also to contact the Police Service or the Environment Protection Authority, if applicable. Some local councils have event planning policies which include all relevant council regulations, as well as higher level legal compliance requirements.

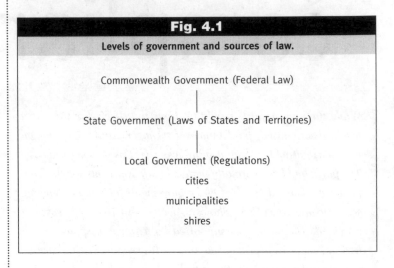

Fig. 4.1

Levels of government and sources of law.

Commonwealth Government (Federal Law)

State Government (Laws of States and Territories)

Local Government (Regulations)

cities

municipalities

shires

Links are provided at the end of this chapter to the Department of Local Government in New South Wales web page where a comprehensive document called 'A Guide to Major and Special Event Planning' can be located. Similar guides are available in other states and territories. In Appendix B, the outline for an event proposal provides prompts for a range of legal requirements, some of which may not be applicable, for example, to the organisation of an indoor event. However, this general outline gives you the main cues for event planning, and for meeting legal obligations.

RELEVANT LEGISLATION

The principles of the major acts and regulations relevant to event management are covered below, in general terms.

Local government acts and regulations

There are a number of local government acts and regulations that may apply to events. These vary considerably from one area to another. Some councils have detailed guidelines, while others have less formal requirements. The size of the event largely determines the detail required in the submission since smaller events tend to have a lower impact on the community.

If an event has already been held in one council area, with approval, it may still be necessary to obtain approval for a second similar event in another location. Likewise, if the event covers more than one jurisdiction, additional proposals may need to be submitted.

If the event requires the building of permanent structures, a development application would most likely be required, and this would link to the Local Environment Plan (LEP), which is the community's vision for the future of the area. Application for the use of the premises and property for entertainment may also be necessary. Plans would need to be developed for the erection of temporary structures and approval would need to be sought for them.

Approvals are required by most councils for:

- using loudspeakers or amplifiers in public spaces
- installing amusement devices
- singing or providing entertainment in public places (fees would also apply)
- using a building or structure for entertainment (change of approval classification)
- building a temporary structure.

Councils are also very concerned about cleaning programs during and after the event, noise and disturbance of local residents, and traffic management.

Business registration

A business can take the form of a sole trader (where you operate on your own), a partnership, a proprietary limited company (Pty Ltd company) or an association. Every business must be registered with a business number. The name of the business must also be registered. Small business development is encouraged, so there are agencies which provide advice and assist with the formalities in all states and territories.

Entertainment industry legislation

Licences for the entertainment industry cover agents, managers and venue consultants. The disbursement of fees, as well as trust accounts for performers, are covered by this type of legislation. There is also a code of ethics. Entertainment industry legislation allows for complaints to be heard and resolved regarding payments to performers, agents, managers and venue consultants.

Music copyright

The right to use music in a business or commercial operation requires a licence from APRA (Australian Performing Rights Association) for the copyright in the song, composition or lyrics. A licence is also required from PPCA (Phonographic Performance Company of Australia), the association representing music publishers and record companies. Therefore, if a sound recording were to be played at an event, the event company would need to apply for licences from both APRA and PPCA. The fees, while nominal, recognise the copyright and commercial value of the music. They vary according to the use of the music (from background music, live performance, music played or sung at sporting venues or function centres, to karaoke).

To clarify, there are two copyrights in each recording: firstly, the copyright in the sound recording of the recorded performance and, secondly, the copyright in the song, composition or lyrics. There are usually at least three copyright issues in a music video clip, namely, copyright in the cinematographic film that embodies the recorded performance, copyright in the recorded performance itself and copyright in the song (i.e. composition or lyrics).

Copyright on text is generally held by the writer, artist or publisher, and permission is required from the copyright holder of any text or image that you wish to reproduce. In the same way, you hold the copyright in your own work. Logos and trademarks must be registered separately.

Deal on Games songs near

Australian songwriters are expected to settle out of court with SOCOG tomorrow after a long-running court battle over licence fees for music used during the Olympic Games.

Before the Games, SOCOG put $1.5 m in a trust fund as a sign of good faith to local songwriters for the use of their songs at Olympic venues. But post-Games negotiations stalled when SOCOG made an amended $100,000 offer in response to the Australian Performing Rights Association claim for $2 m.

Sun Herald, 5 May 2001

Liquor licensing

In general, this legislation covers the age of drinkers, the venues and the situations (for example, with meals) in which alcoholic drinks can be served, as well as the legal hours of alcohol service. Liquor must be correctly labelled and sold in legal measures. A sign must be displayed to say that it is an offence to sell or supply liquor to, or obtain liquor on behalf of, a person under the age of eighteen years. The licensee must be able to show that reasonable steps (including requests for identification) have been taken to ensure that minors have not been served alcohol. Complaints about noise or indecorous behaviour can be made to the Licensing Board.

A liquor licence is required to serve alcohol.

Trade Practices

The Trade Practices Acts aim to ensure that advertised goods and services are provided in accordance with the advertising. For example, at one concert in Sydney featuring an overseas performer, the stage design was so poor that many members of the audience could neither see nor hear. As a result, the event management company was forced to refund the money paid for the tickets to those who had been affected. The staging problem was resolved to everyone's satisfaction before the next performance.

The Trade Practices Act (Commonwealth) and the various state Fair Trading Acts protect the consumer against misleading advertising and deceptive conduct. A consumer (or a client) can sue under common law, under the Trade Practices Act or under the relevant Fair Trading Act. This means that one cannot engage in conduct that is liable to mislead the public as to the nature, the characteristics, the suitability for the purpose or the quality of any services. The contract for services to be provided in the organisation of an event thus needs to be extremely explicit.

Anti-discrimination legislation

This act protects employees and customers from discrimination on the basis of factors such as age and religion.

Clean air legislation

Prosecution for allowing pollution of the air would be the result of any breach of this legislation.

Noise legislation

Noise is a troublesome problem for festivals and events since by their very nature they attract crowds, entertainment events being particularly problematic. It is therefore essential to check noise limitations in terms of allowable decibels and the times during which loud music is permitted.

Clean water acts

Discharge of sewage, oil and other waste into water systems is illegal and our waterways are protected by a number of acts of the various states and territories.

Safe food handling

Food acts provide guidelines for safe food handling. Every contract caterer is required to develop a food safety plan covering food safety at all stages of delivery, preparation and service. This is necessary to guard against bacteria which may develop if food is left standing after delivery, or during preparation and service, and not kept at an appropriate temperature. Buffets where food is left unrefrigerated are notorious for high bacteria levels. Generally, food needs to be kept cool or heated to a hot temperature. The mid-temperature range is the most dangerous. A qualified caterer should know all about food hygiene and should follow correct procedures to avoid contamination. A food safety plan should be part of any catering contract, which should also include menus and prices.

Safe plating of food.
These trollies are designed to be
stored in refrigerators.

Charitable fundraising legislation

The aims of this legislation are to:

1 promote proper management of fundraising appeals for charitable purposes
2 ensure proper record-keeping and auditing
3 prevent deception of members of the public who desire to support worthy causes.

A person who participates in a fundraising appeal which is conducted unlawfully is guilty of an offence. Authority is required to conduct a fundraising appeal and this is obtained by applying to the relevant body in your state or territory.

Insurance

The most important insurance required by an event management company is public and product liability insurance. Claims against this insurance can be reduced by careful risk analysis and prevention strategies. One council requires a $5 million level of insurance for minor events and a $10 million level of insurance for major events. The average householder has a $1 million public liability insurance cover. As with most local government requirements, these may change from one council or municipality to another. Assets and motor vehicles also need to be insured.

The following disclaimer is aimed at reducing the liability of a race organiser:

1 *I, the undersigned, hereby waive any claim that I might have arising out of my participation in this event and fully accept all the risks involved.*
2 *This waiver shall operate separately in favour of all bodies involved in promoting or staging the event.*
3 *I hereby attest and verify that I am physically fit and have sufficiently trained for this event. I agree to be bound by the official rules and regulations of the event.*
4 *I hereby consent to receive medical treatment that may be deemed advisable in the event of injury or accident.*

Essentially, the person who signs this disclaimer is taking responsibility for his or her actions. However, from a legal point of view, there is nothing to stop the contestant from making a case for negligence against the race organiser. Clearly it would have to be shown that this negligence led directly to the injury, and the extent and impact of the negligence would then be investigated. In other words, an event organiser cannot avoid liability for negligence by having participants sign a disclaimer. The person has the right to sue in any circumstances and the case would be judged on its merit.

In addition to public liability insurance which must be taken out by the event management organisation, all contracts signed with subcontractors, such as a company which erects scaffolding, should also include a clause requiring the subcontractor to hold a current policy covering them against liability for incidents that may occur. As you can see, there are a number of different stakeholders who are potentially liable and the event organiser needs to limit their own liability by managing risk and ensuring that subcontractors are also insured. In the following article, the honorary vice-president of Clowns International advised 70 members to take out insurance against potential claims for custard pie injuries!

Clowns gathered at a special Big Top conference last week — to discuss the legal risks of chucking pies. They got serious as they discussed whether circus audiences sitting in the front row were willfully placing themselves in the line of fire. Clowns fear they could be liable for compensation if a member of the public got it in the face.

INTERNATIONAL EXPRESS, 10 APRIL 2001

Other insurance policies which should be considered are professional indemnity (for any claim for breach of professional duty through any act, error or omission by you, your company or your employees) and insurance against rain and other climatic occurrences that might have an impact on the event. Clearly, rain insurance is extremely expensive and the process of demonstrating the impact of climatic conditions on attendance is quite onerous.

Security legislation

This legislation provides for the licensing and regulation of persons in the security industry, such as crowd controllers, bouncers, guards and operators of security equipment. In general, there are different levels of licences requiring different levels of training.

Summary Offences Act

Summary Offences legislation covers issues such as desecration of public and protected places, shrines, monuments, statues and war memorials.

Occupational Health and Safety

This legislation is designed to prevent workplace accidents and injuries. The legislation has specific requirements for employers to provide safe work places and safe work practices. This topic will be covered in detail in Chapter 15.

Workers compensation insurance

Workers compensation insurance, which is obligatory, covers treatment and rehabilitation of injured workers. Volunteers and spectators are covered, in most cases, by public liability insurance since they are not paid workers.

Taxation

For anyone running a commercial business (fee for service), compliance with taxation rules is essential. All businesses must be registered and this can be done by contacting the Australian Taxation Office (ATO). Advice will be provided on all types of taxation applicable, including deductions of PAYE for paid employees. Deductions for superannuation must also be made. All commercial businesses must pay GST, although charitable bodies and some educational institutions are exempt from GST.

STAKEHOLDERS AND OFFICIAL BODIES

Some of the following bodies may require detailed plans or briefings depending on the extent of their involvement in an event.

Transport Authority

Any impact on traffic because of an event must be discussed with the relevant authority, which is generally the Road Transport Authority (RTA). The staging of an important party in Melbourne proved problematic when all the visitors arrived in limousines. The driveway was too small to accommodate them and the traffic backed up for miles, resulting in the event program being delayed. This had implications for the VIPs invited, including senior members of local and overseas governments, who missed flights and other engagements.

Police Service

Police patrols, if required, are charged to the user at an hourly rate, except in such circumstances as charitable fundraising events.

State Emergency Services and St John Ambulance

Both these bodies need to be briefed. St John Ambulance is staffed primarily by volunteers and they should be included in staff recognition programs in order to acknowledge their important role.

CONTRACTS

This final topic is the most important in this chapter and could become a book in its own right. The effectiveness of the contracts between the parties involved in an event is crucial. Specifications need to be incredibly detailed in order to avoid disputes. Clarity and agreement between all parties is essential. The contract provides the basis for variation in price every time the customer has new demands. For this reason, time invested in the writing of the contract will reap rewards and often resolve legal disputes. Professional legal advice is essential for a new event management business.

CONTENT OF CONTRACT/AGREEMENT

- parties to contract
- deadline and deposit
- specifications (for example, space booked, timing, food and beverage, accommodation)
- services to be provided
- special requirements
- schedule of payments
- insurance
- cancellation
- termination/non-performance
- contingency
- consumption
- confidentiality
- arbitration
- warranties
- signatories
- date

Many events involve a range of contractors for services such as catering, cleaning, sound, lighting and security. While it is tempting for an event organiser to take on all roles, the benefits of employing contractors are many. Specialist organisations generally have more expertise and better equipment, they generally carry their own insurance and they have a lot of experience in their particular field. By dealing with a range of contractors and using professionally prepared, well-negotiated contracts, the event organiser can dramatically reduce risk and liability. On the day, the main role of the event organiser is to monitor the implementation of the agreed contracts.

Case study

You and your friends are planning to have a party to celebrate the end of the college year. Your plan is to hold the party at the local football oval, but if it rains you will hold it in your garage. Invitation has been informal and your whole year has been invited. Everyone will bring their own alcohol, although a few of the people will be under eighteen. A friend with a sound system is bringing it along and you have decided to charge everyone who attends $5 to cover your costs. Another friend who runs a catering company will do a spit roast and charge $2 for a beef roll.

- Is permission required to use the football oval? If so, from whom?
- What are the implications of charging an entry fee? Would you recommend this?
- Should the police be told about the party? (Is there any chance that uninvited people may turn up?)
- Do you need a liquor licence if alcohol is not sold?
- Who is responsible for under-age drinking?
- What would happen if a fault in the wiring caused someone to be electrocuted?
- What are the limitations on the use of a sound system, either at home or at the football oval?

Activity
Investigate two venues that offer weddings and compare their advertised services/products, contracts and checklists from the point of view of the customer and the owner of the business. In addition,

SUMMARY

This chapter dealt with legal and related issues that must be considered during the planning of an event, including licensing and approvals. Legal compliance is one of the major risk issues for organisers of an event and research into these requirements is essential. Tight contractual arrangements with the client and subcontractors are equally important as these can ensure the financial viability of an event or completely derail it. Insurances of various types are also required, including workers compensation and public liability, while workplace health and safety should be a major consideration of any event organiser.

compare the contracts of the two venues in terms of the potential for misunderstandings to develop and legal disputes to follow.

Links

http://www.dlg.nsw.gov.au/97-65.pdf (Department of Local Government)

http://www.apra.com.au (Australian Performing Rights Association)

http://www.ppca.com.au (Phonographic Performance Company of Australia)

CHAPTER FIVE

marketing

A record crowd of music lovers are headed to Australia's country music capital, Tamworth, with more than 50,000 expected at this week's festival. At least 20,000 revellers lined the streets yesterday, with ticket sales to among 2500 events up 20 percent on last year.

The festival highlight is the annual Golden Guitar awards next Saturday, with country legend, Slim Dusty in the running for a staggering eight awards, including song and album of the year.

The event is being sponsored for the eighth year by Carlton and United Breweries.

SUNDAY TELEGRAPH, 21 JANUARY 2000

On completion of this chapter you will be able to:

- describe the features of event marketing, including intangibility, variability, inseparability and perishability
- establish the features of an event product
- understand market segmentation
- analyse consumer decision-making processes
- establish ticketing programs where required
- promote and publicise an event
- attract sponsorship for an event
- evaluate the marketing effort.

The Carlton Country Music Festival is one of Australia's best examples of an event that goes from strength to strength, gaining in popularity from year to year. It continues to enhance Tamworth's image as a tourist destination. There are many music festivals in Australia, but few have had as much impact as this one. The reason for its success has a lot to do with marketing and what is known as the marketing mix — the combination of product (country music festival as opposed to rock festival), price, promotion and place. The choice of messages and the channels of communication with the event audience are also important and together these factors form part of the marketing strategy.

Marketing is important because it helps to attract an audience without which any event will turn out to be a non-event! The event audience makes decisions about cost and effort to attend and weighs these against the benefits of attending. An understanding of the decision-making processes of the audience is therefore essential for anyone planning and promoting an event.

NATURE OF EVENT MARKETING

Event products generally include a combination of goods and services and so provide a challenge for those involved in event marketing. Some industries market products without a service component, for example, soft drinks where the focus would be on the product. In marketing computer equipment, however, there would be goods and services aspects of the product which might include hardware and back-up service. On the other hand, when marketing something purely intangible, such as 'Come for the atmosphere' or 'Do you just want to have fun?', there is a large service component. In some respects it is far more difficult to market something that the customer cannot take home or physically consume.

The first feature of services marketing that makes it challenging, then, is its **intangibility**.

Another feature of services marketing is that there is a higher degree of **variability** in the service provided, as well as in the response to the service provided. The service and the service provider are also distinguished by their **inseparability**. This means that as an event organiser you are very reliant on your staff, performers and athletes to meet the needs of the audience. You have far less quality control than you would over tangible goods (such as soft drinks) — unless your training is first rate.

In summary, the three features of services marketing are:

*   Intangibility (such as fun, entertainment, information)
*   Inseparability (such as the usher's service approach to the customer where product and provider are inseparable)
*   Variability (such as different levels of service provided by different ushers or different responses from two or more customers to the same experience).

Some goods and services components of a conference are illustrated in Fig. 5.1 opposite.

There is one final important consideration for the event marketer. A restaurant in a good location can rely on a level of passing trade. So, too, can a general store. This is not the case with an event, as the decision to attend or not attend is generally made shortly before the event and is irrevocable. If a customer decides not to attend, revenue

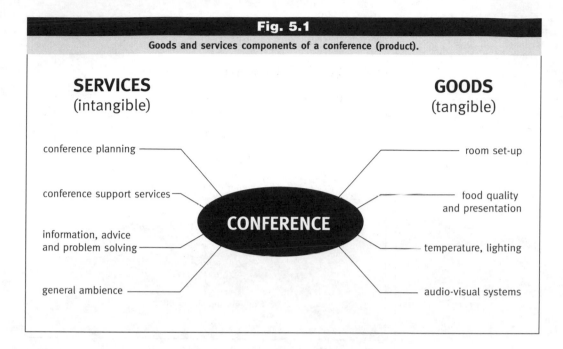

Fig. 5.1

Goods and services components of a conference (product).

SERVICES
(intangible)

GOODS
(tangible)

conference planning — room set-up

conference support services — food quality and presentation

CONFERENCE

information, advice and problem solving — temperature, lighting

general ambience — audio-visual systems

to the event organiser is completely lost. This is not the case for the restaurant owner or shopkeeper who may see the customer at a later date.

An event, whether it is one-off or annual, is highly **perishable**. Unsold tickets cannot be put out on a rack at a reduced price!

Services provided at events, then, are intangible, inseparable, variable **and** perishable, presenting a number of marketing challenges as value for money is generally an issue for the consumer.

PROCESS OF EVENT MARKETING

The event marketing process is summarised in Fig. 5.2 on the following page. Ultimately the aims are to enhance the profile of the event (and associated sponsors), to meet the needs of the event audience and, in most cases, to generate revenue. Some festivals are fully funded by government bodies, and although they are not expected to raise revenue, they aim to attract a high level of attendance or interest as a minimum expectation.

Establish the features of the product

Each event offers a range of potential benefits to the event audience. These may include one or more of the following:

• a novel experience

Fig. 5.2

Event marketing process.

establish the features of the product

↓

identify customers (segmentation)

↓

plan to meet audience needs

↓

analyse consumer decision-making processes

↓

establish price and ticket program

↓

promote the event

↓

evaluate marketing efforts

- entertainment
- a learning experience
- an exciting result
- opportunity to meet others
- chance to purchase items
- dining and drinking
- inexpensive way to get out of the house
- chance to see something unique.

Many marketing experts are unable to see past the main motivating factor for the event, which may be the opportunity to watch an international cricket match. There may, however, be some members of the audience who have little interest in cricket, but are motivated by some of the other features of the product such as the opportunity to see and be seen. Generally, people attending an event see the product as a package of benefits. Convenience and good weather, for example, could be benefits associated with an event product.

When marketing an event, therefore, alignment between the product benefits and the needs of the audience is necessary to guide the design of the event and the promotional effort. Pre-match and mid-match entertainment are good examples of adding value to the main benefit offered by a sporting event product.

Having fun and meeting friends are all part of the enjoyment of attending the Australian Grand Prix.

Identify customers

Market segmentation is the process of analysing your customers in groups. Some groups may enjoy a particular type of country and western music. Others may enjoy line dancing. Yet others might visit just for the excitement and the atmosphere. It is absolutely essential to analyse the different motivations of the event audience and to develop a profile for each of these groups.

As the Mayor of Tamworth, Warren Woodley, says about their festival audience:

The festival is a cultural event the whole nation can be proud of. That's why tens of thousands of fans and families come here every year — the young, the old, the diehards and the curious.

It's a safe haven with a carnival atmosphere made even more enjoyable by the alcohol-free zone in the heart of the city.

Tamworth is an amazing soundscape of different styles: contemporary, traditional, acoustic, bush music, country rock, rockabilly, blue grass, western swing, blues, urban country, comedy and gospel — not to mention astonishingly popular bush poetry.

Plan to meet audience needs

Once you have identified your customer groupings, it is then necessary to ensure that all their needs are met. With the Tamworth example, there may be a generation of older music enthusiasts who

are looking for a certain type of entertainment as well as a younger group (say aged ten to fourteen) which needs to be entertained, too, so that they can gain something from the experience. As another example, a 'Symphony under the Stars' concert would attract many fans of classical music. However, many others would come 'for the atmosphere' and some just for the fireworks at the end. None of these customer segments' needs can be ignored. All audiences need food and facilities, but food and beverage may or may not be a high priority of a particular event audience. For some the fairy floss is the highlight; for others the food is unimportant.

Decisions, decisions, decisions.

Analyse consumer decision-making

The next step is to analyse the customer's decision-making process. Research conducted here will produce information which is very useful in guiding promotional efforts.

Competitive pressure (positioning)

Competition from other forms of entertainment for a person's disposable income would need to be considered. The economic environment would also need to be scanned in order to understand factors that might have an impact on discretionary spending on tickets, as well as possibly on travel and accommodation.

Motivation

Customer motivation has already been mentioned under market segmentation. Potential customers may have positive responses to some aspects of an event and negative responses to others, such as the distance to be travelled, crowding and the risk of bad weather. Customers can be divided into decision-makers, followers, influencers and purchasers. While in most cases the person who decides to attend (and perhaps take his or her family or friends) is the one who makes the purchase, there are situations in which the decision to spend money on an event is influenced by others. For example, if a teenager wished to go to a concert, they might exert pressure on their parents to make the purchase on their behalf. In this case, both the needs of the teenager and those of the parents would need to be met. As teenagers would generally discourage their parents from attending, promotional efforts would need to ensure that parents perceived the concert to be a 'safe' environment. Those who tag along to an event are the followers. Each of these, the influencer, the decision-maker, the follower and the purchaser, would generally have different expectations of the event and would evaluate it differently.

Timing

This is the most important aspect of consumer decision-making since it has implications for the promotions budget. The issue is: when does the consumer make the decision to attend? If the decision will be made two months before the event, you need to deploy all marketing initiatives at that time. If, on the other hand, the decision will be made the week, or the day, before the event, this will have important implications as to how and when the advertising and promotions dollar will be spent.

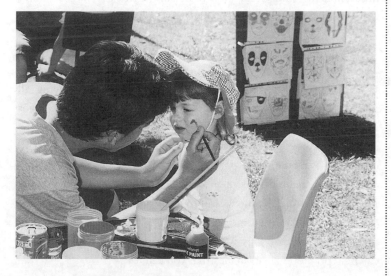

The decision to attend a fete or festival is often impulsive and made on the day.

Purchase or attendance

Finally, the desire to attend needs to be translated into a purchase action. If it is perceived that getting good tickets is going to be difficult, some consumers might not make the effort. In fact, for some festivals, there are no advance sales of tickets. This means that the decision to attend is considered impulsive and that it would generally be made on the day. Clearly, advance ticket selling means a better opportunity to plan for an event as well as a substantial boost to cash flow.

Establish price and ticket program

Sale and distribution of tickets has been mentioned briefly above. Now it is necessary to consider that event attendance could be tied in to tourist travel to a destination. If this were the case, it would involve negotiations with a tour wholesaler, extending the time-line for planning. Plans would need to be finalised long before the event, with price determined, brochures printed and advertising done (sometimes overseas) well in advance. This package tour might also include airfare and accommodation.

Promote the event

Having made the decision as to when it is best to promote the event, the next question is how to promote it.

Differentiation

An event, whether a concert, festival or surf carnival, needs to be differentiated from other related leisure options. The consumer needs to know why this event is special.

Packaging for effective communication

The messages used to promote an event are extremely important. Usually there is only limited advertorial space for convincing all market segments to attend. Thus the combination of text and images requires a lot of creative effort. If there is time and sufficient budget available, trialling the effectiveness of communication messages with consumers is recommended.

There are many forms of promotion, including personal selling; brochures; posters; banners; Internet advertising; news, radio and television advertising; and press releases. Balloons and crowd pleasers (people balloons with moving arms) are examples of eye-catching promotional strategies that you can use.

Evaluate marketing efforts

The effectiveness of all promotional efforts needs to be carefully monitored. With an annual event, for example, customer responses to the various types of promotion will guide promotional efforts in future years. Evaluation needs to be done systematically by asking questions such as 'Where did you find out about the event?' or 'When did you decide to attend this event?'

There are three stages at which research can be conducted: prior to the event, during the event and after the event. The research can be qualitative, such as focus groups and case studies, or quantitative. In the latter case, the research generates statistics such as customers' expenditure at the event.

THE MARKETING MIX

In the final analysis, the marketing efforts need to be analysed in terms of the marketing mix (see Fig. 5.3 on the next page). In other words, was the event positioned well, priced well, promoted effectively and distributed through different channels efficiently. All these factors must work together if success is to be the outcome.

Positioning

The questions to ask are: 'Was the choice of event appropriate and was it positioned correctly in terms of competition?' For example, one would hesitate to run a food and wine festival in a small town when there was already a Spring Market Festival in a larger town nearby.

Price

Pricing for an entertainment event is very tricky. It depends on the size of the potential audience and the selected venue. If the ticket price is too high, and the featured artist not as popular as expected, then the half empty venue will result in a dismal financial outcome. Pricing of food and beverage items is also an important consideration because customers become annoyed if mark-ups are excessive.

Promotion

Promotional activities need to be chosen carefully and timed effectively. Promotion is a costly exercise, radio and television advertising being two of the most expensive. Overall, the most cost-effective methods of promotion are feature articles in local newspapers and banners. Many events are promoted by tourism bodies and by tourism information offices at minimal cost. And increasingly, the Internet is being used as a source of information by the event audience.

Distribution

Tickets can be distributed as part of package tours, through ticket sellers (who take commission) or at the venue. In many cases, the event product is produced, distributed and consumed at the venue. This contrasts for example with goods that are imported for sale and ultimately consumed by the customer at home.

The effectiveness of the channels through which an event is promoted and sold is a crucial aspect of its success.

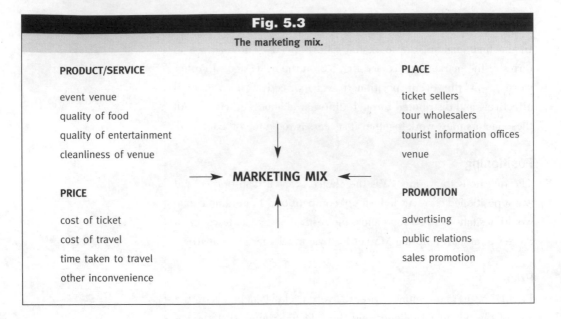

Fig. 5.3

The marketing mix.

PRODUCT/SERVICE	PLACE
event venue	ticket sellers
quality of food	tour wholesalers
quality of entertainment	tourist information offices
cleanliness of venue	venue

MARKETING MIX

PRICE	PROMOTION
cost of ticket	advertising
cost of travel	public relations
time taken to travel	sales promotion
other inconvenience	

SPONSORSHIP

Sponsorship is one of the most common funding sources for staging an event. In some cases, the sponsor is happy to provide cash to support the event in exchange for increased profile and sales of their products. In other cases, the sponsor provides 'value in kind'. This means that the sponsor will provide free goods and services, again with the expectation that this will have a bottom line benefit. For example, a newspaper sponsor may provide free advertising space. Some sponsors use an event to promote a new product and, in this case, the whole event is aimed at developing customer awareness and loyalty. In all of these situations, the marketing messages must be consistent with the event and must be clear to the audience. An expensive party to celebrate the release of a new product is a waste of money if the audience cannot recall the name of the product a few weeks later, much less purchase it.

An exception to this expectation of profit is, for example, the support of Australia Day by Penrith Panthers Club, a non-profit organisation featured below. In this case, the expectation would have been the creation of a positive impact on their image to raise their community profile.

In our Centenary of Federation, Australia Day takes on an extra significance and we hope you will have a wonderful day reflecting on

all the great things that are represented by Australia. At Panthers we recognize the privileged place we have within our community. We also understand the vitally important role the Club Movement has played within our State for decades. Combining these gives us the pleasure of delivering to you the types of entertainment, dining, recreational and leisure activities that the community demands, and delivering it in an environment that is reflective of the friendly, easy-going Australian spirit.

We need to take every step we can to protect that spirit and enhance it. There are an enormous number of ways we at Panthers try to achieve that goal. From donating to worthy and charitable causes, to supporting a Penrith District rugby league team in the NRL competition or a Bathurst team in the Group 10 competition; from providing scholarships for potential elite athletes to nurturing junior sport development.

This protection and enhancement of the spirit within our community is enabled by the fact that we are owned by our members and our profits are earmarked for the community, rather than for distribution to private individuals.

Essentially, the sponsor identifies with the event, mainly through the use of their name and logo, and expects a return on their investment. It is thus essential to evaluate both the sponsor profile and the sponsor's sales, or any other sponsorship objectives, after the event to ensure that the sponsorship has been successful and that the sponsor's relationship with the event will continue.

The QANTAS and Coca-Cola logos are often seen at major events.

There are a number of questions to ask before approaching a potential sponsor.

What are the benefits?

Can the sponsor's involvement lead to some benefit for the organisation in terms of increased profile or increased sales? What other benefits are there? At what cost? Will it be time-consuming for their staff?

How long will the association last?

Is it possible to build a long-term alliance with the sponsor? Can an agreement be reached for perhaps a five-year sponsorship?

How much exposure will the sponsor achieve?

Will the sponsor's logo appear on all advertising? Will they have naming rights to the event or will specific prizes be awarded for particular events by their senior staff. Will the winning athlete wear one the sponsor's caps when interviewed by television crews? Will the sponsor be named in the prize-giving ceremony?

Will the sponsorship be exclusive?

Will this sponsor be the only one and thus clearly associated with the event? Or will there be a large number of sponsors?

Is there compatibility?

Have the potential sponsor's competitors agreed to provide sponsorship and will this lead to a conflict of interest? Is there compatibility between the sponsor's product and the event purpose (for example, if the purpose of the event was promoting a healthy lifestyle)?

Will there be ambush marketing?

Are there organisations which will attempt to gain advertising mileage and sales from the event, despite their lack of sponsorship or other commitment? Will competitors' products be on sale at the event or in a nearby area?

Ultimately, the most important question of all concerns the sponsor's benefit from their involvement in the event. This needs to be negotiated early in the arrangement and a process for measuring sponsor objectives, such as recognition or purchase of their products, needs to be put in place prior to, during and after the event. Where clearly audited records or professional surveys can demonstrate sponsorship outcomes, renegotiating sponsorship arrangements for subsequent events, or different events, will be much easier since success has been demonstrated in a tangible way. At the end of the day, the sponsor needs a report detailing all promotional efforts and the ensuing benefits, as well as photographs and success stories for post-event publicity.

Case study

Using the concepts in this chapter, develop a very brief marketing proposal for each of the following events. When complete, analyse the differences in the approaches you have suggested.

1 Ballarat Winter Festival, Victoria
   Festival held each year to promote the arts, heritage, food and
   beverage, and recreation in Ballarat.
   http://winterfest.ballarat.net.au/

2 Melbourne MOOMBA Festival
   Annual festival featuring performers and entertainers from
   Melbourne and around the world.
   http://moomba.wittingslow.com.au/

3 Melbourne International Comedy Festival
   Long-running annual festival of fun and laughter, rated as one of
   the world's three major comedy fests (with Edinburgh and
   Montreal).
   http://home.vicnet.net.au/~comfest/

4 Melbourne Writers' Festival
   Annual event featuring workshops and talks by both Australian
   and international writers.
   http://www.mwf.com.au/

5 Moonlight Cinema
   Movies under the stars in Sydney, Melbourne and Adelaide.
   http://www.moonlight.com.au/

6 Perth International Arts Festival
   Western Australia's leading cultural event.
   http://www.perthfestival.com.au/

SUMMARY

In this chapter we have discussed the marketing mix for event marketing, including product, price, promotion and place (distribution). Identification of consumer interest in the product and their decision-making processes form a key part of the planning of promotional efforts. Since most promotional budgets are limited, the expenditure must be timed carefully to ensure maximum impact. Sponsorship is one way of attracting funding or 'value in kind' and this is an important element of the marketing strategy. Evaluating the marketing effort is essential as it will facilitate planning of future events.

7 Blessing of the Fleet, Ulladulla, New South Wales
Calls on divine providence to safeguard ships and crews from the danger of the seas.
http://www.blessingfleet.asn.au/

8 Boulia Desert Sands, Queensland
Australia's Premier Camel Racing Festival.
http://www.camelraces.asn.au/

Links

http://www.tamworth.nsw.gov.au/tcc/cmf/index.html (Tamworth Country Music Festival)
http://www.panthers.com.au (Penrith Panthers Club)

CHAPTER SIX

promotion

We are delighted to present the 2001 Royal Easter Show — our 158th Show since the foundation of this great exposition.

In 1997 the Board and the Staff of the Royal Easter Show put together plans to ensure that the Show would have relevance in the twenty-first century. Those well-laid plans have paid off, ensuring that the first Show of this new millennium is very much alive and well and bursting with colour, excitement and the vibrancy unique to the Royal Easter Show.

The new look commercial halls all have a theme: Home Improvement, Information & Technology, Food & Wine and Market Stalls, each with interesting and interactive trade presentations from a wide variety of companies, all keen to present their own brand of expertise.

In the Food & Wine Hall a huge test kitchen will feature some of New Zealand's best chefs and talks from experts on matching food and wine.

Children will enjoy the innovations in the Faber-Castell Children's Art and Entertainment Area and the super line-up of children's book authors who will read from some of their most successful publications.

The main Art Hall has a wonderful new layout to feature Pottery, Ceramics, Painting, Photography, Wood-turning, Ikebana, Asian, Indian, Maori and Pacific Art, Mouth and Foot Painting, Stone Sculpture and Spinning. Various demonstrations from artists of note will be scheduled throughout the Show.

The fabulous Te Vaka, a multi-racial, hugely talented and original group of artists, acclaimed internationally, will headline

On completion of this chapter you will be able to:
- plan the promotional strategy for an event
- develop a brand or image for the event based on the theme
- develop advertising materials and place them appropriately
- manage publicity
- manage public relations.

entertainment at the Show. Te Vaka will be supported by a wonderful array of talent both on the stage and within the Street Theatre.

In the main arena Rodeo and Show Jumping share the spotlight. On the last five days of the Show, international pole climbers will vie for the team trophy. Nearby Farmworld, distinctively presented, offers petting pens, rare breeds, hand-milking, shearing demonstrations and some unique working vintage farm engines.

The Sports Hall hosts Aerobics, Three on Three Basketball, Breakdancing, Karate and Judo — see the timetable for days and times.

The two huge carnival areas once again offer every thrill ride available in New Zealand as well as family rides, and in front of the Commercial Halls some lovely gentle rides are specially assembled for the youngsters.

We are looking forward to sharing what promises to be — the best ever Royal Easter Show.

KEVIN CHOLMONDELEY-SMITH
MANAGER — ROYAL EASTER SHOW

The New Zealand Royal Easter Show is an example of an annual event that is held in most countries and major cities. Agricultural shows continue to appeal to a wide audience ranging from rural farmers to city dwellers. For young children, the baby animal area is always popular, while side shows and stalls are perennial favourites. For rural exhibitors, these events provide the opportunity to have their livestock judged, thus increasing exposure and prices for breeding. The New Zealand event is particularly interesting, with new and exciting ideas capturing current interest in information technology, wine and cuisine. Their promotional information is available on the website listed at the end of this chapter.

Promotion and public relations are a crucial part of the marketing of any event, as we have mentioned in previous chapters, and they will be discussed below in some detail.

As part of the marketing strategy, event promotion involves communicating the image and content of the event program to the potential audience. Broadly, the aim of a promotional strategy is to ensure that the consumer makes a decision to purchase and follows up with the action of actually making the purchase. It is essential to turn intention into action and this is often the biggest obstacle of a promotional campaign.

There are a number of elements involved in promotion, including:

- image/branding
- advertising
- media relations/publicity
- public relations.

IMAGE/BRANDING

The first step for most events is the development of a name, logo and image for the event. This includes the colour scheme and graphics that will appear on all event material ranging from registration forms to tickets to merchandise. Image and logo are closely linked and need to be agreed on well in advance. Together they are referred to as 'branding'. Where sponsors are involved, it is essential to obtain their approval of the branding, otherwise there could be conflict over the use of colour or the positioning and size of logos. The design must meet the needs of all stakeholders, as well as appealing to the event audience, particularly if the design forms the basis for merchandise such as T-shirts and caps. A slogan is sometimes developed as part of the image for an event and incorporated wherever possible. The result should be a consistency in theme and colour scheme for all promotional materials. In most cases, the colour scheme is also carried through to the décor, including signs, fencing, flags, table settings, banners and posters.

ADVERTISING

Advertising is the second element of the promotional strategy. It may take many forms, the following being some of the options:

- print
- radio
- television
- direct mail
- outdoor advertising
- brochures
- Internet.

One form of advertising.

As part of the marketing plan, it is necessary to identify the market to be reached and then to establish where these people live and which of the media would be most likely to reach them. When selecting the most appropriate media, cost is generally the biggest issue. Then you need to decide when to advertise — a month before, a week before or the day before? Faced with budget limits and potentially expensive advertising, these are all crucial decisions.

When preparing an advertising budget, you should be aware that different time slots on radio and television cost vastly different amounts, as do different positions on the pages of print media. Local newspapers and local radio stations are always more cost effective than national ones and are generally a most effective way to reach a local audience. Larger events may aim to attract international audiences and, if this is the case, you will need to clearly identify the potential overseas audience and perhaps develop a tourist package to include accommodation and other attractions. Partnership arrangements can often be reached with travel companies and the assistance of state and national tourism bodies obtained to support and promote the event.

The content of advertisements must be informative but, most importantly, it must inspire decision-making and action to attend or purchase. Let's look at the following advertisement by an event company for their wedding hire products and services:

We provide six-arm gold candelabra in the Victorian style, silk flowers, tea lights, fairy lights, table overlays (in organza, Jacquard and cotton), chair covers with sashes and ceiling drapes. We set up for you.

In this advertisement there is a lot of information but absolutely no inspiration. A number of descriptive adjectives would certainly have enhanced the text, as well as the possibility of customers buying their services!

In contrast, the advertisement for an unusual event on the opposite page is much more creative.

It would be very difficult to attract an event audience if only the facts of a blood donation were presented, and the promotional team has realised this by making this event into something not to be missed.

The advertising message needs to meet the motivational needs of the audience, at the same time assisting the decision-making process by supplying the necessary facts.

> # WE WANT YOUR BLOOD!
>
> *Greendale Clinic Big Bleed Week*
> *May 10–15 with the grand finale (don't miss this) on May 15*
>
> *Greendale Clinic's last Big Bleed was a huge success. This year our target is 3000 units of blood. Sponsors have donated ten major prizes as well as minor prizes for all other donors. The biggest prize, a trip to Cannes, will be presented at the grand finale. We will have free health advice, coffee shop and food stalls, a craft fair, children's entertainment, celebrities, races, a jazz band in the late afternoon and fireworks at the close each evening. Attendance is free and all donors receive a sponsor prize, plus go into the draw for the major prizes. Parking is available in Macleay Street. We start at 10 and finish at 9 pm.*

PUBLICITY

Free publicity for an event can be secured by running a careful publicity campaign with the media. This involves developing and despatching press releases to journalists, and following up by telephone. Sometimes interviews with journalists will also be necessary.

There are several points of contact. In the print media, these include the editor, the feature writers, and the editors responsible for individual sections of the newspaper or magazine. In the broadcast media, the people to contact include the station manager, the news announcers and the radio personalities. In each case, the first question asked will be 'What makes this event newsworthy?' and the answer to this must be clear.

The aim of a press release is to stimulate media interest in the event and thus achieve positive and cost-effective publicity. Many large event organisers post their press releases on their web pages (see as an example the press release in this chapter for the Singapore International Jazz Festival). For mega and hallmark events, a launch is usually held prior to the event to which the media and the stars of the show are invited. These occasions are used to distribute the press release. It is essential that a launch be well attended and that the media report the event in a positive way, otherwise it will be counterproductive. In the case of smaller events, sending a press release to a local paper is generally the best option. Since the staff working on these smaller publications are extremely busy, it is advisable to provide them with a ready-to-go article, including photos, logos and quotations where possible.

The following is an example of the sort of press release/article that would draw the attention of a local newspaper:

WE HOST THE COUNTRY'S LARGEST CYCLE RACE

Thousands Pedal the Peninsula

This year's 54 km race will see 15,000 riders tackle the most scenic mountain and beachside race in the country. The race is the largest sporting event in the state and the largest bicycle race in the country. This indicates a trend towards competitive physical competition for all age groups and cycling is a popular choice. Contestants will be visiting from overseas countries including Japan, Korea, India and Holland. Some riders are fiercely competitive, while others ride as family groups. All age groups are represented, and last year's race was completed by an 84-year-old and his 7-year-old grandson. The race will raise funds for a community parkland project and will be run by five local clubs. An additional $3 million is the target for other deserving causes. To register for the event, contact Richard on 9879 6543 or fax your details to 9879 6544.

The following guidelines for preparing a press release will help to ensure that the reader sits up and takes notice:

- There must be something to appeal to the reader in the first two sentences: he or she must be motivated to read the whole press release.
- All the facts must be covered: what, when, why and how. This is particularly the case for negative incidents. The reader wants to know what happened, when it happened, why it happened and how things will be resolved. When something goes wrong, the facts are important because unsubstantiated opinion is dangerous. If the press release is promoting an event, all information such as the venue, date, time and so on should be included.
- The press release should be short and to the point.
- Layout is extremely important.
- Contact details should be provided.
- Photographs should be captioned.

- Quotes from senior staff and stakeholders (including sponsors) may be included.
- If the press release is promoting an event, it should describe all potential benefits for the audience.
- An action ending for booking or registering should include all necessary information.

Apart from free media publicity, it is also possible to obtain free exposure through a number of official tourism organisations, many of which are listed at the end of this book. They provide tourist information to visitors through tourist information offices or their websites at state or national level. Brochures distributed to such offices or listings on their event calendars can provide valuable information to the potential (and sometimes very hard to reach) event audience. Every effort should be made to ensure that the event is listed as widely as possible.

OUTSTANDING EXAMPLE OF A PRESS RELEASE

The Best of Jazz Comes to Singapore

2 March 2001

For the *first time, renowned jazz musicians from the United States and the Asia Pacific will converge on Singapore, to perform at the Singapore International Jazz Festival from 18 to 20 May.*

The Festival, presented by Singapore Airlines (SIA) and co-sponsored by Heineken and American Express, will showcase top international artists like Lee Ritenour, James Moody, Slide Hampton, Eldee Young, Tuck & Patti and Terumasa Hino, as well as prominent regional musicians such as Eugene Pao, Tots Tolentino and Ireng Maulana. Showcasing more than 50 performances by over 150 musicians on four stages around Suntec City, the Festival promises to be the biggest in Asia this year.

Said Mr Huang Cheng Eng, SIA's Senior Vice President Marketing Planning: 'Singapore Airlines has always been a big sponsor of the Arts. We at SIA hope to bring the Arts to the people of Singapore — something which we also hope to do through this Festival. The Singapore International Jazz Festival is also part of SIA's ongoing effort to help strengthen Singapore's image as a world-class cultural event city. The Festival will serve as a new and exciting attraction to boost tourism to Singapore. We are also happy to have the support of the Singapore Tourism Board.'

Said Dr Les Buckley, General Manager, Asia Pacific Breweries (Singapore): 'The Singapore jazz community has been growing steadily over the years, both in numbers and sophistication. Heineken has helped spur that growth through well-received programmes like the Heineken Green Room sessions, CHIJAZZ and the Heineken Jazz festivals since the mid-1990s. We share the community's excitement over the forthcoming Singapore International Jazz Festival, and our current series of Jazz theme parties at various pubs are part of the build-up to the big event. Heineken remains supportive of Singapore's efforts to reach a world-class stature in the international jazz scene.'

Said Mr Anthony Lee, Area General Manager, American Express International, Inc.: 'American Express is proud to be associated with The Singapore International Jazz Festival. The Festival fits the bill perfectly as a choice event that will bring value to our customers who will appreciate quality entertainment of this genre. We have been in Singapore since 1925 and are very much a part of Singapore and the Singaporean's life — bringing quality products and services, and participating in cultural events. Working with SIA and STB in this jazz sponsorship is further demonstration of American Express' interest and commitment to Singaporeans towards jazzing up the local arts scene. We are pleased to continue the American Express tradition of hosting world-class programmes and events.'

The programme, crafted by Festival Artistic Director Jeremy Monteiro, offers a fabulous mix of traditional and contemporary jazz, catering to the varied tastes of jazz aficionados and those who are not familiar with the genre...

Experience al fresco dining and drinking on the Festival grounds at Suntec City, which will come alive with free performances by regional jazz stars and top local talent on three stages specially set up for the Festival. Great music, close friends, good food and Heineken on the tap all add up to an unforgettable jazz experience.

Other fringe events include jam sessions held each evening at the festival site and late at night at popular local jazz joints. In conjunction with the Festival, there will also be artist workshops and master classes. These are organised as part of the Festival organisers' commitment to giving local musicians the chance to learn from the masters and to build up interest in jazz amongst the young.

Said Mr Huang: 'The idea is to bring jazz music not just to the jazz fans but also the masses. I hope that the Festival will help raise the level of appreciation of jazz music in Singapore and in the region.'

Tickets are priced at $120, $90 and $60, and are available through SISTIC from 31 March. American Express Cardmembers can enjoy priority booking and a 15 percent discount, from 9 March.

For more information on ticketing and other Festival details, please visit the Festival website at http://www.singaporejazzfestival.com

PUBLIC RELATIONS

The role of public relations is to manage the organisation's and the event's image in the mind of the audience and the public. This is mainly done through press releases as described in the previous section. These up-to-date information sources, together with photographs, provide the media with the background information they need to develop stories about the event. Media briefings can also be conducted before and during the event, particularly if high profile people such as celebrities, entertainers and athletes can enhance the publicity.

One of the most critical public relations roles is to inform the media if there is a negative incident of any description. For this reason, an incident reporting system needs to be in place so that senior members of the event management team are fully informed, including the Public Relations Manager, if this is a separate role. It may be necessary to write a press release or appear in an interview if such an incident occurs. In some situations it is essential to obtain legal advice regarding the wording used in the press release. The public relations role can be a highly sensitive one, and in some situations words need to be chosen carefully. A simple expression of regret, for example, would be more tactful than suggesting the cause of an accident.

Another, more positive public relations role is the entertainment of guests and VIPs attending the event, in some cases from other countries. In this public relations role you need to be:

- attentive to the needs and expectations of your guests
- mindful of their cultural expectations
- flexible in your responses to their behaviours
- informative and helpful as a host
- proactive in designing hosting situations to meet the required protocol
- able to make easy conversation.

Particularly with overseas guests or guests of event sponsors, you need to know in advance who they are (official titles, correct names and correct pronunciation) and where they come from. Most importantly, you need to know the reason why your company is acting as host to these guests as often business objectives, such as sponsor product awareness or negotiations, are involved. Research is therefore essential to determine how to meet the needs of the guests and the expectations of, for example, the sponsors.

According to Roger Axtell (1990) the effective multicultural host has the following attributes:

- being respectful
- tolerating ambiguity
- relating well to people
- being non-judgemental
- personalising one's observations (not making global assertions about people or places)
- showing empathy
- being patient and persistent.

As you can see from the above, there are a number of roles for the Public Relations Manager, or indeed for any member of the event team. The opportunity to sell an event occurs every time the telephone is answered or an enquiry is made by a potential customer. Customer relations becomes the role of everyone involved in an event and for this reason training in this area is recommended. This training should focus in particular on the event information likely to be requested by the customer which is more difficult than it sounds since plans are often not finalised until very close to the event. Training ties in closely with the planning process and the distribution of information to all concerned right up until the last minute is very important.

There are a number of situations in which an event manager might become involved in public relations, including:

- making travel arrangements by telephone or email
- meeting and greeting at the airport
- providing transport
- running meetings
- entertaining at meals
- entertaining at events
- providing tours and commentary.

If you have to lead a small group around the venue or the event, there are a number of additional recommendations:

- Plan the tour so that enough time is allocated to see everything.
- Advise your guests of your plan, however informal the group.
- Make sure that there is time for a break and refreshments.
- Provide maps so that people can get their bearings.
- Pause frequently so that the guests can ask questions.
- Be gracious — questions are never trivial or stupid.

- Make sure that everyone can see and hear.
- Treat everyone equally.
- Speak slowly and at an appropriate volume.
- Be patient and speak positively.
- Be flexible and change plans if necessary.
- Be attentive to fatigue or boredom and accelerate the tour if necessary.

In promoting an event, it is essential to analyse and understand the needs of the target market or markets. If, for example, one of the target markets is children aged eight to twelve, it is necessary to understand the motivations of this group and to match the product to these motivational needs. It is also necessary to keep in mind that the person purchasing the product may not be the consumer — in this case, it may be the parent — and promotional efforts need to assist with decision-making processes within the family. Likewise, a sponsor may be making a substantial investment in the event, and may have general, as well as specific, expectations of the event, which may or may not be consistent with those of the event audience.

To summarise, the task of promoting an event to the optimal audience at the most beneficial time is the first challenge. The second is to meet the needs of all stakeholders and to maximise public relations benefits to the satisfaction of customers at all levels.

Case study

South African culture and diversity will be the toast of London when the Celebrate South Africa campaign begins later this month, the High Commissioner to Britain, Cheryl Carolus said yesterday. She said Londoners would have 'their socks knocked off' with South African arts, crafts, music, dance, theatre, film, cuisine and song from April 18 to May 31.

The focus of the six-week programme will be to showcase South Africa as a nation in formation since achieving democracy in 1994. A huge concert will be held in Trafalgar Square to mark Freedom Day.

THE STAR, JOHANNESBURG, 6 APRIL 2001

Using the above newspaper article, and any materials you can find on the history and culture of South Africa, prepare the following promotional materials:

●●●●●●●●●●●●●●
SUMMARY
In this chapter we have dealt with event promotion in more detail, and have seen that branding or image is linked to the event purpose and theme, and that all of these aspects must be consistent and compatible in order to create the greatest impact on the consumer or event audience. There are many media options for advertising and these are often determined by the promotional budget available. Advertising and publicity need to be carefully planned to ensure the highest possible level of attendance at an event. We have also discussed the public relations role, communication with the media and other stakeholders being important during the planning phases and equally important when there are problems or incidents that threaten the success or reputation of an event. A more positive public relations role is the entertainment of guests and VIPs for which certain attributes are essential, including tolerance, patience, persistence, respectfulness and an ability to relate well to people of all cultures.
●●●●●●●●●●●●●●●●●

- a travel brochure promoting the campaign as part of a holiday in London
- a design for a web page (front page only) promoting the six-week program
- a press release to explain the historical background of Freedom Day.

Links to tourism and other websites provided below and in Appendix 1 will assist with your research.

Activity
Select five advertisements for events and analyse the differences, deciding which has the most audience appeal in terms of:
- *attraction*
- *development of interest*
- *assistance in decision-making*
- *ability to lead to action/attendance.*

Links
http://www.royaleastershow.co.nz/
http://www.southafrica.net/

CHAPTER SEVEN

financial
management

The Perth International Arts Festival has posted a deficit of $1.5 million, its main losses attributed to the failure of its extensive film program and newly located festival club, the Watershed.

Doran, who directs the next four Perth Festivals, said the event was conceived and curated as a four-year strategy, with public funds of $12 million from the State's Lotteries and $2 million from the University of Western Australia. The former director of the Belfast Festival was determined that his first festival would make its mark in spectacular fashion. In effect, the overall shortfall for the event was $2.6 million, but a meeting of the festival board last year approved $1.1 million to be amortised across the four festivals to support the new paradigm of the festival in terms of its different marketing, administrative and repositioning initiatives for its future development.

SYDNEY MORNING HERALD, 7 APRIL 2000

On completion of this chapter you will be able to:

- **develop an event budget, including income and expenditure**
- **identify the break-even point in order to make pricing decisions**
- **review and manage cash flow**
- **produce a simple profit and loss account**
- **develop control systems for managing finances within budget.**

Long-term financial results are an important consideration in event management. In the above case, part of the shortfall for the first festival is being amortised (spread) across future festivals but, in general, the aim of financial management is for all expenses to be recouped at the time

Not all events are profit oriented. For example, a promotion for a new product, such as a new brand of perfume, would be part of a major marketing initiative, with the expectation being long-term return through sales. The perfume company would meet the expenses associated with staging the event. Similarly, a party or celebration is usually paid for by the client. Good financial management by the event company will ensure that the quote given to the client at the beginning will at least cover the expenses incurred in staging the party — and hopefully make a profit for the company! In other cases, ticket revenue and other sales (such as from merchandising) are expected to exceed the expenses, thus delivering a profit to the organisers or investors.

The first step in the financial management of an event is to ask the following questions.

Is the aim to make a profit?

There are many events that have a range of objectives that do not include making a profit. For example, street parades or music festivals may be offered to the public free of charge, the expenses being met by government agencies and/or sponsors. Often, goods and services are provided by businesses and individuals to assist in the running of an event, thus making it difficult to accurately estimate the actual costs. However, it is still essential that all other expenses are properly approved and documented.

Where the objective of an event is raising money for charity, a target needs to be set and, once again, both the expenses and the funds raised need to be accounted for correctly.

How much will the event cost?

In the example of the fundraising event above, as indeed for any non-profit event, it is important to estimate how much the event will cost as well as to keep track of the actual expenses incurred. With every event, money changing hands must be properly documented and, in most cases, the financial records should be audited. Expenses, or costs, include fees, hire costs, advertising, insurance, and so on.

What are the revenue sources?

Generally, revenue is raised by selling tickets or charging admission fees. Merchandise sales also contribute to revenue. Merchandising items, such as T-shirts and caps, may be sold by the event organiser or under arrangement with the retailer whereby the event organiser earns a percentage of any sales. The same arrangement may occur with food and beverage sales.

How many tickets must be sold to break even?

This is a critical question. In essence, it relates to whether you decide on a large venue, large audience and low price or a small venue, small audience and high price? This will be discussed in more detail later in this chapter.

What is the cash flow situation?

Events are fairly unique in that, for most, revenue comes in only on the day of the event. This means that all costs, such as salaries, office expenses and fees, have to be met up-front from existing funds. When ticket sales occur long before an event is staged, as they do with major concerts, this puts the company in the enviable position of being able to pay for its expenses from revenue while also earning interest on this money until the remaining bills become due. Very few events fit this category. Cash flow planning is an essential part of the event planning process for the above-mentioned reasons.

What control systems are needed to avoid fraud?

All businesses are accountable and systems need to be put in place to ensure that moneys are accounted for. Systems and procedures are needed so that every transaction will be recorded and all expenditure approved, including payment of invoices, handling of cash, paying of tax and so on. Cash management systems for the day of the event are often lacking and it is not uncommon for registers to be left open, for staff to take handfuls of change without substituting notes and for bags of cash to be left lying around. This is clearly unsatisfactory.

How will legal and taxation obligations be met?

Employing the services of a properly qualified accountant will ensure that your organisation maintains accurate records and meets its legal obligations.

THE BUDGET

Preparing a budget is part of the initial planning stage. A budget includes projected revenue and expenditure from which an estimate of the net profit (or sometimes net loss) from the proposed event can be ascertained. It is a plan based on accurate quotes from all contractors and suppliers and careful research to ensure that no expenses have been overlooked. It provides guidelines for approving expenditure and ensuring that the financial aspects of the event remain on track. The budget is part of the event proposal or the basis of the quote by the event management company to the client.

Several sample budgets are provided in Figs 7.1 to 7.4. As you will see, they vary considerably in the number of expense and revenue items, though the general principles remain the same. Note the differences between fixed costs (these do not alter) and variable costs (these vary in accordance with the size of the event audience).

Management fees

In many cases, an event organiser charges a management fee to oversee an event. As a ballpark figure for planning purposes, this is generally in the region of 10–15 per cent of total costs. While an event might have a low budget, it might still require considerable time and effort in its organisation and the lower end of the range, 10 per cent, would simply not cover management costs.

Prior to contracts being signed, the event organiser should work out the tasks involved in the event, allocate staff to the various roles and determine their pay rates in order to come up with a more accurate estimate of management costs and therefore the management fee to be charged. In some situations, the event organiser might wish to involve themselves in a collaborative entrepreneurial arrangement with the client whereby the management fee is based on income earned or sponsorship raised.

If a management fee is charged, the client is usually responsible for all pre-event payments to venues and subcontractors. The fee is for the management and co-ordination of the event by the event organisers, and for their expertise, from concept through to execution.

Contingencies

Most event budgets include a contingency for unexpected expenses. This ranges from 5 per cent of the costs (if the event organiser is confident that the costs are controllable) to 10 per cent (if there are a number of unknown variables or the costs are uncertain).

Fig. 7.1
Budget items for themed dinner.

Fixed Costs

Band

Dancers

MC

Fig. 7.1 CONTINUED

Stage crew
Costumes
Theme
    Decoration
    Sashes
Signage
    Entrance
Graphics
    Anlmation logo
Artwork and printing
    200 programs
Lighting
Sound
Vision
    Rear projection
    4.2 x 3 m screen
    Data projection
Freight and travel
Labour
    Set-up
    Dismantle
Management fee
    Creation, production, supervision
    Management of evening

Total fixed costs

Variable Costs (based on 200 guests/pax)

Table decoration, say 21	@ $	
Food	@ $	per head
Beverage	@ $	per head
Band/entertainer meals 15	@ $	per head

Total Variable Costs

Contingency
Plus 10% GST

GRAND TOTAL

Reproduced with permission of Events Unlimited.

Fig. 7.2

Budget items for outdoor running event.

INCOME (inc. GST)

Entry — corporate 40 @ $

Stall rental

Merchandising

Raffle

Entry donation

Other donations

Total Income (inc. GST)

EXPENDITURE
Fixed Costs
Hire

Structures

50 team marquees 6 x 6 m (30 pax)

5 fete stalls (food)

3 fete stalls (merchandising)

1 officials structure (6 x 6 m)

6 marshall/official posts

1 children's marquee

50 m synthetic grass

Allowance for under panels for grass

Ticket barrel

3 flag poles

Glassware (4000 @ $0.25)

3 trestle tables

2 urns

5000 paper cups

Cartage

1 information booth 4.8 x 2.4 m

1 site office 6 x 2.4 m

Toilets

20 dual sex toilets — GP and runners

1 disabled toilet

Service attendants

5 hand basins

Equipment

Stage 6 x 3 m, 6 x 0.3 m

Stage roof 6 x 3 m

Fig. 7.2 CONTINUED

Lectern

850 metal racks

150 witches' hats

10 rolls safety marking tape

Cartage

3 x 9.5 cu m coolrooms — VIPs and runners

Govt Stamp Duty @ 2%

Control

Scoreboard

Scoreboard production

Timekeeping

Hire of PC and equipment

500 coded wristbands

Hire of 2 bar code readers

10 radio sets

4 phone lines

50 x 10 prs team numbers

70 marshalls/officials bibs @ $11

PA system for stage and area

Start/finish hooter gas

1 winner's shields @ $110

10 winners' medals with ribbon

500 competitors' medals with ribbon

Staff

MC/announcer

Security

20 control/carpark

Labour, set-up/pull-down

50 marshalls/race officials, incl. relief

St John's first aid

Photographer

Logistics

Garbage bins

Cleaning up and garbage removal

Power

Water

Transport/cartage

AJC staff

Fig. 7.2 CONTINUED

Promotion

    Printing

    Design/artwork

    500 entry forms

    10,000 flyers

    2000 programs

    50 corporate prospectus

    50 competitors' entry kit preparation

    Stationery

    1500 'show bags'

    Signage

    2 banners 6 x 3 m

    20 directional signs

    5 sponsor marquee signs

    50 team names for tents

    Advertising

    Marketing

    Media Launch

Administration

    Couriers, postage

    Phone, fax, email

    Insurance: 3rd party, property, volunteer

    Council permit

    Alcohol licence

    Children's amusements

    Raffle prizes

Management fee

    For collection of team monies and database management; media co-ord; production; co-ord and running of event, including budget

Total Fixed Costs

Variable Costs (based on 40 teams)

Food and beverage

    Catering 1200 @ $

Fig. 7.2 CONTINUED

Buffet tables set-up
Beverage (4 hr package) 1200 @ $
Waiting staff 40 @ $
Health drink for athletes
Health food for athletes

Total Variable Costs

Contingency

Sub-total

10% GST

TOTAL EXPENDITURE

PROFIT

Reproduced with permission of Events Unlimited.

Fig. 7.3

Budget items for exhibition.

Fixed Costs

Venue hire
Costs included in hire budget
Signage
Directional
Large banner with rotating globe
National flags x 32
Lighting
On banners, globe and flags
Name tags
Exhibitors 300 @ $
Visitors other than delegates 500 @ $
Welcome display
Estimate: operates as reception and info desk
Exhibitor manual
Placed on website
Preparation of Intranet site info

Fig. 7.3 CONTINUED

Marketing

    To previous showcase exhibitors

    Promotion to new database in conjunction with promo

Set-up/dismantle

    Incl. scissor lift hire

Exhibition function

    Wine and cheese evening sponsored by

On-site staff

    14 @ $

Public Liability Insurance

    Included in general event insurance

Printing

    Exhibitor manual — 100 copies

    Exhibitor guide — 1000 copies

    Exhibitor lists and floor plan, large layouts

Miscellaneous

    Consumables

    Estimate: postage, phone, email, courier fees, etc

    Storage area

    Internet cafe — stand only with furniture

    Internet cafe — IT equipment

    Internet cafe — coffee bar estimate incl. espresso machine

    Additional supervision/security 36 hrs @ $

    Cost of stand

    Travel, accom. for exhibition and attendance at 8 meetings

Management Fee

Total Fixed Costs

Variable Costs (based on 20 stands)

Shell construction

    6 x 6 m stand per concept description @ $

Catering

    2 days x 6 pax per stand @ $

Total Variable Costs

Contingency

10% GST

TOTAL COSTS

Fig. 7.4

Budget items for music event.

Fixed Costs

Venue hire

Artists

    Speaker

    Actor/scriptwriter

    Singer/composer

    Choreographer

    Technical director

    Set designer

    Make-up designer

    Props designer

Production Team

    Stage manager

    Asst stage manager

    Asst technical

Costumes

    T-shirts @ $ (+10% extreme sizes)

Sound

    Copyright

    Hire

Lights

Vision (for presentation and speaker)

    Based on powerpoint presentation and video

    Preparation of visuals

Staging

    Preparation of production detail

    Set backdrop, paints etc.

    Props materials

    Expendables

    Posters for theatre x 6

    Props

    Laptop and printer

Printing

    Individual group labels

    Invitations

    Programmes — shell plus insert

    Reviews

Onsite staff (catering)

Other hire (catering)

Gifts

Photography (digital camera)

Fig. 7.4 CONTINUED

Video recording

    Video camera hire

    Tapes

Set-up/dismantle

Freight

Airfares

    SYD-AKL return x 1

    SYD-AKL return x 1 (bus.class)

    SYD-MEL return x 5 @ $

Transfers

    Airport

    Coach — Hotel-theatre-hotel

    Coach — Office-theatre-office

    Coach — Airport-theatre-hotel

Accommodation and meals

    AKL 2 x 2 days

    MEL 4 x 2 days, 1 x 1 day

Miscellaneous

    Phone, fax, courier estimate

Contingency

Management fee

Total Fixed Costs

Variable Costs

Catering

Coffee on arrival	@ $	
Morning tea with muffins	@ $	
Lunch — working type	@ $	
Afternoon tea	@ $	
Pre-show canapé and buffet dinner	@ $	
Beverage	@ $	
Total	$	per head
Breakfast for interstate arrivals 15	@ $	

Total Variable Costs

Total Each Location

10% GST

GRAND TOTAL

BREAK-EVEN POINT

To work out the break-even point, the event organiser has to estimate the number of tickets that need to be sold in order to meet expenses (see Fig. 7.5). These expenses include both fixed costs and variable costs. Fixed costs, such as licensing fees, insurance, administrative costs, rent of office space, advertising costs and fees paid to artists, generally do not vary if the size of the event audience increases and are often called overheads. Variable costs increase as the size of the audience increases. If food and beverage were part of, say, a conference package, clearly these costs would escalate if the numbers attending the conference increased. Once the total revenue is the same as the total expenditure (fixed and variable) then break-even point has been reached. Beyond it, the event is profitable.

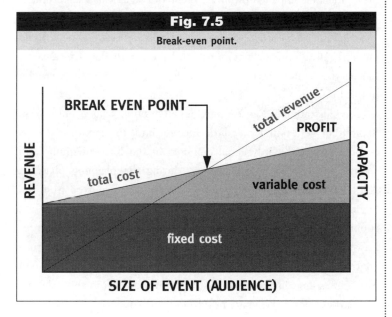

Fig. 7.5
Break-even point.

In the case of an exhibition, the organiser would be using the budget to establish how many exhibitors were needed to break even. The price charged for exhibiting could clearly be quite low if there were a lot of exhibitors; the price charged would have to be high if there were few exhibitors and if the aim were to meet the budget (particularly for fixed costs). However, this is not an altogether feasible way of setting prices or fees since there is a maximum price the market will bear and a minimum level at which the event becomes viable. This iterative process of analysing ticket prices or fees charged and the break-even point is part of the financial decision-making process.

CASH FLOW ANALYSIS

Capital is required to set up any business and even more so in the event business as the planning phase can be quite long and the period for capturing revenue very short. For example, an event team may spend a year planning an event during which period costs will be incurred, all of which have to be paid long before there is an opportunity to recoup any money. Having spent a year planning, it is possible that tickets will be sold at the venue and all revenue will be collected on the one day. This is in contrast to an everyday business where there is a more even cash flow.

In instances where the client is paying for the event, a deposit is generally negotiated. However, payment of the balance may not be paid to the event management company until at least a month after the event. Ideally, complete upfront payment, or a significant establishment fee, should be negotiated to alleviate cash flow problems.

In summary, monthly expenses and projected revenue need to be entered into a spreadsheet to establish how cash flow can best be managed. A funding crisis, just days before an event, is not uncommon in this industry.

The illustration in Fig. 7.6 provides an example of an event held in September generating very little income until the month and days before the event. Only small amounts in the form of grants and sponsorships are shown as income during the planning phase in April, May and June. Meanwhile, expenses were incurred from the beginning of the planning process, peaking in July and August when suppliers were becoming demanding. Expenses include salaries for staff, office expenses, deposits and up-front payments to sub-contractors for catering and equipment hire. The gap between expenditure and income is the cash shortfall, which in this example was particularly problematic in July and August.

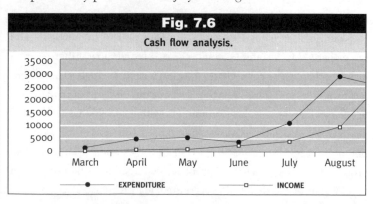

Fig. 7.6

Cash flow analysis.

PROFIT AND LOSS STATEMENT

This is a list of an organisation's revenue, expenditure and net profit (or net loss) for a specific period. In many cases the profit and loss statement (or income statement) is prepared after the event.

In a perfect world, the profit and loss statement would match the budget. The budget is the plan, and if everything went to plan this would be reflected in the profit and loss statement. In the event industry, the budget is generally prepared before the event and the profit and loss statement afterwards, while in most ongoing business operations, budgets and profit and loss statements are done regularly and routinely. In an event management company, a profit and loss statement would be done for each event, as well as for the ongoing concern, the company itself. Alternatively, each event could be shown as a different cost centre.

On the profit and loss statement, the most important source of revenue, such as sales of tickets, appears as the first item. If the event is paid for by a single client, this will be the first item as it is the predominant source of revenue. **Gross revenue** is the total revenue before any costs have been deducted. This is a similar concept to gross (not unpleasant) wages, the amount you would receive if there weren't all sorts of deductions such as tax, superannuation and the like before it reached your pocket.

If you deduct the **cost of goods sold** (also known as direct costs) from the gross revenue, you get the **gross profit**. If the gross revenue from an event were $750,000 and direct costs of $520,000 were deducted, this would result in a gross profit of $230,000. Cost of goods sold are those which relate directly to the revenue earned. They could include cost of venue hire, labour and equipment rental. After calculating the gross profit, you would then deduct your **overhead costs**, such as administration costs and rent, of $165,000 and you would be left with an **operating profit** of $65,000. Finally, your **net profit** is your profit after all other costs and tax have been deducted, in this case $41,000. This is illustrated in Fig. 7.7 on the following page.

BALANCE SHEET

While the profit and loss statement captures results for a given period, such as a financial year, the balance sheet gives you an idea of what a business is worth at a certain point in time. Where the owners of the

Fig. 7.7	
Profit and loss statement.	

Profit and Loss Statement as at 30 June 2001

Gross revenue	$750,000.00	
Less cost of goods sold	$520,000.00	
Gross profit		**$230,000.00**
Less adminstrative and other overhead costs	$165,000.00	
Operating profit		**$65,000.00**
Less other income expenses (such as interest)	$6,000.00	
Profit before tax		$59,000.00
Less tax	$18,000.00	
Net profit for the year/event		**$41,000.00**

business have acquired assets, such as sound and lighting equipment, this becomes very relevant. Likewise if there were outstanding bills to be paid. The balance sheet shows what the result would be if all bills were paid and everything were sold (the assets minus the liabilities). This result is the owner's equity in the business. The problem for many event management companies is that their assets, such as their reputation, are intangible!

FINANCIAL CONTROL SYSTEMS

All purchases must be approved and usually a requisition form is used for this purpose. This means that the manager has the opportunity to approve costs incurred by employees. Once goods are ordered, or services provided, checks must be made that they meet specifications before the bills are paid. Fraud could occur if an employee had authority to make purchases, record and physically handle the goods, and pay the bills. This is why these roles are usually carried out by different people. In any case, the system should have checks and balances to make sure that:

- purchases or other expenses are approved
- goods and services meet specifications
- payment is approved
- accounts are paid
- incoming revenue is checked and banked

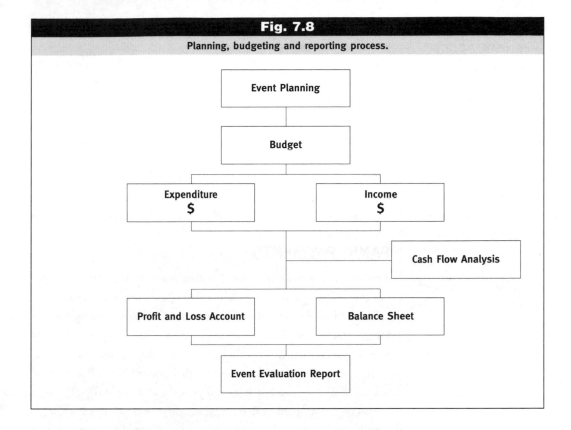

Fig. 7.8

Planning, budgeting and reporting process.

- revenue totals are recorded correctly
- debts are met
- all transactions are recorded and balanced
- taxation requirements are met
- financial matters are correctly reported to stakeholders.

The following article quoting Leo Schofield illustrates the Sydney Festival's aim of making a profit on box office events while ensuring that free outdoor events were well attended. This is a good example of a major event with several objectives which was successfully staged and financially well managed.

Thrilled by the festival's success, Mr Schofield yesterday said it had exceeded the $2 million box office target 'handsomely'. The number of people attending the festival had also been 'an extraordinary' success, he said. The surplus would be in addition to $500,000 which had been put aside as a 'war chest' to ensure future festivals were in good financial shape.

'When I came to the festival it was $500,000 in the red and I'm leaving it the same amount in the black,' Mr Schofield said. 'This year we have done a significantly impressive box office … enormous considering the range, and in the end I'm a subscriber to the view that every artistic decision is a financial one. We've had no event falling below the projected box office.'

'The big free outdoor events characterising the festival this year have been stronger than they have ever been.' Symphony in the Domain, always popular, had drawn 120,000 last weekend while Jazz in the Domain attracted 105,000 people earlier in the festival.

DAILY TELEGRAPH, 24 JANUARY 2001

PANIC PAYMENTS

This unusual accounting term is not exclusive to the event industry, but this industry is one in which inflated panic prices are often paid. In an ideal world, the event manager has all quotes sewn up and the budget locked in long before the event. There should be few unforeseen contingencies — but don't forget this line in your budgets!

In reality, Murphy's law dictates that something will always go wrong. And the closer it is to the event, the more difficult it is to negotiate a reasonable price for what you require to put it right. In fact, if it is a last-minute crisis, it could easily lead to a price with a high premium — a panic payment. Essentially, the supplier has the event manager over a barrel. Careful planning and detailed contracts negotiated well in advance can prevent this situation occurring.

Case study

Your event business, Rave Reviews, has the opportunity to quote for two major parties. Having experienced some financial difficulties in your first year of operation, you want to ensure that you choose the most feasible of these for which to prepare a proposal and produce the winning quote.

The first party is for a top celebrity and will be held at her waterside mansion. The party will be outdoors and the brief is to transform the garden through the use of a spectacular theme. The party will be attended by 350 guests and a lavish dinner is expected.

The second party is much larger, as 500–600 people will be invited. The company is giving the party to celebrate its 50th year of tractor and farming equipment operations. The party will be held in a large airport hangar in the country. Food will be pretty basic and alcohol will be very plentiful. Décor is not important, but entertainment is.

Discuss which of these two events you would choose in terms of its ease of financial management and its potential profitability.

Activity

Prepare a budget for the promotion of a local fundraising event. You can use any number of promotional strategies, including various forms of advertising. Make sure you include the time taken to prepare the communication messages and designs for these materials. In the case of brochures, there may be print costs as well as distribution costs. Your budget should comprehensively cover all activities and expenses associated with promotion, including any salaries or wages involved.

SUMMARY

This chapter has covered the important subject of financial management. We have learnt that the budget developed prior to an event must anticipate all revenue and expenditure and that steps should be taken to finalise contracts as early as possible to ensure that expenses do not exceed budget forecasts. The event manager also needs to take into account the cash flow situation in the lead-up to an event since most expenses occur early in the planning process while the bulk of the revenue is generally collected close to, or during, the event. We have touched on profit and loss statements and balance sheets and have emphasised the importance of financial control systems for managing expenditure and revenue from sales. Reporting systems need to be in place so that complete and accurate records are available for the final post-event report.

CHAPTER EIGHT

risk
management

On completion of this chapter you will be able to:

- **identify the risks associated with an event**
- **assess the risks and prioritise the risks**
- **manage the risks by prevention or contingency planning**
- **develop a risk management plan.**

Exhibition Park in Canberra is where street machine enthusiasts meet, display and strut their mechanical stuff. It's the place to find the most highly customised, modified and faithfully restored cars from early model street machines through to the cutting edge, late model, 'techno' cars.

Exhibition Park offers the opportunity to cruise the kilometres of roadways, and stretch performance to the maximum, in the outrageous Burnout and Go-Whoa competitions on the world's first and only purpose-built burnout facility. Entrants' cars, tortured on the Chassis Dyno, search for the Summernats Horsepower Hero, while grass driving events provide the stage to demonstrate those proudly held driving abilities.

The Top 80 Show, Car Audio Sound Off, and Miss Summernats combine with entertainment and displays to bring Exhibition Park to life with a high-spirited, automotive, New Year atmosphere.

SUMMERNATS CAR FESTIVAL

While not everyone's choice of event, this car festival is extremely popular, attracting a crowd of enthusiastic rev heads to the world's only purpose-built burn-out facility. This crowd has been described as high spirited, so the organisers insist on the following rules in an effort to minimise risk: no alcohol to be brought in; no glass bottles; no pets; no fireworks; no weapons; and no illegal drugs.

All event organisers face a range of risks, and in this chapter we will look at ways in which these risks can be identified, analysed, prioritised, minimised and monitored. Firstly, however, it is essential to define risk management.

Risk is the chance that something will go wrong. Event organisers often think of risk in terms of safety and security, but risk is much broader than that. It may include a cash flow crisis, a staff strike, poor publicity or, of course, bad weather. The last of these is the event manager's greatest risk. Even if it does not have a direct impact on the event, poor weather will reduce the number of people attending an event unless adequate weather protection is provided. Rainy or stormy weather also has an impact on people's mood and motivation, making it a serious concern for which careful planning is required. **Risk management is the process of identifying such risks, assessing these risks and managing these risks**.

In the case of the Summernats Car Festival, the potential for bad crowd behaviour, and the negative publicity that could result, is no doubt the reason for the organisers establishing such strict rules of entry to this event. The organisers, in this instance, have adopted a risk prevention strategy. At a broader level, any negative behaviour and publicity could have a negative impact on the profile of Canberra, where the festival is held, as an event destination.

The following risks need to be considered if relevant to the event you are planning.

Natural disasters

Heavy rain is a disaster for an outdoor event, as too are hail, snow and extreme heat. Flooding can affect event venues, particularly temporary ones, and it can also cause damage to electrical wiring — potentially a very serious risk. Of course, fire is one of the risks most venue managers fear, and must plan for, since evacuation of large crowds is extremely difficult.

Financial risk

Financial risk may involve unforeseen costs, lower than expected revenue, high exchange rates, general decline in economic circum-stances and disposable income, fraud, fines and cash flow problems.

Legal risk

Legal risks include disputes over contracts between the event organiser and the client and/or between the event organiser and a subcontractor. These can occur if expectations are unrealistic or if a gap develops between what the client had in mind and the product the event organiser can produce for the price negotiated. Disputes can also occur if the venue hired does not meet the required standards in terms of such things as reliable electricity supply and suitable access for delivery vehicles. Breach of legal requirements is another form of legal risk, an example being a venue losing its liquor licence for a violation of the liquor laws, such as selling alcohol to under-age drinkers.

Technology-related risks

Technological failure is an increasing risk for high-profile events that are extremely reliant on computer programming and computer networks operating successfully. For example, a problem with guest registration at a trade exhibition would prevent the successful capture of attendee data, which is essential information for all stall holders. For the exhibition organiser, the attendance list (generated during registration) is their most valuable asset. It would be made available to current exhibitors wanting to follow up contacts, as well as being used by the event organiser in the advertising drive for the next event of a similar nature.

New Year's Eve fireworks displays are probably one of the events that are most reliant on highly sophisticated technology. No doubt the pyrotechnics planners for the New Year's Eve fireworks in Sydney on 31 December 1999 had any number of back-up systems for the Y2K situation which could have left Sydney in darkness. This event attracted a worldwide audience, not only for the fireworks but also because it was thought that Australia might be the first to feel the effects of Y2K.

Technology-related risks of this magnitude are of increasing concern for the event management team.

Mismanagement

A successful event requires good management, detailed planning and sound interpersonal relationships at all levels. Mismanagement can prevent an event reaching its objectives so, too, can people-related problems, such as disputes at the top management levels, leading to the dismissal of key personnel. Both are potentially serious risks.

Safety and security risk

Accidents, riots, terrorism and sabotage are all safety and security risks. Safety and security measures will be described in Chapter 15 in more detail.

Bike races carry risk both for the competitors and the audience.

Risk at sporting events

While the risks associated with most community, commercial and entertainment events are largely financial, with sporting events there is the additional risk of danger to the sports men and women involved and, in some cases, to the audience. For example, most bike and car races carry the risk of injury to both drivers and spectators, whether on the track or off-road. Bike races and even fun runs, such as the City to Surf held annually in Sydney, generally experience a number of medical emergencies and the occasional fatal heart attack. The challenge for organisers of such events is to reduce risk to an acceptable level by careful planning and by introducing new procedures and technologies where available, as safety standards change over time. Working out the safety standards for a particular sporting event at a particular time involves looking at a number of factors:

- perceived level of acceptable risk of participants and audience
- current legislation and legal precedents

- availability of risk management solutions
- development and implementation of plans, procedures and control mechanisms.

The last of these is extremely important for event organisers, for if they can show that their procedures for managing risk were well considered and well implemented, this would stand them in good stead if a charge of negligence were laid.

From the following interview with Mr Max Mosley, President of the Federation Internationale de l'Automobile (FIA), reported on the Australian Grand Prix website, it is evident that the issue of risk is always on the agenda for the organisers of this race and that change is something that they have to deal with.

Q: *Just going back to safety quickly … a couple of issues, separate, but possibly disastrous if combined. There are suggestions a number of teams have failed crash tests. That is the first part. The second part is: almost a quarter of the field will be made up of rookies this year. Are they concerns for you?*

Mosley: *The crash tests, that's very worrying for the team concerned, because when they fail, they have to do it again. But what is happening is that the teams want to build the chassis as light as they possibly can, but still pass the crash tests, and sometimes they overdo the lightness and then they have to strengthen it and come back and do the tests again. Inconvenient for them, but it isn't really an issue for us. The question of the rookies is always a slight problem, but don't forget that the great majority of these people have a huge fund of experience in other forms of racing, so it shouldn't present a problem. But inevitably, in any sport, you're going to have new people coming in all the time and at this level in Formula One we do have the safeguard of the lower formulae. But it is a process which is bound to happen and I think the experienced drivers will take account of this, and I hope the rookies will be very careful.*

Another important risk issue for sporting event organisers concerns temporary fencing and seating. Recently, a theatre company was fined $40,000 for two breaches of the Occupational Health and Safety Act because a temporary seating stand collapsed at a play resulting in four people being hospitalised. According to *Workcover*

News, Issue 16, the judge determined that the theatre company had not obtained a report from a structural engineer and had not taken steps to ensure that correct safety standards had been met.

This sporting venue is well designed, not only for the comfort and convenience of the audience and the sportspeople, but also for the excellent facilities provided for the organisers and contractors. First-class facilities help to improve safety.

PROCESS OF RISK MANAGEMENT

Risk management involves a three-step process:

1 Identify risks and hazards.
2 Assess the risks and hazards.
3 Manage the risks and hazards.

This process allows the event organiser to establish and prioritise the risks, to take steps to prevent problems occurring and to make contingency plans if problems do occur.

Identifying risks and hazards

The first step is identifying the risk or hazard and ascertaining when and how a problem might occur. It is important to view risks broadly, in terms of the risk factors listed at the beginning of this chapter. The next step is to analyse the likelihood of problems arising, as well as the resulting consequences. As an example, mismanagement by a senior staff member, such as the person responsible for sponsorship, could have dire financial repercussions; on the other hand, poor performance by a junior member of the event team could probably be managed and resolved without serious consequence.

In terms of hazards that represent potential risk, these include:

- fire
- plant and equipment
- hazardous substances

- electrical equipment
- spills
- stacking of unbalanced heavy items
- temporary fencing, staging, seating and other venue features
- moving vehicles.

Brainstorming by the event management team will help enormously in identifying potential risks. Research of written material and website information, such as current leglislative requirements, as well as conversations with organisers and managers of similar events will also contribute to a detailed list of possible problems. For major events, a risk management consultant is recommended.

Assessing the risks and hazards

Once potential risks and hazards have been identified, their likelihood of occurring needs to be evaluated. This allows the team to prioritise the issues for attention. It is a good idea to set up a committee to manage risk, safety and security issues, and to establish operational guidelines for operating equipment, testing schedules and the like. The following questions need to be asked (you might wish to consider heavy rain as an example of a risk factor when looking at each of these questions):

- What is the likelihood of this happening?
- Who will be exposed to the risk?
- What impact has this risk had in similar circumstances?
- How will people react to this risk/hazard?

With hazards that might pose a risk to health and safety, the following three classifications are recommended:

Class A hazard This has the potential to cause death, serious injury, or permanent disability or illness.

Class B hazard This has the potential to cause illness or time off work.

Class C hazard The resulting injury or illness will require first aid.

While this classification refers mainly to injury, the principle of looking at potential consequences is well illustrated. The potential consequences of fire, flooding, bombs and computer failure can be evaluated in the same way.

Managing the risks and hazards

Once the risks and hazards have been prioritised, the final step is to look at the most effective ways of managing them. Control measures include:

1 Elimination plans to eliminate the risk altogether (for example, erecting covered walkways to protect spectators from rain).

2 Substitution plans (such as looking for a better designed grandstand).

3 Isolation plans (for example, isolating dangerous or noisy equipment).

4 Engineering controls (for example, using safety barriers and fences to limit access and control crowds).

5 Administrative controls (for example, erecting warning signs and training staff well in procedures).

6 Contingency plans (for example, developing evacuation plans for situations where risk cannot be completely avoided).

Here, fencing has been erected to limit access to machinery and equipment.

INCIDENT REPORTING

Incident reporting is an important risk control process, and it is essential that every member of the event team is familiar with this process. An incident report card similar to the one included in Fig. 8.1 on the next page should be completed for every problem that occurs, from customer complaints to slips and falls. On receipt of the incident report cards, management staff can look for patterns in the incidents and ways in which these risks can be better managed.

There are several reasons for maintaining all documentation relating to risk:

• to demonstrate that an appropriate process was in place
• to provide a record of incidents and responses
• to allow for monitoring, review and improvement.

Fig. 8.1

Sample incident report card.

INCIDENT REPORT CARD

Time

Date

FUNCTIONAL AREA/DEPARTMENT

YOUR POSITION

YOUR NAME

NAMES OF PERSON/S INVOLVED IN THE INCIDENT

CONTACT DETAILS OF PERSON/S INVOLVED IN THE INCIDENT

NAME AND CONTACT DETAILS OF WITNESS/ES IF ANY

INCIDENT DETAILS

TIME OF INCIDENT

LOCATION OF INCIDENT

CAUSE OF INCIDENT

CONSEQUENCES OF INCIDENT

CAN ANY ACTION BE TAKEN TO PREVENT REOCCURRENCE?

DATE AND TIME RECEIVED AND LOGGED

OUTSTANDING ACTIONS

The results of such an approach include:

- reduction in problems, accidents and incidents
- improved legislative compliance
- decrease in potential liability
- improved workplace performance
- customer satisfaction
- avoidance of controversial issues and negative media exposure.

EMERGENCY RESPONSE PLANS

Every event or venue should have an emergency response plan. This is usually referred to by the acronym ERP or in some cases VERP (venue response plan). It is usually developed in conjunction with professional consultants who also train staff on procedures, such as evacuation, and the roles of everyone involved. This plan will be discussed in more detail in Chapter 16, 'Crowd Management and Evacuation'.

An example of a simple risk management plan is shown in Fig. 8.2. This plan shows the risks anticipated by the the event organiser, the potential impact of such risks, and management strategies and contingency plans put in place to control them.

Fig. 8.2

Risk management plan.

Priority	Identification: Nature of Risk	Assessment: Impact of Risk	Management: Control	Management: Contingency Planning
1	Weather: rain or extreme heat	Rain will result in poor attendance and low on-site sales; problems with queuing; potential electrical and other equipment failure.	Monitor weather reports. Provide cover (also at entrance) for spectators. Needs to be part of event promotional material. Electrical hazards must be avoided through careful planning, competent subcontractors, control systems for safety and continuous supply.	Roving staff sell ponchos if it is wet, or drinks and water if it is very hot. Provide staff with free wet weather gear or water, as appropriate. Establish task force to maintain electrical supply and back-up systems.
2	Fire and evacuation	Impact would be extremely serious, however risk is not high due to venue design.	Establish VERP. Continuously monitor and control, using checklists (e.g. fire equipment, access and exits). Staff training.	VERP to identify clear communication with emergency services. Senior staff appropriately deployed.

Fig. 8.2 CONTINUED

Risk management plan.

Priority	Identification: Nature of Risk	Assessment: Impact of Risk	Management: Control	Management: Contingency Planning
3	Crowd control	Biggest potential impact is on entry to venue due to transport delays.	Use promotional material and ticketing process to advise audience on transport and parking. Provide ushers, signage and crowd control barriers to avoid congestion.	Ticketed patrons to be allowed into the venue once game has started without ticket checking through turnstiles. Senior staff deployed to deal with resulting problems of gate-crashers.
4	Financial management	Financial failure for event organiser, bankruptcy, breach of contract.	Financial control systems: limited authority for purchasing and expenditure. Contract and cash flow management by finance committee. Control of ticket revenue and revenue from programs and catering. Security provided for transporting cash. Staff training on procedures.	Limited. Short-term money market. Sponsorship and VIPs.
5	Staff management	Poor staff selection and training which would have impact on level of service and satisfaction. Impact on event ambience.	Development of job descriptions and specifications, recruitment drive, training and support materials provided. Leadership and control systems training for supervisors. Performance appraisal system for senior staff. Policies and procedures for staffing, performance management, dismissal, health and safety.	Agency staff. Pay for volunteers. Work experience student group. Loyalty payment on completion. Certificate of participation.
6	Occupational health and safety	Costs of litigation, poor publicity, fines.	Development of policies and procedures to reduce risk as part of workplace practice. This includes the use of licensed subcontractors, fulfilling requirements for equipment maintenance, and building temporary structures that meet required standards. Documentation and regular review, including inspections.	Reporting and documentation system for recording incidents relating to health and safety, including witnesses to any incidents. Emergency response plan. Legal advice.

STANDARDS FOR RISK MANAGEMENT

Both Australia and New Zealand have standards for risk management, AS/NZS 4360:1999 Risk Management, which provide the following definition of risk management.

Risk management is recognised as an integral part of good management practice. It is an iterative process consisting of steps which, when undertaken in sequence, enable continual improvement in decision-making. Risk management is the term applied to a logical and systematic method of identifying, analysing, evaluating, treating, monitoring and communicating risks associated with any activity, function or process in a way that will enable organisations to minimise losses and maximise opportunities. Risk management is as much about identifying opportunities as avoiding or mitigating losses.

You can find further information about these standards from the website at the end of this chapter.

Case study

Conduct a risk management analysis using a table format and appropriate headings (see Fig. 8.2 as an example) for at least two of the following events:

- Outdoor launch of a soft drink product, with entertainment, for a target audience of children aged nine to fourteen.
- Minor/local surf carnival (run, swim, paddle) for all age groups, with a handicapping system based on heat times.
- Wedding ceremony on the beach followed by a reception at the local RSL Club.
- School swimming competition for high school students of the Asia-Pacific region.

Activity

Consider some of the social and legal issues relating to the use and abuse of alcohol and drugs at events. Identify some of the factors that increase the level of this risk for the event organiser. Identify ways in which this risk can be minimised and managed.

SUMMARY

This chapter has looked in detail at some of the risks associated with the staging of events. The weather is often a significant risk as it can reduce attendance, even at indoor events. More serious risks include fire and accidents. Failure of any key system, such as event registration, ticketing, scoring or sound, can have a major impact and can lead ultimately to financial ruin. The development of a risk management plan that anticipates and prioritises all of the major risk factors is essential. With this as a guide, risks can be managed and contingency plans developed to deal with almost every issue that occurs.

Links

http://www.crowdsafe.com (Crowdsafe website)

http://www.bigdayout.com (Big Day Out event)

http://www.airm.org.au/index.cfm?L1=1&L2=30&Item=15 (Australian Institute of Risk Management)

http://203.32.220.220/docushare/dscgi/admin.py/View/Collection-79 (Insurance and Risk Management)

http://www.standards.com.au/catalogue/script/Details.asp?DocN=std s000023835 (Australian and New Zealand Standards for Risk Management)

CHAPTER NINE

planning

Successful event management involves many people undertaking separate tasks in a coordinated manner. In Mosman this involves staff from every section of Council, staff in several other State agencies, staff of companies and clubs, as well as volunteers. Events must be managed in accordance with not only Council's own policies, but also various state laws and regulations.

Only a small portion of this effort is visible to the general public. Even if the event runs smoothly there will be some negative feedback as some degree of inconvenience is inevitable. If the event is poorly managed, however, the impact can be profound with damage to property and to the natural environment, with public safety threatened, and with widespread dissatisfaction by visitors and local residents alike.

MOSMAN MUNICIPAL COUNCIL
SPECIAL EVENT MANAGEMENT OPERATIONS MANUAL

A s this statement from a special event operations manual so clearly illustrates, planning and organisation are the key elements that determine the success of an event. For most event organisers, the first stop is the local council. The local council will provide guidelines on the possible impact of your event, such as the impact of noise. This may be a factor even if your event is not being held at a public venue. Another useful contact is the local tourism office. This office, with links to corporate offices in each state and territory, plays an important part in the strategic management of events and, in many cases, provides support in a number of other ways, such as listing events on their website.

On completion of this chapter you will be able to:

- identify the purpose, aims and objectives of an event
- develop an event proposal or outline
- identify the team and the stakeholders involved in staging an event
- plan the location and layout of an event using maps/illustrations
- use charts and run sheets to develop timelines
- develop management control systems, such as checklists.

Effective planning ensures the provision of all necessary services and amenities at an event.

However, before making these contacts, you need to develop the event concept. As we learnt in Chapter 2, this involves defining the event's purpose and aims, as well as the specific objectives on which the success of the event will be measured. Funding for your event may come from grants or from sponsors, but all stakeholders have to be provided with a good understanding of the event concept before you proceed further. If your client is the one funding the event, the provision of a clearly developed concept, plan and evaluation strategy will generally avoid problems down the line, including legal ones.

DEVELOP A MISSION/PURPOSE STATEMENT

The first step is to develop a simple statement that summarises the purpose or mission of the event. Too often, the purpose of the event becomes less and less clear as the event approaches. Different stakeholders have different interests and this can sometimes lead to a change of focus of which most stakeholders are unaware. The purpose of an event could be, for example, 'to commemorate the history of our town in an historically authentic parade that involves the community and is supported by the community'. In contrast, a sporting event may have as its mission statement 'to attract both loyal team supporters and first-time spectators (potential regulars) in an effort to improve ticket sales and thus the viability of the competition and venue'.

The mission statement should ensure that planning and implementation do not go off the rails and that the initial intent is realised.

ESTABLISH THE AIMS OF THE EVENT

The purpose can be broken down further into general aims and specific measurable objectives. An event could have any one, or more, of the following aims:

- improving community attitudes to health and fitness through participation in sporting activities
- increasing civic pride
- injecting funds into the local economy
- raising funds for a charitable cause
- increasing tourist numbers to a specific destination
- extending the tourist season
- launching a new product
- raising revenue through ticket sales
- providing entertainment
- building team loyalty
- raising the profile of the town or city
- celebrating an historical event
- enhancing the reputation of a convention organiser/venue
- conducting an inspirational ceremony
- providing a unique experience
- increasing product sales
- acknowledging award winners (for example, tourism awards or staff awards)
- producing media coverage
- highlighting the main point of a conference.

Aims vary widely from one event to another, and this is one of the challenges for the event manager. One event might have social impact aims while another might be profit oriented. It cannot be stressed enough that everything to do with the event must reinforce the purpose and the aims. Choice of colours, entertainment, presentations, and so on must all work together in order to fulfil the purpose and aims of the event. A client may arrive at a meeting with an event organiser and say, 'I want a banquet for 200 people with a celebrity entertainer', and it may only emerge through questioning that the aim of the event is to recognise key staff, to present awards and to reinforce success. This is something that must be established early in the negotiation process and remembered during all the planning stages.

The Sydney Gay & Lesbian Mardi Gras is an event with predominantly social impact aims, starting as it did in 1984 as a protest march. Today this event attracts 600,000 spectators to the parade along Oxford Street and more than 1 million viewers on national television. The broadcast was recently sold to a US cable network which reaches 54 million households. In 1998 the Mardi Gras celebrated its twentieth anniversary, 'From Riot to Revolution', with the biggest festival line-up ever. A comprehensive economic impact study of the 1998 Sydney Gay & Lesbian Mardi Gras revealed a total economic impact of $99 million on the city of Sydney. However, while the Mardi Gras may achieve significant economic and tourism impact, this is not its primary aim.

The commitment statement for this event reads as follows:

We are committed to:
- *human rights and social justice*
- *lesbian and gay coalitionism*
- *reconciliation with indigenous Australians (as outlined in the Reconciliation Statement)*
- *excellence and innovation*
- *accessibility and accountability*
- *enabling individuals and groups in the lesbian and gay communities to discover, express and develop their artistic, cultural and political skills and potential*
- *passionately and unashamedly affirming the pride, joy and dignity of gays and lesbians and their diverse communities, and strengthening the lives and rights of gay and lesbian people nationally and internationally.*

In order to maintain our activities and sustain the organisation for the future, we operate as a community business enterprise that is financially responsible and continues to invest in the development of the diverse lesbian and gay communities.

In all our activities we respect equally the participation of our artists, members, staff and volunteers.

In contrast, Canberra's annual Floriade aims to enhance the perception of that city as a tourist destination and to achieve targets for attendance by domestic and international tourists as part of its more specific objectives. In 1999 this event attracted 162,000 visitors, over half of whom came from interstate or overseas.

The aims of an event provide the foundation for many aspects of the planning process. An event organiser who becomes distracted from the stated aims is likely to clash with the organising committee and other stakeholders. When working with clients, it is therefore essential to identify the aims early and to use them to inform the planning process. Too often, enthusiasm for the theme or the entertainment overrides the aims and planning goes awry. If, for example, the aim were to increase consumer recognition of the main sponsor, it would be necessary to develop specific objectives and to take steps to ensure that they were achieved. At the end of the event, there should be one or more measures in place to indicate the outcomes of the event, in this case the results of a survey indicating percentage levels of sponsor recognition by the event audience. As an event manager, you need to show, in a measurable way, how the aims have been achieved. Developing objectives helps you to do this.

ESTABLISH THE OBJECTIVES

The aims are used to develop detailed and specific objectives. Ideally, objectives should be realistic and measurable. Targets, percentages and sales are generally the factors used to measure objectives. As an example, an objective could be 'to increase the participation level in the local community's fun walk to 3,500, including a cross-section of age groups, ranging from 15 to 60 plus, this target to be reached by the 2005 event'. The number of participants and the ages of participants would be measures of this objective, while a survey on training undertaken in preparation for the walk would indicate less tangible outcomes such as changes in community exercise patterns and attitudes towards fitness and health. As a second example, one objective of an event organiser might be to increase awareness of a sponsor's products, whereas the main objective might be to translate this awareness into sales totalling $3 million, which would be an even more successful outcome. Surveys of spectators and television viewers are used to demonstrate changes in awareness of a sponsor's products.

Evaluation of event outcomes will be covered in more detail in Chapter 17. However, evaluation is not possible if the aims and objectives are not clear in the first place.

Objectives are generally evaluated by measures such as:

- size of audience
- demographics (age, country, place of origin, etc.) of audience
- average expenditure of audience
- sponsor recognition levels
- sales of sponsor products
- economic impact of event
- profit.

SMART objectives are specific, measurable, achievable, realistic and time related.

PREPARE AN EVENT PROPOSAL

A complete outline for an event proposal is included in Appendix B. At this stage of event planning, however, the proposal should include the purpose and the aims and objectives of the event, as well as details on organisation, physical layout and the social, environmental and economic impact, if applicable. The relevant headings are shown in the outline included in Fig. 9.1 (opposite). Maps and models are extremely useful in illustrating the event concept and more detailed plans will ensure that the client's expectations are realistic.

MAKE USE OF PLANNING TOOLS

Organisation charts, maps and models, Gantt charts, run sheets and checklists are useful tools for presenting material and information to your clients, members of your staff and stakeholders. These are described and illustrated in the following sections.

Maps and models

Maps are a useful way to represent an event, particularly to contractors who may be required to set up the site. It may be

---

Fig. 9.1

Example of an event proposal in the early planning stage.

EVENT PROPOSAL

EVENT DESCRIPTION

Event name

Event type

Location, suburb and council

Date(s)

Duration/timing

Overview and purpose/concept

Aims and objectives

EVENT MANAGEMENT

Management responsibility

Major stakeholders and agencies

Physical requirements

    Venue

    Route for street events

    Event map

    Event layout (indoor)

Audience

Impact

    Social

    Environmental

    Economic

---

necessary to develop more than one map or plan, using CAD (Computer Assisted Drawing) software, since different parties involved in the event will require this material for different purposes. The various people might include:

- builders and designers
- telecommunications and electrical contractors
- emergency response teams
- spectator services hosts
- artists, entertainers and exhibitors
- event audience.

Models are also extremely useful, as most clients find it difficult to visualise three-dimensional concepts. A model can also assist in many

---

Fig. 9.2

CAD perspective views of an exhibition stand.

Colour presentation   The end product

Reproduced with permission
Exhibition Hire Service, Sydney.

aspects of event management, such as crowd control. In this instance, bottlenecks and other potential problems are likely to emerge from viewing a three-dimensional illustration. Most CAD software can also present the information in this way, allowing the event management team to anticipate all design and implementation issues. Examples of maps and models are illustrated in Figs. 9.2 and 9.3.

Fig. 9.3

Sample map of a sporting stadium.

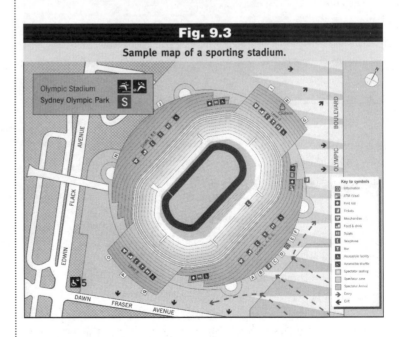

Gantt charts

A Gantt chart is generally used in the **early planning days** and **in the lead-up** to an event. In this type of planning sheet, dates are listed across the top of the chart and rules (or blocks) are used to illustrate how long each task (listed at the side of the chart) will take. The benefit of this type of chart is that the interdependence of the tasks can be clearly seen. For example, once you have plotted the process of recruiting, inducting, training and rostering staff for an event, you may realise that the recruitment process needs to start earlier than expected to enable staff to be completely ready for the big day.

Another aspect of planning is identifying the critical path: those elements of the plan that are essential to the successful outcome of the event and therefore high priority. Critical path analysis is beyond the scope of this text, however the general principle of identifying planning elements on which all else is dependent can be done with a Gantt chart.

In the case of arrangements with sponsors, for example, these need to be finalised before any work can be done on print or promotional material as sponsors need to approve the use of their logos. If one sponsor pulls out of the arrangement, this will have an impact on print production which will, in turn, affect promotional activities and ticket sales.

Project planning software, including specialised event planning software, is available, while for smaller events a spreadsheet is probably sufficient. The trick is to identify the tasks that can be clustered together and to choose the ideal level of detail required in planning the event. At the extreme, the chart can be expanded to a point where even the smallest task is shown (but at this stage it will fill an entire wall and become unmanageable). As with maps, the Gantt chart must be a user-friendly planning tool in order to be effective.

Another point to take into account is that change is an integral part of event planning and it may be necessary to make significant changes that immediately make all your charts redundant. An experienced event manager is able to ascertain the level of planning required to ensure that everyone is clear about their roles and responsibilities, while remaining reasonably open to change.

A high-level planning chart for an event is illustrated in Fig. 9.4 (see over). It provides a broad overview of the main event tasks and a general time-line.

Fig. 9.4

Sample Gantt chart for planning an event.

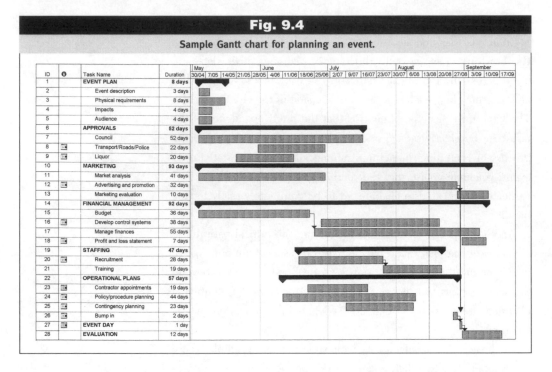

Each of these major tasks could also be used as the basis for a more detailed plan. This has been done in Fig. 9.5, which shows the planning process for recruiting and training staff for the above event. This Gantt chart is clearly an example of a fairly detailed level of planning although, even here, the training aspect is not covered fully as there would be many steps involved, including writing training materials and seeking approval of the content from the various functional area managers.

Fig. 9.5

Sample Gantt chart for planning staffing for an event.

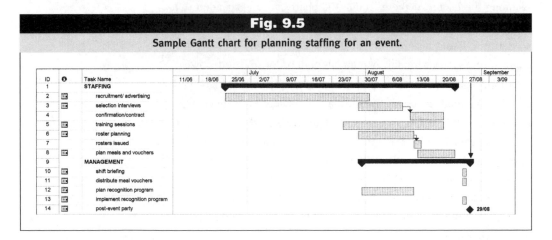

Run sheets

The run sheet is an indispensable tool for most event managers. It is the program, or schedule, of events. In the preliminary stages of planning, the run sheet is quite simple, with times allocated only to specific elements of the event (see the run sheet for a gala dinner in Fig. 9.6). This overview of proceedings forms part of the event concept briefing.

Fig. 9.6
Preliminary run sheet for gala dinner — concept stage.

1900	Guests arrive. Pre-dinner drinks in foyer.
1930	Doors to Royal open. Guests move to tables.
1935	MC welcome.
1940	Entrée served.
2000	First 'Championship' (demonstration dance routine).
2010	Main course served. Band starts playing.
2050	Band stops. Second 'Championship' (demo dance routine). Guests drawn onto dance floor at the end.
2115	Dessert served. Band plays.
2140	Band stops. ABTA Awards Presentation (1 award, with 2 finalists).
2225	Ms & Mr Sparkly awarded. Dancing for guests starts properly.
2355	MC announces final winners (all!) and last dance.
2400	Guests depart.

Reproduced with permission Events Unlimited.

As planning progresses, however, the run sheet becomes even more detailed with, for example, timings for dancers, technicians and other staff. This is illustrated in Fig. 9.7 (see over) where bump-in and bump-out are also shown.

Fig. 9.7

Complete run sheet for gala dinner.

0800	Lay dance floor and stage, and lower vertical drapes.
	Scissor lift ready.
	Audio subcontractor commences bump-in.
	Rear projection screen set.
0900	Dance floor and stage set.
	Stage designer bumps in for stage decoration.
1000	Production meeting.
1100	On-stage set-up commences (audio and video).
1230 (approx)	Band set up.
1430	Technical set-up complete.
	Table set-up can commence.
1500	Technical run-through.
1730	All decorations complete.
1745	Rehearsal with MC and SM (probably walk through with music). Band sound check.
1830	All ready.
1845	External sign ON.
1900-1930	Guests arrive. Pre-dinner drinks in foyer.
1900	Dancers arrive. Walk-through and music check.
1915	Pre-set lighting ON.
1925	Walk-in music ON.
1930	Doors open. Guests move to tables.
	All dancers ready.
1935	MC welcome.
1940	Entrée served.
2000	First 'Championship' (Demonstration dance routine).
2010	Main course served.
	Band starts playing.
2050	Band stops.
	Second 'Championship' (Demo dance routine).
	Guests drawn onto dance floor at the end.

Fig. 9.7 CONTINUED

Complete run sheet for gala dinner.

2115	Dessert enters and is served. Band plays.
2140	Band stops. Awards presentation (1 award, with 2 finalists).
2225	Ms & Mr Sparkly awarded. Dancing for guests starts properly.
2355	MC announces final winners (all!) and last dance.
2400	Guests depart. Bump-out commences.
Tue 0230	All clear.

Reproduced with permission Events Unlimited.

Finally, an even more detailed run sheet can be developed (at this stage called the script) to identify each person's role and cues. This is illustrated below in Fig. 9.8 in which the timing of meal service and the cues for recommencement of the 'championships' after the main course are outlined in detail.

Run sheets are an important tool for all stakeholders and participants, from the venue management team through to the subcontractors.

Fig. 9.8

Script for part of gala dinner.

2010	Main course served.	
As main nearly cleared		MC and dancers stand by. Dance 2 music ready.
When clear 2050	Band stops and exits.	MC mic ON. Band Off. MC spot ON. House down.
	MC: Welcome to our next championship, The Self-Booking Samba. Amazingly the finalists are our previous winners. Please welcome them back.	Vision — Self-Booking Samba. Dance floor ON.
	Dancers run on. (2nd dance routine 10 min). Dancers pause at end.	MC spot OFF. Music 2 On. MC mic OFF. When music 2 finished cue music 3.

Fig. 9.8 CONTINUED

Script for part of gala dinner.

MC: And once again it's a tie, isn't that fantastic!	MC spot ON. MC mic ON.
Now I know that there are some aspiring champions out there who are probably thinking 'I could never do that'! Well our champions have graciously agreed to teach you some of their steps, so come on up and join in...	
MC somehow coaxes people up. When enough on dance floor he cues music with: **OK. Let's dance!** (About 10 minutes dance coaching)	House UP ½.
	Music 3 ON. MC mic OFF. Kitchen advised 10 min to dessert.
At end	Dance music 3 OFF. Cue march in — SB track 14. Kitchen 1 min to dessert.

Reproduced with permission Events Unlimited.

Organisation charts

An organisation chart is another important tool used in planning. Once all tasks have been identified and grouped logically, the staffing requirements for an event become much clearer and can be represented on an organisation chart. This will be described and illustrated more fully in Chapter 12. However, we have illustrated an event committee structure, as an example of an organisation chart, in Fig. 9.9 opposite.

Checklists

At the most detailed level of planning, a checklist is indispensable. It is a control tool which ensures that the individual performing the tasks has not forgotten a single detail. For example, when checking fire-fighting equipment and emergency exits, it is imperative that a specific checklist be followed, and that it be signed and dated on completion. This is part of the record-keeping process, aimed not only at preventing potential problems, but also at reducing the risk of litigation if anything should go wrong. Detailed and correctly implemented plans reassure the client, allow the event team to work

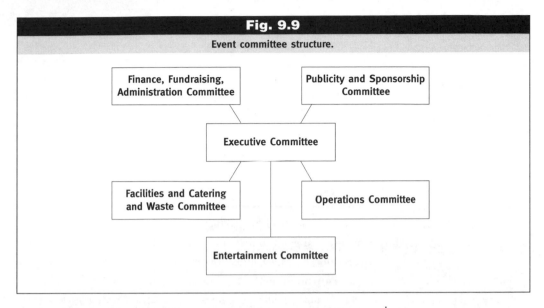

Fig. 9.9
Event committee structure.

Finance, Fundraising, Administration Committee

Publicity and Sponsorship Committee

Executive Committee

Facilities and Catering and Waste Committee

Operations Committee

Entertainment Committee

effectively and build confidence in achieving the objectives of the event. A safety checklist is illustrated in Fig. 9.10.

Fig. 9.10
Daily safety checklist.

DAILY SAFETY CHECKLIST

Name _____ Today's date and time _____

Task	Check ✓ ✗	Comment	Follow up required ✓
First Aid kit fully equipped			
Flammable goods signage correct, storage away from combustible materials			
Extinguisher visible, free of obstruction			
Cleaning products labelled and stored correctly			
All electrical appliances tested and tagged within last six months			
Extension cords tested and tagged within last three months			
Extension cords not presenting a hazard over walkways			
Boxes, rubbish, etc. not obstructing exits or fire-fighting equipment			
Gas cut-off valve visible and not obstructed			

• • • • • • • • • • • • • • •
SUMMARY

In this chapter we have explained the differences between the purpose, the aims and the objectives of an event, and have stressed the importance of these being clearly stated and adhered to. Using maps, diagrams, charts and checklists, the event manager can show how they can be achieved within the allocated time period. Unlike most other projects, deadlines in event management cannot be postponed since the date must be advertised and the event venue booked. The planning tools described and illustrated in this chapter will help to meet these deadlines, particularly as each aspect of an event is generally contingent upon another. Nevertheless, planning needs to remain flexible since this is a very dynamic industry in which change is inevitable.
• • • • • • • • • • • • • • •

The nature of the event business is that most of the time is spent in planning and very little is spent in the execution phase. In fact, it often comes as a shock when the event is over so quickly. Things can go bad in an instant in the event environment but good planning can prevent this happening. In the best cases, the plans have been so thoughtfully developed that the event manager's role is simply to ensure that procedures are correctly implemented, resulting in minimal incidents and satisfied clients.

Case study

As the organiser of a product launch for a prestige motor car company, you need to reassure your client of your capacity to plan a successful event. Develop an **overview** of the event (event concept), a brief **run sheet** and a series of illustrations showing the event and staging layout. Finally, prepare a time-line or **Gantt chart** to show the planning process in the lead-up to the event.

Activity

The concept, 'chain of events', is very relevant to event planning. Review three different types of event (such as a product launch, fete and sporting competition) and identify potential weak links in the planning process that could jeopardise each event if they were not thoroughly considered. For example, the lack of a back-up system for electrical supplies at an outdoor venue could jeopardise the event.

Links

http://www.un.org (United Nations)

http://www.adc.nsw.gov.au (Australia Day Council)

http://www.exhibitionhire.com.au (Exhibition Hire Service, Sydney)

CHAPTER TEN

protocol

The ceremony is a major state function, with the Royals granting an audience at the event, hence certain restrictions regarding the observation of the ceremony are unavoidably necessary. They apply to all persons who are not actual participants in the ceremony. The Royal Household requests the kind co-operation of all visitors to this ceremonial event to observe the following:

- Dress code for international media. Members of the Press are requested to dress in formal business attire with 'Press/Media' accreditation. For men: shirt, jacket and necktie. For ladies: blouse and skirt or dress. (Please refrain from wearing trousers or pants.)
- Photographers must have their cameras and accreditation passes checked by Security at approximately 09:00 am at tent number 19.
- Photographers who are authorised to take photos at the event must be dressed in a business suit with the appropriate press accreditation status. Other unauthorised photographers will be excluded.
- After 11:30 guests and tourists must remain within the tents assigned.
- Photographers are not permitted to walk into or with the procession. Photographing is permitted only from both sides of the procession. Three specific locations with elevated seating have been prepared for photographers at the eastern side of the procession.
- Following the arrival of the Royals at the gala luncheon, guests and individuals without Media accreditation are not permitted

On completion of this chapter you will be able to:

- **explain the concept of protocol**
- **identify protocol associated with a range of events**
- **identify sources of information regarding event protocol**
- **avoid a breach of protocol**
- **use national symbols correctly.**

to take photos. Photographers are allowed to take photos from the designated vantage points.

The above example illustrates the protocol for a Royal ceremonial procession. If VIPs and dignitaries are present at an event, protocol is an important aspect of planning. The formalities outlined below are among those you might be called upon to put in place when managing events.

Rolling out the red carpet is usually associated with formal or ceremonial events.

ORDER OF PRECEDENCE

Outlined in Table 10.1 (opposite) is an abbreviated version of the order of precedence for Australian commonwealth, state and territory dignitaries. Besides these basic requirements, there are additional rules for more complex situations, such as establishing order of precedence based on the date of taking or leaving office. Those dignitaries included range from the Governor-General to ex-ministers of state to those who retain the prefix 'Honourable'.

An event planner would consult the order of precedence in order to make seating and other arrangements, and would also need to contact state or federal government protocol officers for any specific information on protocol. Asher Joel's book, *Australian Protocol and Procedures* (1988), is a very useful reference on this subject.

Table 10.1

Abbreviated order of appearance for commonwealth, state and territory dignitaries.

The Governor-General

The Governor of the State
The Governor of the other States according to their date of appointment
The Administrators of the Northern Territory and Norfolk Island

The Prime Minister

The Premier within his/her own State
The Chief Minister of the Northern Territory and Norfolk Island

The President of the Senate and the Speaker of the House of Representatives according to seniority of appointment

The Chief Justice of Australia

Ambassadors and High Commissioners
Chargés d'affaires en pied or en titre
Chargés d'affaires and acting High Commissioners

Members of the Federal Executive Council under summons

The Administrators of the Northern Territory and Norfolk Island

The Leader of the Opposition

Former Governors-General
Former Prime Ministers
Former Chief Justices of Australia

The Premiers of the States according to the population of their States
Chief Minister of the Northern Territory and Norfolk Island

The Lord Mayor within his/her city

TITLES

Style guides, available in most public libraries, provide guidelines on the correct titles for people such as Prime Ministers ('Right Honourable') and Commonweath Ministers ('Honourable').

Correct titles used in Canada are summarised in Table 10.2 (see over). If high-ranking overseas visitors were attending an event, an event organiser would contact the relevant embassy to obtain information on the table of precedence and the titles to be used.

Table 10.2

Correct titles used in Canada.

1 The Governor General of Canada to be styled 'Right Honourable' for life and to be styled 'His Excellency' and his wife 'Her Excellency', or 'Her Excellency' and her husband 'His Excellency', as the case may be, while in office.

2 The Lieutenant Governor of a Province to be styled 'Honourable' for life and to be styled 'His Honour' and his wife 'Her Honour', or 'Her Honour' and her husband 'His Honour', as the case may be, while in office.

3 The Prime Minister of Canada to be styled 'Right Honourable' for life.

4 The Chief Justice of Canada to be styled 'Right Honourable' for life.

5 Privy Councillors of Canada to be styled 'Honourable' for life.

6 Senators of Canada to be styled 'Honourable' for life.

7 The Speaker of the House of Commons to be styled 'Honourable' while in office.

8 The Commissioner of a Territory to be styled 'Honourable' while in office.

9 Puisne judges of the Supreme Court of Canada and judges of the Federal Court and of the Tax Court of Canada, as well as the judges of the Courts in the Provinces and Territories, to be styled 'Honourable' while in office.

10 Presidents and speakers of Legislative Assemblies of the Provinces and Territories to be styled 'Honourable' while in office.

11 Members of the Executive Councils of the Provinces and Territories to be styled 'Honourable' while in office.

12 Judges of Provincial and Territorial Courts (appointed by the Provincial and Territorial Governments) to be styled 'Honourable' while in office.

13 The following are eligible to be granted permission by the Governor General, in the name of Her Majesty The Queen, to retain the title of 'Honourable' after they have ceased to hold office:

- Speakers of the House of Commons

- Commissioners of Territories

- Judges designated in item 9.

Source: http://www.pch.gc.ca/ceremonial-symb/english/prt_precedence.html

STYLES OF ADDRESS

Styles of address for foreign dignitaries are summarised in Table 10.3. Again, style guides can assist you with this form of protocol, as well as with the correct form of address for the clergy.

Table 10.3
Styles of address for foreign dignitaries.

Dignitary	Salutation	Final Salutation	In conversation
A King/An Emperor	Your Majesty/Sire:	I have the honour to remain, Your Majesty's obedient servant,	'Your Majesty' first, then 'Sire'
A Queen	Your Majesty/Madame:	I have the honour to remain, Your Majesty's obedient servant,	'Your Majesty' first, then 'Ma'am'
A Prince/Princess With title 'Royal Highness'	Your Royal Highness:	I remain, Your Royal Highness, Yours very truly,	'Your Royal Highness' first, then 'Sir/Ma'am'
With title 'Serene Highness'	Your Serene Highness:	I remain, Your Serene Highness, Yours very truly,	'Your Serene Highness' first, then 'Sir/Ma'am'
Without title 'Highness'	Prince:	Yours very truly,	'Prince' first, then 'Sir' 'Princess' first, then 'Madam'
	Madame:	Yours very truly,	
A President of a Republic	Excellency:	Yours sincerely,	'Excellency' first, then 'President' or 'Sir/Madam'
The President of the United States	Dear Mr. President:	Yours sincerely,	'Mr. President' or 'Excellency' first, then 'Sir'
A Prime Minister His/Her Excellency (full name) Prime Minister of (name) Address	Dear Prime Minister:	Yours sincerely,	'Prime Minister' or 'Excellency' first, then 'Sir/Madam' or 'Mr./Mrs./ Ms./Miss (name)'
Ambassadors/High Commissioners of foreign countries	Dear Ambassador/ High Commissioner:	Yours sincerely,	'Your Excellency' or 'Excellency'

Source: http://www.pch.gc.ca/ceremonial-symb/english/prt_precedence.html

DRESS FOR FORMAL OCCASIONS

The appropriate dress for formal occasions should be included on the invitation. This might include morning dress for formal day functions or black tie (or sometimes white) for formal evening events. Protocol also needs to be observed as to the correct insignia to be worn at ceremonial events.

PROTOCOL FOR SPEAKERS

Speakers need to be briefed in advance and provided with a list of the guests to be welcomed, in order of precedence. The timing and length of speeches needs to be discussed with the speakers before the event and must also be canvassed with the chef so that food production coincides with the event plan and speakers are not disturbed by food service or clearing of plates.

SEATING PLANS FOR FORMAL OCCASIONS

Correct seating arrangements for occasions such as awards ceremonies and formal dinners must be observed by the event organiser. The guest of honour always sits at the right of the host unless the Governor-General or Governor is present, in which case, the guest of honour sits at the left of the host. If other government dignitaries are present, the table of precedence outline in Table 10.1 is then followed.

The seating plan illustrated in Fig. 10.1 is designed for an event at which all dignitaries are male and accompanied by their spouses. If some of the dignitaries are female, or some are unaccompanied, this adds to the level of difficulty in planning the seating. In general terms, those with higher rank sit closer to the official party, and the guest of honour sits at the right of the host. As mentioned above, protocol officers based at federal and state government level are an invaluable source of information, as are their counterparts in other countries.

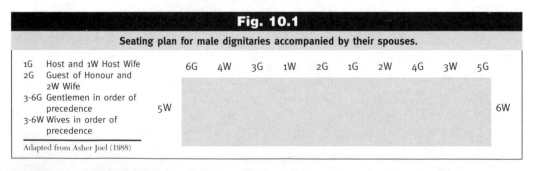

Fig. 10.1

Seating plan for male dignitaries accompanied by their spouses.

1G	Host and 1W Host Wife
2G	Guest of Honour and 2W Wife
3-6G	Gentlemen in order of precedence
3-6W	Wives in order of precedence

Adapted from Asher Joel (1988)

| 6G | 4W | 3G | 1W | 2G | 1G | 2W | 4G | 3W | 5G |

5W

6W

RELIGIOUS AND CULTURAL PROTOCOL

Formalities attach to most religious and cultural ceremonies, although these may or may not be observed by the client. The event organiser may therefore be required to assist with the protocol for such an event or to provide advice if the client wants a more relaxed arrangement.

Following are examples of traditions associated with a number of wedding ceremonies from around the world.

Scottish wedding

The stag night is a tradition of Scottish — and Australian — weddings, male friends taking the groom out to celebrate with lots of drinking and practical jokes at the expense of the groom. Another old Scottish custom requires the groom to carry a basket of stones on his back until the bride can be persuaded to kiss him. The groom and his groomsmen often wear kilts to the wedding (traditionally with no undergarments), and the groom may present the bride with an engraved silver teaspoon on their wedding day as a pledge that they will never go hungry. A traditional sword dance is sometimes performed at the wedding reception.

Greek Orthodox wedding

There are two parts to this service: the betrothal ceremony and the marriage ceremony. During the marriage ceremony, the priest crowns both bride and groom three times and all three parade around the altar table three times. The entrance of the families of the bride and the groom to the reception area, as well as the arrival of the bride and groom at the reception, are greeted with a fanfare.

Japanese wedding

The bride's wedding gown is often a traditional wedding kimono. The first sip of sake drunk by the bride and groom at the wedding ceremony symbolises the official union of marriage. The ceremony is generally quite small and is held at a Shinto shrine or in a chapel. Guests invited to the wedding reception make gifts of money to the couple and they, in turn, are given a gift to take home.

Macedonian wedding

Prior to the wedding ceremony, an unmarried relative or friend of the family makes a loaf of bread and decorates it with sweets. Once the bread is cooked, the family members dance and sing, and then give the loaf to the best man who carries it to the reception. Towards the end of the reception the bread is taken apart by all the single males. The story goes that if they eat some and keep some under their pillow they will see their future wife.

The day a Sydney woman married a Zulu warrior

When talk turned to ritual sacrifice, the Cogley family from Sydney wondered what kind of wedding they were in for. They had flown to South Africa to see their daughter, Sofi, 31, marry Robert Ntshalintshali, also 31, a Zulu from a small village in the foothills of the spectacular Drakensberg mountain range.

The night before the April 18 ceremony they were summoned to the spirit hut to witness the village chief call upon his ancestors. Three boys held down a bleating goat while a man slaughtered it, collecting the blood. With a piece of dried sage burning and the skinned goat strung from the ceiling, the chief called the names of his ancestors, one by one, telling them about Sofi, about the wedding and asking them to accept the couple into the family.

He sprinkled bile on Ms Cogley's forehead, arms and legs, then rolled a thin piece of goat skin around her wrist, a symbol that she was now a member of the family.

Custom dictated that Mr Ntshalintshali should give Ms Cogley's family 11 cows for her hand in marriage. Not surprisingly, both families were relieved to quietly drop the whole subject — not just because of the unwanted excess baggage for the Cogley family but because the cost is prohibitive for the average Zulu.

The Cogleys tried to get some idea of the number of guests who would attend the festivities, only to be met with a shrug. 'Maybe 100, maybe 300, maybe 1,000 — it depends who hears about it', their daughter said. 'There are no invitations here. The word spreads and people start coming.'

DANIELLE TEUTSCH, *SYDNEY MORNING HERALD*, 13 MAY 2001

The formalities for weddings of different nationalities can often be found on the Internet (see one such website at the end of this chapter) or from the many books on wedding etiquette available in bookstores.

For the modern bride and groom there are many variations on the old traditions and these must be discussed with them before the ceremony. For the organiser of the wedding, the most crucial elements are the timing of the music, the speeches and the meal at the reception. From a planning perspective, there are many details which need to be agreed upon, including:

- décor
- seating plans for the bridal party (see Fig. 10.2) and other guests

- timing and duration of the reception
- menu and special food requirements
- beverages and payment for beverages
- timing of food service, speeches, dancing, etc.
- music, sound system and microphones for those giving speeches
- rooms where the bride and groom can change.

Fig. 10.2

Seating plan for bridal table.

Chief Bridesmaid	Groom's Father	Bride's Mother	Groom	Bride	Bride's father	Groom's Mother	Best Man

A run sheet (see Chapter 9) for a wedding reception would need to include the following steps and the timing of these steps:

- music on arrival
- arrival of guests
- drink service commences (generally champagne, wine, beer and soft drinks)
- arrival of bride's and groom's families
- guests seated
- entry and introduction of the bridal party approximately half an hour later
- entrée served, starting with the bridal table
- main course served, starting with the bridal table

Approximately two hours after commencement:

- all guests are served champagne in anticipation of the speeches and toasts
- speeches by father of the bride, the groom and the best man (this may vary)
- cutting of the cake
- bridal waltz
- dessert and coffee served
- dancing
- throwing of garter and bouquet
- farewell of bride and groom through an arch formed by guests
- close bar and music stops
- guests leave.

Note that an open bar (which does not generally include spirits) may extend only for a number of hours, after which guests pay for their drinks.

PROTOCOL FOR SPORTING CEREMONIES

There are a number of formalities for sporting events, including the awarding of trophies, cheques or medals at the ceremony held soon after the event has finished. Traditionally, in team sports, the press interviews the team captain of the runner-up before the winner is announced. However, different sports have different conventions. For example, at motor racing events, champagne is sprayed over spectators by the winner and this ritual is followed by a press conference at which the drivers remain seated. Press interviews for a number of other sports take place in the locker rooms. Generally, there is a major presentation at the end of the season. An outline of the procedure at a sporting award ceremony is illustrated in Fig. 10.3. The briefing provided for the MC lists the order of precedence of those attending so that the MC can make the appropriate introductions (see Fig. 10.4 opposite).

Fig. 10.3

Order of ceremony for a sporting awards evening.

6 pm	Arrival of guests
	Pre-dinner drinks
6.25 pm	Guests seated
6.30 pm	MC welcomes everyone
	President's welcoming speech
	Junior sportsman award presented by Vice-President
	Junior sportswoman award presented by Vice-President
7 pm	Entrée
7.20 pm	Official of the year presented by Sport & Recreation representative
	Administrator of the year presented by Sport & Recreation representative
	Coach of the year presented by Life Member
	Team of the year presented by Life Member
7.40 pm	Main course

Fig. 10.3 CONTINUED
Order of ceremony for a sporting awards evening.

8.10 pm	Introduction of new Life Member by the President
	Presentation to state players selected in national squads
	by former Australian representative
8.40 pm	Dessert
9 pm	CEO thanks all sponsors and presents a small token of
	appreciation to major sponsor
	Speech by major sponsor
	Sportsman of the year presented by major sponsor
	Sportswoman of the year presented by major sponsor
9.30 pm	MC thanks all presenters, congratulates all winners and
	wishes everyone the best for the next year
9.35 pm	DJ plays music

State Sports Award Presentation © Jennifer Anson. Reproduced with permission.

Fig. 10.4
Briefing notes for presenters at a sporting awards evening.

- MC will announce title of next award and will welcome the presenter to the stage.
- Walk to the stage, proceed up centre stairs and then to the lectern.
- MC will shake right hands and pass the envelope to you with the left hand.
- At the lectern announce the nominations for the ... award are ...
- The award goes to ...
- As the winner proceeds to the stage the awards assistant will hand you the award.
- Meet the winner in the centre of the stage.
- Shake right hands and present the award with the left hand.
- Face the front for official photographs.
- The awards assistant will direct the winner to return to their seat.
- You will either return to lectern for second presentation or return to your own seat.

Briefing notes for awards assistant
- All awards are set up on the presentation table in the order of

Fig. 10.4 CONTINUED
Briefing notes for presenters at a sporting awards evening.

proceedings to the side of the lectern.

- All envelopes are placed under the appropriate award.
- Hand envelope to MC as the presenter moves to the stage.
- Hand award to presenter as the winner moves to the stage.
- As the official photographer and family/friends finish taking photographs, indicate to the winner to return to their seat.
- Indicate to the presenter to return to their seat or, if they have a second presentation to make, hand them the next envelope.

Briefing notes for MC
Guests in order of importance:

- Major sponsor
- State Sport & Recreation representative
- Former Australian representative
- Life Member
- President
- Vice-President
- Board Members
- Athletes (members of Association)
- Staff of Association
- Family and friends

State Sports Award Presentation © Jennifer Anson. Reproduced with permission.

RULES OF FLAG FLYING

There are many conventions involved in flying the national flag and the flags of other nations. Take, as an example, an international sporting event staged in Australia. The Australian flag, as Australia's national emblem, should take precedence over all flags of other nations and should always be presented properly (it should not be used as a tablecloth or seat cover!). When flying with flags from other countries, the Australian flag should be in the position of honour, for example, immediately opposite the entrance to the stadium; when carried in procession, the Australian flag should lead. The Australian flag may be used for advertising purposes, although it must be displayed clearly and be unobscured by other logos or images (Joel, 1988).

Activity

You have been asked to run an event with an Australian theme for a senior American executive who is about to return to the United States after working in Adelaide for three years. This event will be held outdoors and up to 400 staff members will attend. The Australian theme should be evident in all aspects of the event, including the décor, music, food and beverage. (A link to a recipe for 'dogs in blankets' is provided at the end of the chapter.) Since this is a large multinational company and the media will no doubt attend the event, you must observe the correct protocol for use of Australian symbols. You also need to ensure that you do not breach copyright in your use of images, music, etc. and seek permission for usage, or pay licensing fees as necessary.

- *Expand on the approach to the theme of this event.*
- *Explain how you will use Australian images and music.*
- *Illustrate your use of the Australian flag.*

Links

http://www.dfat.gov.au/protocol/index.html (Australian Department of Foreign Affairs and Trade)

http://members.tripod.com/virtaus/volume3/cuisine (site with 'dogs in blankets' recipe)

http://fotw.digibel.be/flags/ (flags of the world)

http://www.pm.gov.au/aust_focus/nat_symbols/flag.htm (Australian symbols)

http://www.chicagomarriage.com/wedding_traditions.htm (wedding tradition)

http://www.pch.gc.ca/ceremonial-symb/english/prt_precedence.html (Canadian protocol and events site)

SUMMARY

This chapter has dealt with the topic of event protocol. Protocol encompasses the traditions associated with government functions, official ceremonies, sporting events, weddings and the like. Such rules and guidelines assist event planners in working out seating arrangements, making introductions, and protecting the privacy and security of VIPs, such as overseas dignitaries. Our national symbols often form part of event décor and an event manager needs to be aware of the rules pertaining to their use. Awareness of the importance of protocol and the ability to locate the relevant information prior to the event will ensure that the event runs smoothly.

CHAPTER ELEVEN

staging

On completion of this chapter you will be able to:

- evaluate an event site to assess its suitability
- select a theme and plan the décor
- plan all staging elements, including lighting and sound
- plan all event services, such as catering
- understand the roles of staging subcontractors.

More than two thousand of the world's leading artists and performers, from 23 different countries, participated in the New Zealand Festival which was a three-week, multi-arts event in Wellington, the capital of New Zealand, from 3 to 26 March 2000.

The Festival commissioned the best of New Zealand's own dramatic talent to produce five new theatre and music works, making up the <u>Outstanding Aotearoa</u> series. The 2000 Festival was the biggest ever held in New Zealand. More than 265,000 tickets were sold, to 121 ticketed events, including the Edinburgh Military Tattoo (in its first-ever foray outside Scotland), Wynton Marsalis and the Lincoln Center Jazz Orchestra, the National Dance Company of Spain, French aerialists Les Arts Sauts, and many more.

As well, over a quarter of a million people enjoyed the Festival's extensive programme of free events, which included the famed Urban Dream Capsule (four men living in a shop window in Wellington's Cuba Quarter, for sixteen days).

New Zealand Festival 2000 was the eighth international arts festival in New Zealand. The next Festival will run from 22 February to 17 March 2002.

http://www.nzfestival.telecom.co.nz/

The New Zealand Festival, with 121 ticketed events, provides an introduction to the issues associated with staging. The staging of an event incorporates all aspects of the event that enable the performance to go ahead. Broadly speaking, by performance we mean entertainment: the sport, the parade, the ceremony. The topics

Jackie Clarke in the stage adaptation of 'The Underwatermelon Man' by Fane Flaws — New Zealand Festival.

Reproduced with permission.

covered in this chapter, such as theme, venue, sound and lighting, as well as all the essential services, are relevant to every one of the free and ticketed events of the New Zealand Festival. For every event in that festival, the organisers would have had to look at issues such as capacity, seating arrangements, emergency access, stage requirements and staffing.

Staging is an ancient concept: the Roman gladiatorial events were staged in spectacular, albeit gruesome, fashion, but these events certainly had the enthusiastic atmosphere every modern event organiser aspires to, although the modern audience would be unlikely to enjoy the same level of bloodshed.

CHOOSING THE EVENT SITE

Selection of an event venue must take the needs of all stakeholders into account. Stakeholders include emergency services, catering staff, entertainers, participants and clients.

Frequently, the client has an unusual idea for a venue, but however imaginative this may be, selection of the site must be tempered with rational decision-making. While a parking lot could be transformed into an interesting place to have a party, it would have no essential services, such as electricity, and would present enormously expensive logistical problems. An existing event venue, such as a conference centre, could more easily lend itself to transformation using decoration and props. Table 11.1 and Fig. 11.1 (see over) illustrate useful information, such as hall size and capacity and layout of facilities, that is available from venues and convention centres on the Internet.

Choosing a venue that is consistent with the event purpose and theme is essential. It can also lead to cost savings as there is far less expense in transforming it into what the client wants.

Table 11.1

Example of information, such as hall size and capacity, provided by venue providers on the Internet.

CAPACITIES	AREA Sq m	AREA Sg f	THEATRE	BANQUET	CLASSROOM
Hall A	430	4628	540	300	210
Hall B	430	4628	540	300	210
Hall C	430	4628	500	300	210
Hall D	430	4628	500	300	210
Halls A&B	860	9256	1080	650	420
Halls C&D	860	9256	940	650	400
Halls B&C&D	1290	13884	1540	720	N/A
Great Hall A&B&C&D	1720	18512	2330	1300	730
Hall 2 (Auditorium)	1470	15817	5000	N/A	N/A
Hall 2 (Flat floor)	1470	15817	N/A	1080	630

Reproduced with permission Cairns Convention Centre.

Fig. 11.1

Layout of halls and facilities of a convention centre available on the Internet.

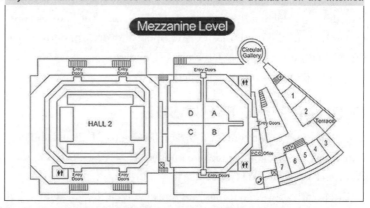

Reproduced with permission Cairns Convention Centre.

Cairns Convention Centre Hall 2 (above) used for conference banquet dinner.

Reproduced with permission.

The major considerations for selecting an event venue include:
- size of the event (including the size of the audience)
- layout of the site and its suitability for the event
- stage, field of play or performance area
- transport and parking
- proximity to accommodation and attractions
- supply issues for goods and services providers, such as caterers
- technical support
- venue management.

An inspection of the site should reveal any limitations, the aspects to consider including:
- compatibility with the event theme
- audience comfort
- visibility for the audience (line of sight)
- storage areas
- entrances and exits
- stage area (where relevant)
- equipment
- cover in case of poor weather
- safety and security
- access for emergency vehicles
- evacuation routes.

In viewing a potential event site, there are three major stakeholders who need to be considered and whose perspectives could be quite different: **the performers**, **the audience** and **the organisers**. By performers we mean those in the limelight, whether this involves providing an educational talk, dancing in a parade, presenting an award or scoring on a try line. Performers have specific needs that are fundamental to their success, such as the level of intimacy with the audience (often the result of the distance from the audience) or the volume of the sound. Secondly, the audience has needs, the primary one being to see what is going on! An illustration of line of sight is shown in Fig. 11.2. The level of lighting and sound, as well as access to and comfort of the seats also contribute to audience satisfaction. Catering and facilities are generally secondary. Finally, from a management perspective, the venue must help to minimise risks, such as adverse weather, power failure, accidents and emergencies.

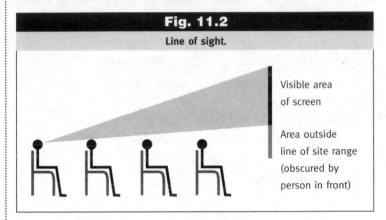

Fig. 11.2
Line of sight.

Visible area of screen

Area outside line of site range (obscured by person in front)

DEVELOPING THE THEME

As we have mentioned several times, the theme of an event must be supported in every aspect, including the décor, lighting, sound and special effects. The theme may be quite subtle: for example, in the case of a high-tech theme for a conference, the audience would only be subliminally aware of aspects of the theme, such as the colour scheme. In more dramatic cases, guests might be asked to support the theme by dressing appropriately or participating in entertainment that is consistent with the theme. Themes may be tried and tested, or quite unique.

A theme can be reinforced through such creative elements as:

- colour
- landscape and/or location
- film/theatre/art/dance
- humour
- fantasy.

Following are important aspects of the theme that need to be carefully considered by the event organiser. As you will see, there are many decisions to make!

Entertainment

There is a wide range of acts that can be used to enhance the theme of an event, and corporate events, in particular, often employ interesting performers such as snake charmers, hypnotists and belly dancers. Entertainment companies have a wealth of ideas and these can be investigated on the website listed at the end of this chapter. Such companies need to be briefed in the early planning stages so that they become familiar with the event purpose and the event audience. They can then look at the event theme and come up with a range of concepts to suit the theme. If a band is recommended, the specific technical requirements should be discussed at this stage. (One event organiser illustrated the importance of briefing the entertainment provider with her own experience in organising an event for a young audience. When the teenager's parents heard that one of the band members had stripped, they were furious with her!)

Décor

Lena Malouf is one of Australia's foremost event designers and her work has recently earned her two awards, the first for Best Event Produced for a Corporation or Association (overall budget US$200,000 to US$500,000) and the second for Best Theme Décor (décor budget over US$50,000). Her guests were submerged in a magical 'underwater' world reminiscent of the fantastical journey in the children's classic, *Bedknobs and Broomsticks*. Malouf's events are characterised by extravagant displays, including imaginative moving art pieces that tie in perfectly with the chosen theme, her main aim being to surprise and transport the audience. She is now the President of the International Special Event Society (ISES). Her book, *Behind the Scenes at Special Events* (1998), is recommended for those interested in specialising in event design.

Décor encompasses many things, from the colour scheme to the drapes, props and floral arrangements. The challenge is to bring them all together into a cohesive theme. Staging rental companies can be extremely helpful with this task.

Layout

The layout of the event venue is clearly integral to the success of the event. Anyone who has worked on conferences and formal dinners knows that table layout is something that needs to be negotiated with the client well in advance. With large dinner events in large venues, all too often the audience at the back of the room has very limited vision of the stage. If this is compounded by poor sound and too much alcohol, it does not take long before the presenter is drowned out by the clink of glasses and the hum of conversation. This can be very embarrassing.

The limited space offered by a marquee emphasises the need for effective planning of seating.

When planning an event at which guests are seated around a table, it is essential to plan the layout according to scale. If the dimensions of the tables and chairs are not considered, as well as the space taken by seated guests, there may prove to be no room for waiters or guests to move around. A number of common table and seating layouts are illustrated in Fig. 11.3. For each of these, a scale drawing would be used to calculate the capacity of the room and the appropriate use of furnishings.

Fig. 11.3

Table and seating layouts.

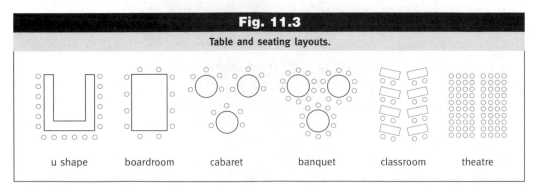

| u shape | boardroom | cabaret | banquet | classroom | theatre |

Lighting and special effects

Lighting can be used to spectacular effect, and for this reason, events held at night provide the opportunity for more dramatic results than those held during the day. Lighting can be used both to create the general ambience and to highlight particular features. It is often synchronised with sound for special effect at dances and fireworks displays, and can also be used to highlight sponsor advertising. As with sound, lighting is used to create a particular mood, although it is important to remember that this must be consistent with the event theme. Subtlety is required, for there has been a tendency recently to use some of the latest patterning techniques too often. Professional advice from a lighting designer is recommended as lighting is more often than not one of the main contributors to staging a successful event.

Sound

Music is a powerful creator of mood. It can excite or calm an audience, while particular pieces can be highly emotive. The volume needs to be pitched at just the right level, and all members of the audience need to be able to hear clearly, particularly if the event is being staged in a large stadium. Professional sound engineers can be relied upon to give advice on equipment and the acoustic qualities of a venue. For example, a concrete venue with little or no carpeting or curtaining has a negative effect on sound, but this can be remedied by the incorporation of drapes in the design.

Vision

Vision incorporates all projected images, such as replays of sporting highlights on large screens or scoreboards. Video projectors, slide projectors and data projectors can project images onto screens for dramatic effect, and this can be extended to live broadcasts with satellite links. A wall of monitors can be used to project one large image across the whole monitor wall, achieving the effect of a large screen. The splitting of the image between monitors is done by computer programming.

Back-up projectors and duplicate copies of videos, slides, and so on are essential. Most business and academic presentations use computer software packages to improve the visual quality of the images.

BUSINESS PRESENTATIONS

Computer-generated slide shows

While computer-generated slide shows look highly professional, there is a tendency for some users to become too excited by the features provided, changing colours and effects all too often. Bullet points coming in from all directions can bamboozle the audience, while the use of multiple fade-in and fade-out effects only adds to the problem, resulting in a most distracting presentation.

Another pitfall is a presentation that is too large to save onto a floppy disk (this often occurs if a lot of graphics have been used), requiring the presenter to bring his or her own laptop to the event. It is useful to keep in mind that there is a saving technique which minimises the memory required and results in the presentation being 'ready to go'. This software also allows the printing of notes pages, which include a reproduction of the slide and room for note-taking.

There are a number of alternatives to computer screen shows, such as flip charts and slide shows, and these are returning to favour as their novelty value increases and the wow factor of computer screen shows diminishes.

Overhead transparencies

Transparencies are useful for simple presentations and for back-up in case of computer incompatibility. Always ensure that presenters have their slide shows printed on overhead transparencies in case of emergency.

Flip charts

While flip charts are considered quite old-fashioned by some, they are thought essential by others as they allow the full participation of the audience when developing ideas and trying to reach a consensus. Some trainers use flip charts extensively, as they are more interactive and more educationally beneficial than pre-prepared presentations.

Stage

The stage is used for many reasons, including performances, prize-givings and presentations. Equipment rental companies can provide advice on the size and shape of the stage, as well as on screens and other devices on which to project images from the rear of the stage.

However, the needs of the audience are the most important consideration, particularly the line of sight, which must be considered when deciding on the size and shape of the stage and the placing of lecterns or screens.

Set

The set includes all objects on the stage: props, flats, lecterns, stairs, curtains, and so on. Sometimes these are hired; at other times they must be built.

The **cyclorama** is the drape at the back of the stage used to create a sense of distance, special lighting of the cyclorama providing different coloured backgrounds. **Borders** are used to mask parts of the rigging system and to trim the sightlines so that only the set may be seen by the audience. A **traveller** is a type of curtain that moves along a track. Often it is used as the main stage curtain, being configured so that one operating line moves curtains from both sides of the stage simultaneously.

Field of play

Each sporting event has specific requirements. These may include gymnastic equipment, which must be properly set up to very clear specifications, or simply a good quality pitch and wicket. In fact, there is nothing simple at all about a good quality wicket, as cricket fans would know only too well! The quality of the grassed field is important for most sports. The 2000 Olympic Games soccer semi-final held in Canberra was threatened with cancellation due to the poor quality of the newly laid turf. Fortunately the problem was solved in time for ticket-holders to enjoy the eagerly awaited match. Problems of this nature are not uncommon. For this reason, sporting fields are often covered when they are used for other events. However, while the cover protects the surface, it also blocks out the light so that damage can still be caused to the field. These days, professional grass specialists can replace the entire field within hours, but this is a costly exercise.

Line of sight is clearly important for sporting enthusiasts, and one cannot afford to sell seats from which visibility is impaired. The placement of media equipment is often the cause of this type of problem, and discussions must be held before tickets go on sale to establish the proposed position of cameras and sound equipment. The same holds true for processions and street parades where an elevated position is preferable for camera crews. This may require authorisation by the local authority, and accreditation may be necessary for those eligible to enter the media area.

Finally, the use of giant screens with rear screen projectors, such as those used at the Mahler 8 concert at the Sydney Superdome in

2000, need to be considered for large venues where there is a risk that members of the audience will not be able to readily see the stage or field of play.

THE TECHNICAL TEAM

The production, or staging, of an event involves many specialists. As an example, members of the technical team supporting a performance would include:

- Artistic Director
- Production Manager
- Technical Director
- Stage Manager
- Choreographer
- Scriptwriter
- Lighting Designer
- Lighting Operator
- Sound Designer
- Sound Operator
- Vision Designer
- Vision Operator
- Front of House Manager
- Floor Manager

The following staff would support the performance indirectly:

- Venue Manager
- Operations Manager
- Logistics Manager
- Catering Manager
- Cleaning and Waste Manager

CONDUCTING REHEARSALS

The importance of rehearsal cannot be underestimated. This is the opportunity for all involved to integrate their efforts — everyone from the stage manager (who calls the shots for the presentation) to the technical support staff (who follow the appropriate cues for lighting and sound). A technical run-through allows the staff involved to test the set-up and to make sure that all elements work satisfactorily. Technical glitches at an event are unprofessional, to say the least, so a back-up plan for all aspects of the presentation is absolutely essential. This includes two copies of each video or sound clip, slide presentations in more than one format and multiple microphones. Every potential problem should have a ready solution. The final aspect, over which the event manager has little control, is the quality of the presentation given by the speaker, particularly at business and academic conferences. Giving some basic advice and encouragement beforehand can assist a presenter enormously. If rehearsals have been conducted and everything is under control, speakers are far less nervous and far less likely to feel uncomfortable under the spotlight. A 'ready room' where the speaker can set up and test the presentation before going on stage is recommended.

Rehearsal leads to perfection.

STAGING TERMS

Performance

Management and agent	Take care of performers' interests
Talent	Person who is not the main performer (demeaning term)
Green room	Area where performers wait and watch monitors
Dressing room	Area where performers dress and are made up
Wings	Area used for assembling performers and props
Stage-in-the-round	Circular stage allowing 360 degree views for the audience
Proscenium arch	Traditional theatre style, curtains at side and above
Thrust	Stage projecting into the audience, such as at fashion parades
Tracks	Fixed tracks used to move props
Lectern	Stand for speaker

Lighting

Mixing desk	Where the lighting engineer controls lighting effects, adjusting colours, brightness and special effects; also where the sound engineer controls sound, including volume and switchover between music and microphone
Rigging	Overhead truss
T-stand/tree	Upright stand for lights
Floodlight	Wide light
Spotlight	Narrow light
Fresnel	Circular soft-edged beam (can go from spot to medium flood)
Cyclorama	Curved white screen at the back of the stage for light projections
Parcan	Fixed beam with soft edge, cheaper than floodlight, usually above the front of the stage and usually used in groups of four
Lighting gels	Slip-over colours used to change the colour of spotlights and parcans
Wash light	General area cover
Key light	Used for highlighting an object
Back light	Rear lighting effect (should use for speakers)
House light	Lighting provided by venue

Sound

Sound spec sheet	Specifies the sound requirements for a particular group or performance
Sound amplifier	Used to project the sound (microphones are plugged into amplifiers which power up the sound and send it to the speakers)
Out-front speakers	Speakers which face the audience
Fold-back speakers	Positioned on stage, facing the performers, to help performers hear themselves
Microphones	Include battery, stage (dynamic voice), headset and lectern

STAGING TERMS CONTINUED

Exhibitions

Floor plan	Two-dimensional layout of the venue
CAD drawing	Computer-generated, three-dimensional drawing of the design for a stand
Booth	Usually 3 m x 3 m stand at an exhibition
Corinthian	Walling covered with fabric to which Velcro will adhere
Pit	Service duct located in the floor, providing power and telephone cables (for some indoor and outdoor events, water and compressed air and gas can also be provided in this way)
Tracker/reader	Device for scanning visitor cards to capture their data

General

Pyrotechnics	Fireworks
Three-phase	Power for commercial use comes in three-phase (lighting, sound and vision equipment requires three-phase) and single-phase for domestic use

PROVIDING SERVICES

The supply of water, power and gas, a communications network and transport and traffic management are essential to the staging of most events.

Essential services

Essential services include power, water and gas. While the provision of these may sound simple, various different electrical sources are often required, including three-phase power for some equipment and power back-up in case of emergency. Providing the venue kitchen with gas can also be a challenge. The choice of a complex site can add to the difficulties of providing these essential services to the event venue.

Communications

Many events have particular requirements for communications, which may even include the installation of a complete telephone and communications network. Where there is a high level of demand on the communications network, the issue of band width must be resolved, particularly if there is a significant amount of data being transmitted. A stadium often requires its own mobile phone base station owing to the number of people using mobile telephones, particularly at the end of an event.

Transport and traffic management

Transport to the event, including air, rail, bus, train and taxi, all need to be considered. So, too, does the issue of parking and its impact on local traffic. In some cases, streets have to be closed, traffic diverted, and special permission sought for this purpose, the event plan being an important part of the submission to the relevant authorities. Thought must also be given to access for people with disabilities, marshalling of crowds and notifying of businesses affected by any disruptions. A link to a traffic management planning guide for events is provided at the end of this chapter.

ARRANGING CATERING

A catering contractor usually does the catering for an event, taking care of food orders, food production and service staff. These contractors (or the venue catering staff) should provide menus and costings relevant to the style of service required. Photographs of previous catering and food presentation styles can be helpful in making a decision.

There are many approaches to event catering, the most common being:

• set menu, with table service
• buffet
• finger food
• fast food.

The style of cooking and the type of service have the main impact on cost. Food that is prepared off site and heated or deep fried on site can be very cost effective. If fully qualified chefs are to provide quality fresh food with superb presentation, and the guests are to be served by silver-service-trained waiting staff, then clearly the costs will escalate enormously.

When discussing catering contracts, the event organiser needs to be very explicit about food quantities, speed of service and type of food required. Despite expression of interest in healthier food at sporting events, findings show that the old favourites, such as pies and chips, are still popular and that fruit salad and sandwiches do not sell well.

A food safety plan is another essential item when planning an event. Food safety involves protecting the customer from food poisoning by implementing a plan to prevent cross-contamination and other factors that cause bacterial growth. For example, food needs to be kept at the correct temperature all the way from the factory/market to the store, into the kitchen and onto the buffet. Food safety plans look at every aspect of food handling and, if well implemented, ensure the measurement of temperatures at key points in the process in accordance with the guidelines of the plan. The best kitchens have refrigerated delivery areas and separate storage for vegetables, meat, seafood and other products at the correct temperatures. Planned food production processes, including plating food in a refrigerated area, can further reduce the risk of bacterial growth. Finally, it is essential for the food safety specialist to consider the length of time taken for the food to reach the customer (perhaps at the other side of the stadium) and the length of time before it is consumed. Health authorities in the various states and territories monitor food safety.

Catering for an event is extremely demanding for those in the kitchen. Producing several hundred hot meals is not for the faint-hearted. The chef should be aware of the planned time for service of all courses and this should be confirmed at an early stage of the planning. Most floor managers will ask the chef how much notice is needed for service of the main course and they will monitor proceedings and advise the chef accordingly.

Beverage supplied at functions and banquets usually comes in the form of beverage packages ('packs') which are available in a range of prices, depending mainly on the quality of the wine. A pack includes a specific range of wines, beers and soft drinks, and does not generally include spirits. The client may choose a selection of beverages, but this will clearly be more expensive, and may also specify a time limit for an open bar.

ORGANISING ACCOMMODATION

For many conferences, exhibitions, shows and sporting events, accommodation is an essential part of the package. The packaging of air travel and accommodation demands that planning for such events occurs well in advance in order to acquire discounted air fares and attractive room rates. If such rate reductions are essential to favourable pricing of the event, it is preferable to hold the event in an off-peak season. However, as soon as an event such as the Formula 1 Grand Prix in Melbourne reaches a significant size, discounted rates are out of the question as accommodation in the destination city will be fully booked.

The following extract illustrates the response of many accommodation providers as soon as they get wind of an event, although this approach to pricing is generally counterproductive. The negative image created by overpricing can have an impact on tourism in the long term.

The normally sleepy town of Mongu (in Zambia) is about to come alive this weekend for the Kuomboka ceremony. The ceremony stretches back several centuries and is about moving Lozi people from the flooded Zambezi Plains to the plateau. Hotel owners in Mongu say they immediately hiked room rates as soon as the announcement of the event was made, by between 600 and even 1000 percent in some cases. They are also quoting their room rates in United States dollars as they expect more than 5000 tourists to witness Zambia's foremost traditional event.

The holding of the ceremony is dictated by the amount of rain that falls in a particular season. So much rain has fallen this year that staging the ceremony was never in doubt.

SUNDAY INDEPENDENT, SOUTH AFRICA, 25 MARCH 2001

This is a most unusual event — most event organisers dread the prospect of rain, while those organising this event require rain to ensure its success!

MANAGING THE ENVIRONMENT

One of the legacies of the Sydney 2000 Olympic Games is an increased awareness of environmental issues in Australia. For example, because of the enormous amount of take-away food it was estimated would be consumed at the Stadium, the Sydney 2000 organisers knew that they had to come up with a plan for its disposal. Their solution was the development of plates and cutlery from cornstarch and other biodegradable products so that all food waste would be able to go into one bin for composting. In contrast, the foil pie plates and polystyrene containers used at other events generally end up as landfill.

Waste management is an important consideration for all event organisers.

Pollution

Methods for reducing the environmental impact of noise, air and water pollution should be part of the planning process and advice on these can be obtained from the Environmental Protection Agency which has offices in each state. Professional contractors can advise you on the correct disposal of cooking oils and other toxic waste that could affect our water supply. As we all know, clearly marked bins should be provided to facilitate recycling of waste products. With regard to air pollution, releasing helium balloons into the atmosphere has been shown to be environmentally unfriendly and this practice is slowly dying out around the world.

Toilet facilities

Toilet facilities include those at the venue and any temporary facilities required. The number and type of toilets to be provided at an event, including the number allocated to men, women and people with disabilities, is another part of the decision-making process. The composition of the event audience — the number of men and women attending — and the average time taken by each also need to be considered! Theatre management has been working on this for years. Every woman has faced the problem of long queues during intermission and, believe it or not, there is a formula for working out how many toilets are required! Too many events provide substandard toilet facilities that cannot meet the demand.

It is essential to discuss the requirements for any event you are planning with a toilet facilities hire company as they are the experts.

Cleaning

There are a number of cleaning contractors which specialise in events, including Cleanevent, the company most widely used for events in Australia. In most cases, cleaning is done before and after the event. Maintaining cleanliness during peak times is challenging, particularly if there is only a short changeover time between event sessions. This means that you have to get one audience out, the cleaning and replenishment of stocks done, and the next audience in on time. The timing of this is part of logistics planning, which we will cover in detail in Chapter 14. Cleaning staff should be treated as part of the event staff and receive appropriate training so that they can answer questions from the people attending the event.

As you can see from the above, staging an event involves a myriad of tasks for the event organiser. With some events, the staging process may even include managing the fans who queue for days before the

SUMMARY

In this chapter we have looked in detail at the staging of an event, including layout, décor, sound, lighting and vision. The staff and subcontractors have also been identified, and the services required at an event, including catering, cleaning, waste management and communications, have been discussed. Staging an event is probably the most creative aspect of event management and there is enormous scope for making an event memorable by using the best combination of staging elements. The selection of the right site for an event is essential as this can have an enormous impact on the cost of staging the event and the level of creativity that can be employed in developing the theme.

event for places at the event. At the Academy Awards, for example, the area designated for fans is occupied for up to two weeks before the big night, as one of the fans receives a free grandstand seat overlooking the red carpet. According to the *London Daily Telegraph*, 20 April 2001, 'The commitment of Oscar followers makes Wimbledon campers look like amateurs. A thriving industry has developed around their needs, from food stands to camping equipment.'

Case study

As an introduction to an academic awards ceremony in the Town Hall, you have been asked to organise a performance by contemporary or indigenous dancers. Unfortunately, the Town Hall is a large space, with limitations in terms of lighting effects. There will also be a significant difference between the requirements of the performance and the requirements of the awards presentation, which is a formal, traditional daytime event.

Investigate the options for props and drapes and/or create a model of the stage set-up for the dance production. Remember that the set will have to be easily removed or somehow integrated with the awards presentation.

Activities
- *Develop a checklist for a venue inspection and then visit two or three venues and compare their various merits and limitations. In order to do this, you will need to have a specific event in mind, for example, a sporting event, a party, a conference or a wedding.*
- *Watch a video of* Gladiator *and review the staging and the audience response to the events portrayed.*

Links
http://www.cairnsconvention.com.au (Cairns Convention Centre)
http://www.specialevents.com.au (on-line special events magazine)
http://www.greatoutdoorlighting.com.au
http://www.gweep.net/~prefect/pubs/iqp/iqp.html (technical theatre handbook)
http://www.onsiterentals.com.au (rental equipment)
http://www.ises.com (International Special Events Society)
http://www.rta.nsw.gov.au/traffic/se_manv3.pdf (traffic management planning guide)

CHAPTER TWELVE

staffing

There were two training sessions for volunteers. The first was very general and did not answer any of my questions. In fact, I was so confused I almost didn't return for the second session. All I really wanted was a realistic idea of where I would be and what I would do. Instead we were told about reporting relationships, incident reporting and emergency evacuation. When they started to talk about the VERP and the chain of command I was totally lost. The final straw came when the manager talked about the contractors 'attempting to claw back service in response to price gouging'. I had absolutely no idea what he was saying. All I really wanted was a map and my job description.

EVENT USHER

On completion of this chapter you will be able to:

- **develop an event organisation chart**
- **write job descriptions and specifications**
- **conduct recruitment and selection**
- **plan induction and training**
- **manage volunteers**
- **plan recognition strategies**
- **prepare staffing policies**
- **manage industrial relations and occupational health and safety.**

This comment, made by a newly employed usher, illustrates the importance of effective communication and understanding the listener's needs and expectations. In this chapter we will look at two important staff planning processes: developing organisation charts so that people understand their reporting relationships and developing job descriptions so that people understand their specific roles, thus avoiding situations such as the one outlined above. The human resource functions of recruitment, selection, training and performance management will then all fit into place.

DEVELOPING ORGANISATION CHARTS

Organisation planning for events can be complex as generally several organisation charts are required, one for each different stage or task.

Pre-event charts

Prior to the event, the focus is on planning and, as we know, this lead-time can be quite long. The charts required during this period show:

- All those responsible for the primary functions during the planning stage, such as finance, marketing, entertainment, catering and human resource management. For example, the core event team for the Melbourne Comedy Festival includes the Festival Director, General Manager, Marketing Manager, Development Manager, Marketing Executive, Marketing Co-ordinator, Ticketing Manager, Office Manager, Production and Technical Manager, Artist Co-ordinator, Senior Producer and Producer's Assistant.
- Small cross-functional teams which manage specific issues such as safety and customer service.
- The stakeholders committee (including external contractors, suppliers and public bodies).

Charts during the event

When staffing levels for an event expand to the requirements of a full-scale operation, the size of the organisation generally increases enormously. In some cases, there may be more than one venue involved, so each of the functional areas, such as the catering manager for each event venue, needs to be indicated on the chart. Charts should show:

- Full staff complement, together with reporting relationships for the overall event operations.
- Emergency reporting relationships (simplified and streamlined for immediate response).

Post-event chart

After the event, the team frequently disperses, leaving only a few individuals and a chart showing key personnel involved with evaluation, financial reporting and outstanding issues.

An organisation chart can also include a brief list of tasks performed by individuals or the people performing each role. This clarifies roles and improves communication. An organisation chart for a team involved in a product launch is illustrated in Fig 12.1.

In Fig. 12.2 on page 162 is the organisation chart for Clean Up Australia. More than 300,000 volunteers turned up for the first Clean Up Australia Day and this number continues to rise each year.

Fig. 12.1

Organisation chart for a product launch.

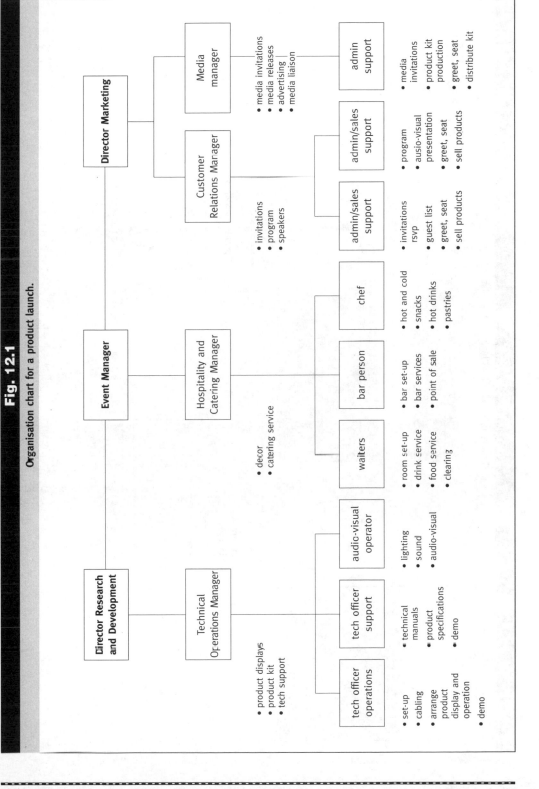

Fig. 12.2

Organisation chart for Clean Up Australia.

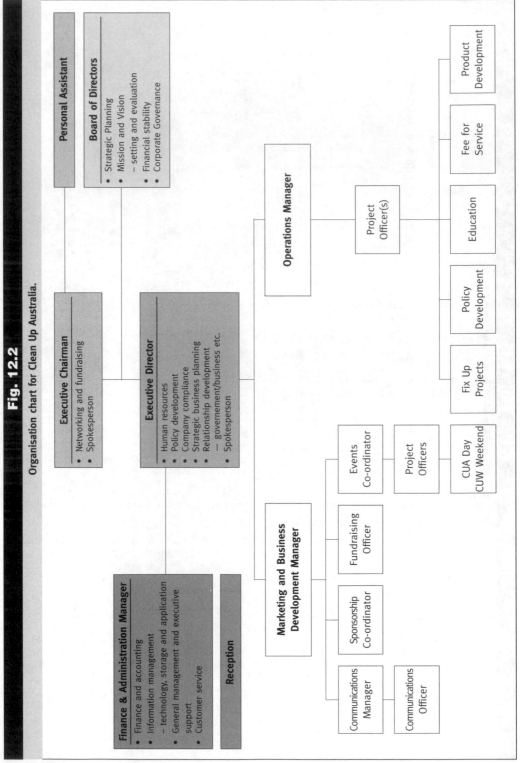

Reproduced with permission Clean Up Australia.

PREPARING JOB DESCRIPTIONS

A job description, outlining the tasks that need to be performed, is required for each role. This document should show the position title, the reporting relationships and the duties. A position summary is optional. In addition to the sections shown in the job description for a Catering Services Manager in Fig. 12.3, there should be a section showing the terms and conditions of employment. This job description would indicate the salary applicable, while those for many other positions would show the award and the pay rate under the award. As this position is likely to be a temporary one, the job description should also show the start and finish dates.

As you can see from the job description, this person will not have a direct role in catering. Instead, he or she will be managing catering subcontractors. This means that experience in selecting organisations to tender for the catering contracts and managing supply of the products promised in the contracts would be essential.

Fig. 12.3
Sample Job Description

Job Description

Position title: Catering Services Manager

Reports to: Venue Services Manager

Responsible for: Sub-contracts with caterers/concessionaires

Position summary:
To meet the food and beverage needs of all customer groups through the selection and management of appropriate subcontractors and concessionaires. To ensure compliance with the negotiated agreements regarding menus, pricing, quality and service.

Duties:
- Develop tender documents for provision of food and beverage, including bars, fast food, coffee stalls, snack bars, VIP and staff catering.

- Select subcontractors and confirm agreements regarding menus, pricing, staffing and service levels.

- Develop operational procedures with special attention to integration of services, food hygiene plans, supply and storage of food and beverage, staffing and waste management.

- Work with venue operations on the installation of the required facilities and essential services (including power, water and gas) for food and beverage outlets.

- Monitor performance of contractors.

- Deal with daily operational and customer complaint issues.

Once the job description is complete, it is necessary to develop a person specification, as shown in Fig. 12.4. This identifies the skills, knowledge and experience required for the role, and is used to inform the selection process. In this case, experience in a similar role, particularly in relation to tendering and contract management, would be required. In addition, knowledge of menu planning and costing would be essential, as would knowledge of food hygiene planning.

Fig. 12.4

Sample Person Specification.

Person Specification

Position title: Catering Services Manager

Reports to: Venue Services Manager

Responsible for: Sub-contracts with caterers/concessionaires

Position summary:

To meet the food and beverage needs of all customer groups through the selection and management of appropriate subcontractors and concessionaires. To ensure compliance with the negotiated agreements regarding menus, pricing, quality and service.

Knowledge:

- Legal contracts (with professional advice where necessary)
- HACCP (food hygiene plans)
- RSA (responsible service of alcohol)
- Catering for large numbers
- Installation and management of bar and kitchen facilities

Skills:

- High level negotiation skills
- Verbal and non-verbal communication skills
- Preparing budgets and planning
- Development of operational procedures
- Problem solving

Experience:

- Managing large-scale catering subcontracts, multiple subcontractors, concessionaires
- Menu planning and catering control systems for large-scale catering
- Operational planning for new installations

Desirable:

- Experience in an event environment

As you can see from the requirements for the position, experience in an event environment is desirable. However, experience in managing multiple contracts, such as in a resort, hotel or catering organisation, may be relevant in the absence of event experience.

The actual position description for a volunteer for the Australian Blues Music Festival in Fig. 12.5 is an excellent example.

Fig. 12.5

Excellent example of a position description.

AUSTRALIAN BLUES MUSIC FESTIVAL
VOLUNTEER POSITION DESCRIPTION

DETAILS OF THE JOB

Date of Establishment	October 2000
Date Last Reviewed	October 2000

GENERAL DESCRIPTION

1.1	Position Title	Australian Blues Music Festival Volunteer
1.2	Division	Corporate & Planning Services
1.3	Role	To assist with the operations of the Australian Blues Music Festival
1.4	Accountable to	Tourism Manager/Events Officer
1.5	Accountable for	Provision of information on the Australian Blues Music Festival, and sale of Blues Festival merchandise and tickets
1.6	Delegated Authority	Customer Service

AWARD/SALARY PROVISIONS

2.1	Work Hours	Applicants for this position will be required to work a minimum of 35 hours, which will be accrued in the lead-up to and during the 2001 Australian Blues Music Festival.
		This position is subject to an open spread of hours, and will include day, weekend and evenings as part of the employment.

Fig. 12.5 CONTINUED

Excellent example of a position description.

| 2.2 | Remuneration | This position is voluntary and successful applicants will not be paid a wage. They will however receive the following benefits in return for their work. |

- Two Official Festival Volunteer T-Shirts
- One Australian Blues Music Festival Cap
- Pass to the VIP section at the Chain Awards at the Tattersall's Hotel on Sunday, 11 February 2001. Opportunity to meet the bands.
- One-day Festival Pass, for a time the applicant is not scheduled to be working.
- Official Australian Blues Music Festival Certificate of Appreciation, and Statement of Work.
- Meal vouchers for the periods that the applicant is scheduled to work.
- Complimentary CD from the artist of the applicants choice, within the range of the Australian Blues Music Festival 2001 merchandise.
- Two invitations to the post Festival volunteers BBQ.

SELECTION CRITERIA

Essential
- Passion for Australian Music
- Excellent communication and time-management skills
- Sales focus
- Strong customer service ethic
- Evidence of self-motivation
- Flexibility
- Ability to work as a member of a team
- Ability to work under pressure
- Must be 18 years of age or over

Desirable
- Previous experience in a Festival environment

Fig. 12.5 CONTINUED

Excellent example of a position description.

- Knowledge of tourism product available in the Goulburn District.
- Cash handling skills
- Love of Blues Music

KEY TASKS/PERFORMANCE MEASURES

Key Tasks — Customer Information Provision
- Applicants need to have an accurate knowledge of the Festival programme, venues, merchandise items and costings, ticket structure and bands.
- Provide existing and prospective ticket holders with up-to-date information on the 2001 Australian Blues Music Festival.

Performance Measures — Information Provision
- Minimal complaints received from customers.
- Volunteer attends compulsory training session prior to the Festival.

Key Tasks — Sales & Bookings
- Sale of Australian Blues Music Festival tickets and merchandise.

Performance Measures — Sales & Bookings
- Sale of tickets and merchandise at the Goulburn Visitor Information Centre, Blues vans and various Festival venues, as specified by Festival organisers.
- All details are recorded accurately, and sales rung up through the Point of Sale machines immediately.
- Tills and stock levels balance at the close of business each day.

Key Tasks — Door Control
- To undertake door control at Festival venues to ensure only patrons with correct wristbands gain entry.

Performance Measures — Door Control
- All patrons in the Festival are wearing the required wristbands on their wrist.
- All wristbands are the appropriate colour/s for the relevant days of the Festival.
- Minimal complaints from Festival patrons, and venues.

DUTIES
1 Supply accurate information on:
   - Accommodation
   - Ticket structure & costs
   - Bands playing at the Festival
   - Key personnel
   - Festival venues
   - Local knowledge
   - Business houses
   - Festival sponsors

Fig. 12.5 CONTINUED

Excellent example of a position description.

- – Market stalls
- – Busking competition
- – Blues Hall of Fame
- – Shuttle buses
- – Chain Awards

2 Attend face to face, telephone, fax enquiries about the Festival.

3 Provide information to visitors and local community.

4 Sale of souvenirs and merchandise, through the POS system.

5 Handling of cash, and assisting with balancing the POS system at the end of shift.

6 Undertake shift stocktake, and provide written report to Goulburn Visitor Information Centre staff.

7 Courteous and efficient ticket and merchandise sales.

8 Distribute promotional brochures and posters to local business houses, and for mailing to regional centres.

9 Assist with the presentation of Goulburn Visitor Information Centre, and ticket/merchandise outlets.

10 Attend compulsory training session, as well as briefing and debriefing for the 2001 Australian Blues Music Festival.

11 Work as part of a team.

12 Perform other duties as required that are consistent with the Principle Objectives of the position.

TRAINING

A compulsory Training Programme will be conducted for all volunteers working on the 2001 Australian Blues Music Festival. Successful completion of this Training Programme will guarantee a volunteer work placement with the Festival.

I agree to the current requirements of the job description as at

_____ 2000.

_____   _____
VOLUNTEER   FESTIVAL ORGANISER

Reproduced with permission.

RECRUITMENT AND SELECTION

Once the job description and person specification have been completed, they can be used to develop advertisements and interview questions.

The most common approach to recruitment is to advertise the position in local newspapers or major newspapers, on the Internet home page for the event or event-related sites, or on notice boards. Examples of advertisements for positions in the event industry are included in the final chapter. Employment agencies can also provide event staff — for a placement fee. This is an attractive method of recruitment as it cuts down your work by providing you with a short list of suitable applicants, as well as managing the administrative side of employment, such as taxes and insurance.

The best places to look for volunteers are volunteer organisations, schools, colleges and universities.

When selecting paid or volunteer staff, questions should be asked to check the candidates' suitability for the position. In the case of the position outlined in Figs. 12.3 and 12.4 (pages 163 and 164), the recruitment officer could focus on, for example, food hygiene legislation and liquor licensing as both are relevant to the position of Catering Services Manager.

DRAWING UP ROSTERS

Staff planning includes the development of work rosters. This can be quite difficult, particularly if multiple sessions and multiple days are involved and interrelated tasks have to be considered, as sufficient time needs to be factored in for each task. For example, if the site crew has not completed the installation of essential equipment for a particular session, work cannot begin on related tasks. Staff scheduled to be on duty will stand idle and become frustrated, knowing that deadlines are slipping. Having got out of bed at 3 am to arrive as scheduled at 4.30 am to set up for the day will contribute further to their frustration. In the event environment there is often limited time for transition from one session or show to the next and there are usually many interrelated jobs to be done, requiring extremely detailed planning and scheduling. A staffing crisis in the hours preceding an event can also contribute to the risk of accidents and poor service, again emphasising the importance of effective planning.

TRAINING

Event staff must be trained in three basic areas: the objectives of the event, the venue and their specific duties.

TAFE NSW volunteer training session for the 2000 Olympic Games.

Reproduced with permission TAFE NSW.

General outline

Staff need to be presented with a general outline of the event, as well as its objectives and organisational structure. They need to be motivated to provide outstanding service and reliable information to every member of the event audience.

Venue information

A tour of the venue enables staff to become familiar with the location of all facilities, functional areas and departments, and the spectator services provided. This is the ideal time to cover all emergency procedures.

Specific job information

Event staff need to know their duties and how to perform them. Maps and checklists can be extremely useful for this purpose, while rehearsals and role plays help to familiarise staff with their roles before the onslaught of the event audience.

Most trainees would rather move from the specific, which is more personally relevant, to the general. However, in some cases, access to the venue is only permitted at the very last minute and training has to focus on the more general aspects first.

Training days provide an ideal opportunity for team building. Team building activities, such as quizzes, games and competitions, should be included in all training so that comfortable relationships will develop. Such activities should be relevant to particular tasks. Event leaders need to accelerate all processes as much as possible in order to hold the attention of the trainee group and develop team spirit.

Reinforcement is essential and, at the end of training, the event manager should be confident that all staff have achieved the training objectives for knowledge, attitudes and skills. Too often these sessions are a one-way process, trainees becoming bogged down with an overload of information. Training materials need to be prepared in a user-friendly, jargon-free format for participants to take home. An illustration of how to use a stopwatch is provided in Fig. 12.6 to show how effectively simple training aids can support learning. A hotline staffed by volunteers who answer staff questions about rosters, roles and transport information is also a good idea.

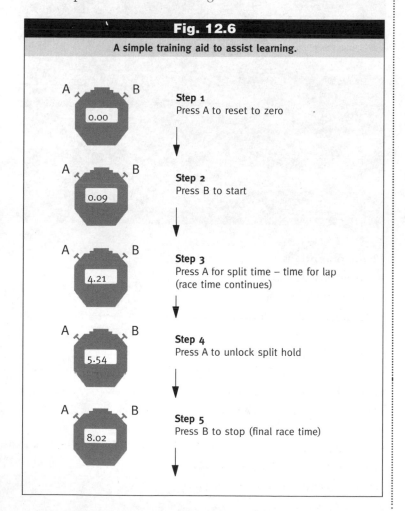

Fig. 12.6
A simple training aid to assist learning.

Step 1
Press A to reset to zero

Step 2
Press B to start

Step 3
Press A for split time – time for lap
(race time continues)

Step 4
Press A to unlock split hold

Step 5
Press B to stop (final race time)

The following checklist covers the type of information that might be included in training manuals and training sessions.

Shift routine and specific tasks

- location of check-in area and check-in procedure
- reporting for shift and briefing
- uniforms and equipment
- incident reporting system
- supervision
- specific roles
- breaks and meals
- debriefing and check-out.

Moving stock quickly and safely from one area to another is an important task for event staff.

Venue operations

- venue organisation and support operations
- staffing policies/rules
- emergency procedures
- radio procedures
- other relevant procedures.

General event information

- event outline and objectives
- event audience expectations
- transport
- related local services information
- contingency planning.

Customer service training is a key component of all event training. As the general principles of quality service are well known, the focus should be on specific information required by staff in order to properly assist customers rather than on general skills (such as the five steps of complaint handling). Most event staff rate training on specific event information for the event audience as being the most relevant to their training needs. Staff, however well intentioned, find themselves helpless and frustrated when asked questions that they cannot answer. Fig. 12.7 shows the attributes of staff that event customers value.

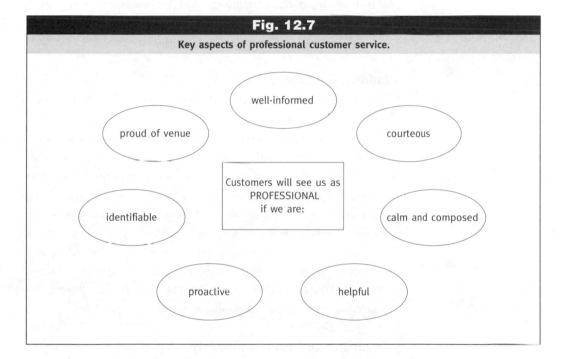

Fig. 12.7

Key aspects of professional customer service.

Volunteers at the Sydney 2000 Olympic Games and Paralympic Games were clearly identifiable by the event audience through their distinctive uniform.

BRIEFING STAFF

Briefing staff prior to every shift is essential. It is an extension of the training sessions and allows the venue or event manager to impart important, relevant information to staff before they commence work. Some information may be new, such as changes to spectator transport arrangements, while other elements may be a reinforcement of key information, such as incident reporting or emergency procedures.

MANAGING LEGAL REQUIREMENTS

Managers in charge of staffing need to be aware of the legal requirements of employing staff. The two main areas of concern are industrial relations and occupational health and safety.

Industrial relations

All paid staff should be remunerated in accordance with the relevant industrial award or agreement. Employers have a range of legal obligations, such as deduction of PAYE tax, that can be explored on the websites at the end of this chapter. Frequently a number of awards apply. This is due to the variety of occupations involved in staging an event, ranging from catering to electrical installation. For this reason, the use of agencies and subcontractors is common in the event industry as it reduces the administrative work of the event organiser. It is also possible to put in place a specific workplace agreement, as was done by the Sydney Organising Committee for the Olympic Games (SOCOG) for the 2000 Olympic Games, though this is not generally feasible for smaller events.

Occupational health and safety

The topic of occupational health and safety is covered in detail in Chapter 15. The most important element of this legislation is the responsibility it places on the event organiser for training and supervision of staff.

Employers have a duty of care for the health and safety of employees. Any issue which places employees in the workplace at risk should be considered a duty of care issue, including matters not typically seen as OH&S issues, such as aggression from customers, working alone at night or working long hours with limited rest periods. An employer's responsibilities include the provision of a safe place of work and training in safe systems of work.

A five-step approach is recommended in implementing an OH&S system. The five steps are:

1 Develop OH&S policies.
2 Set up consultation meetings with employees.
3 Establish training programs and communication plans (including posters).
4 Establish a hazard identification process.
5 Develop, implement and continuously improve risk control strategies.

PREPARING STAFFING POLICIES

Staffing policies should be developed as part of any human resource planning strategy and should cover such aspects as health and safety, misconduct, poor performance, sexual harassment and contravention of safety procedures. These policies are then simplified and summarised as rules for all paid and volunteer staff:

1 Work in a safe manner.
2 Do not endanger the health and safety of others.
3 Report all accidents and incidents.
4 Protect the confidentiality of the event organisation and sponsors.
5 Do not say anything derogatory about any aspect of, or person involved in, the event.
6 Refer media questions to the correct person.
7 Look after equipment, uniforms and other assets.
8 Act in a polite and courteous way to spectators and team members.
9 Use and abuse of alcohol or drugs while on duty is prohibited.
10 Act in a financially responsible manner.
11 Follow reasonable instructions of supervisors and senior event staff.

DEVELOPING RECOGNITION STRATEGIES

Recognition of the work of both paid and volunteer staff can have a huge impact on motivation. One of the most effective strategies is the development of realistic goals for staff as this allows individuals to see that their work has contributed to the success of the event.

Intangible rewards include:

• goal achievement through individual and team targets and competitions
• job rotation
• job enrichment

- meeting athletes, stars, musicians and artists
- working with people from overseas
- providing service and information and performing other meaningful tasks
- praise and verbal recognition
- training and skill development
- opportunities for building relationships and friendships
- media recognition.

Tangible rewards include:
- merchandise
- tickets
- post-event parties
- recognition certificates
- statement of duties performed
- meals and uniforms of a high standard
- badges, memorabilia.

Linking performance to individual or team goals should be considered carefully by those in charge of motivating staff. When recognition is given to individuals, it needs to be done with caution, otherwise it can lead to accusations of inequity. Team targets are more likely to improve team performance and to develop camaraderie.

MANAGING VOLUNTEERS

Volunteer management is particularly relevant to the event business since many events are staffed by volunteers. The Australian Council of Volunteers provides training in volunteer management and the following guidelines summarise the main principles of their training:
- Volunteers have the right to be treated as co-workers.
- They should be allocated a suitable assignment, task or job.
- They should know the purpose and ground rules of the organisation.
- Volunteers should receive continuing education on the job, as well as sound guidance and direction.
- They should be allocated a place to work and suitable tools and materials.
- They should be offered promotion and a variety of experience.

CLEAN UP AUSTRALIA

The first Clean Up Sydney Harbour Day in 1989 achieved an enormous public response with over 40,000 Sydneysiders donating their time and energy in an attempt to clean up their harbour. The next year **Clean Up Australia Day** was born, after Ian Kiernan, AO and his committee thought that if a city could be mobilised into action, then so could the whole nation. Over 300,000 **volunteers** turned out on the first Clean Up Australia Day and the numbers have risen ever since.

The subsequent step was to take the concept of **Clean Up Australia** to the rest of the world. After gaining the support of the United Nations Environment Programme (UNEP), Clean Up the World was launched in 1993. The success of **Clean Up the World** (40 million people from 120 countries took part in the event in 1998) has shown that the environmental effort in Australia has been noticed and the environment is a concern to all people globally.

Every official clean up site needs to have at least one supervisor on **Clean Up Australia Day**.

Site supervisors must be over 18, and should be responsible people who are happy to commit their services for the entire day. Site supervisors are volunteers who report to the local organising committee.

Site supervisors are responsible for the correct registering of volunteers, distributing Clean Up bags, overseeing the site's recycling activities and ensuring participants are aware of safety requirements. On the Day itself the supervisors must arrive prior to the official starting time and must be on duty for the duration of the entire Clean Up.

It is easy to organise a **Clean Up Australia Day** site in your local area. Once you register your interest in joining the national campaign, **Clean Up Australia** will provide you with a step-by-step guide explaining exactly what you need to do to get involved! Simply contact **Clean Up Australia** by telephoning us on 1800 024 890 or e-mailing **cleanup@cleanup.com.au.**

Reproduced with permission Clean Up Australia.

- Volunteers should be heard and allowed to make suggestions.
- They must be adequately insured.
- They should be given a reference at the end of the event.

In return, the event organisation can expect:
- as much effort and service from a volunteer as a paid worker, even on a short-term basis
- conscientious work performance, punctuality and reliability
- enthusiasm and belief in the work of the organisation
- loyalty to the organisation and constructive criticism only
- clear and open communication from the volunteer.

The organisation has the right to decide on the best placement of a volunteer, to express opinions about poor volunteer performance in a diplomatic way and to release an inappropriate volunteer.

The roles most commonly performed by volunteers include:

- usher
- marshal
- time-keeper
- results co-ordinator
- referee
- administrator
- media co-ordinator
- protocol/public relations assistant
- logistics co-ordinator
- transport officer
- information officer
- customer relations officer
- first aid officer
- physiotherapist/sports medicine
- access monitor/security officer
- shift co-ordinator
- uniform/accreditation officer
- safety officer.

From a survey done by the Australian Bureau of Statistics (4441.0, June 1995) it was shown that 2,639,500 persons, or roughly 20 per cent of the Australian population, performed some form of voluntary work. It was also shown that two fields of voluntary work claimed almost half of all volunteer hours: sport/recreation/hobby (24 per cent) and welfare/community (24 per cent).

The personal benefits, as perceived by volunteers, were:

- personal satisfaction
- social contact
- helping others in the community
- doing something worthwhile
- personal or family involvement
- learning new skills
- using skills and experience
- being active.

From another ABS survey (4172.0, 1997) into cultural trends, it was shown that 200,000 people Australia-wide were involved each year in organising cultural festivals. (Note that this does not include events from other categories as discussed in Chapter 1.) The following data revealed by the survey is also interesting: 28.5 per cent of festival involvement was for a duration of one to two weeks and 24.9 per cent involved three to four weeks work. Most people were not paid for their involvement — only 14.2 per cent received any payment for their work.

These findings are useful in understanding the contribution and motivation of volunteers and the importance of developing recognition strategies to meet their needs. In the job description for volunteers for the Australian Blues Music Festival earlier in this chapter, a number of benefits are listed that would meet the stated needs of volunteers for social contact and being active. These volunteers also received rewards in the form of merchandise and meeting musicians. After the Sydney Olympics, IOC President Juan Antonio Samaranch described Australia's volunteers as the 'most dedicated and wonderful volunteers ever'. This was a richly deserved accolade for a country in which volunteering is part of the social fabric. However, not only volunteers embraced the Olympic spirit. An experiment by one of the radio stations showed that a person posing as an American tourist with a map and a puzzled look was offered immediate assistance by those who witnessed his dilemma. The average response time to offer help was 66 seconds (Column 8, *Sydney Morning Herald*, 18 September 2000). This illustrates the positive attitude of most Australian citizens towards tourism and the importance of the role of events in increasing tourist numbers. Intangible rewards, such as achievement of specific service targets, should therefore form part of the motivation strategy for both paid and volunteer staff.

Case study

You have been asked to run a tourism destination promotional forum. The aims are to:

1 raise the profile of your region as a tourist destination
2 provide a platform for the public and private sectors of the local tourism industry to gather, discuss and address regional tourism issues
3 assist in the expansion of marketing networks and opportunities to promote local tourism destinations and events.

The Buyers and Sellers Business Session will enable delegates to

●●●●●●●●●●●●●●●
SUMMARY
Staffing is a very important part of event management and crucial to the smooth running of an event. In order to cover this adequately, we have discussed many topics ranging from the preparation of organisation charts, which allow employees to understand their reporting relationships, to the importance of writing clear job descriptions. Recruitment and selection help to bring staff on line, while induction and training prepare them for their event roles. These topics, too, have been covered, and we have also looked at the management of volunteers and the development of recognition strategies for paid, volunteer and contract staff. Finally, the event manager needs to be able to manage industrial relations and occupational health and safety issues, as well as prepare human resource policies.
●●●●●●●●●●●●●●●●●●

network and conduct business with high-level government officials and representatives of the national, state and local tourism organisations, as well as entrepreneurs, hoteliers, travel agents, tour operators and the media. Break-out sessions, at which all delegates will be invited to voice their opinions, will aim to generate ideas and solutions. Also on the discussion table will be issues such as standards, product ranges, joint promotional efforts, and marketing opportunities and strategies.

You are to invite:
• tourism representatives and tourism information officers
• investors and financiers seeking new opportunities and business partners
• hoteliers, tour operators, ground transport providers and tourism facility operators
• transport operators serving the area
• buyers and tourism suppliers
• media representatives.

You have two major tasks:
• Develop an organisational chart similar to the one illustrated in Fig. 12.1 in this chapter.
• Develop your own job description as 'Tourism Forum Event Manager'.

Activity
Investigate the occupational health and safety legislation in your state or territory by visiting the NOHSC website listed below. In the process of this investigation, identify the particular problems related to workplace health and safety facing employees and their employers in the event industry.

Links
http://www.goulburn.nsw.gov.au/Tourism/Blues_Festival/Blues_Festival.htm (Australian Blues Music Festival)
http://www.dewrsb.gov.au/smallbusiness/default.asp (Department of Employment, Workplace Relations and Small Business)
http://www.wagenet.gov.au/index.html (wages information)
http://www.nohsc.gov.au/other related sites/ (National Occupational Health & Safety Commission)

CHAPTER THIRTEEN

leadership

The volunteer took one look at the uniform, refused to wear it and walked off the job. Of the twenty people I had in my team on the first day, only six remained by day five. Three of my best people were reassigned to another team on the second day. Some of those who remained beyond the second day found the work too hard; others found it too boring. People assume that when they work at a major event they will be directly involved in the action. We were long gone by the time the bike race began each morning, rushing ahead to set up the next night's camp. In reality most event employees work behind the scenes, handling difficult situations such as spectators trying to gain access to secure areas. In our case drunkenness, aggression and general horseplay by both riders and spectators were hard to handle. The work was physically hard too. Holding a team together is a real challenge, especially when there are many other opportunities for them, or nothing to hold them.

CYCLING EVENT MANAGER

This story is indicative of the problems that face many event managers. Staff are often hard to come by owing to the short-term or unpaid nature of the work. In the above scenario, the event manager was struggling to keep the event team together for the duration of a six-day, long-distance bike race. While her team may have been enthusiastic to support the charity involved in the race, as well as excited to be on the road with the cyclists, the harsh realities are often quite different from the team's expectations.

Although the event planning team may work together for months or even years, the bulk of the event team works together for an

On completion of this chapter you will be able to:

- understand the time pressures that have an impact on event leaders and their leadership style
- manage staff by planning, organising and controlling work processes
- manage staff by informing, leading and reinforcing outstanding performance
- accelerate group development processes
- manage diverse and temporary teams
- manage communication effectively
- plan and manage meetings.

extremely short period, ranging from one day to about one month. Staff expectations are hard to manage under these conditions, and there is little time for building relationships and skills. Therefore, the focus of the event leader should be on giving clear guidelines, facilitating efficient work, energising people and celebrating successes. The event must be extremely well planned and the event leader must concentrate on developing tools for organising and controlling activities, as well as on innovative ways to inform, lead and motivate employees and volunteers who may need to reach job maturity within minutes or hours.

DEVELOPING LEADERSHIP SKILLS

The leadership model on which this chapter is based is shown in Fig. 13.1. The two main dimensions of this model are task management and people management, the basis for many other models used in organisational behaviour.

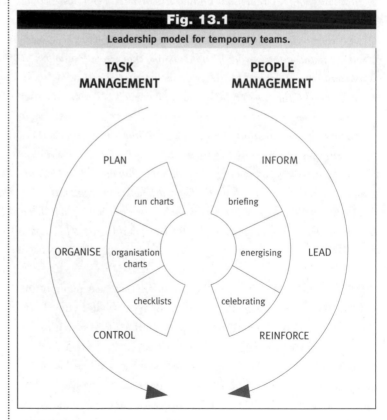

Fig. 13.1
Leadership model for temporary teams.

Task management

Task management involves the skills of planning, organising, co-ordinating and controlling work processes, using tools such as run charts, organisation charts and checklists.

Plan

Planning is probably the most important aspect of event management. It encompasses the development of policies and procedures to cover all situations, from disputes over ticketing/seating to summary dismissal of alcohol-affected employees. Planning is necessary for the development of staff rosters and the provision of meals for paid and volunteer staff, as well as for restocking, careful scheduling of stock being most important for multi-session events. When a venue is still under construction, architectural drawings are used in logistics planning to ensure, for example, that materials and equipment can be unloaded and set up easily.

There are a number of useful tools which can facilitate the planning process. A simplified version of a run chart (see Chapter 9) is helpful for all team members, and charts and maps should be displayed and discussed during training. Sometimes it is necessary to modify them so that they can be easily understood by all event staff. While the event management team needs to focus on the macro level of the event (the big picture), the micro level must not be ignored. It is essential that all members of the team be clear about the specific jobs that they are expected to do, otherwise they will become frustrated and their performance will deteriorate.

Organise

Organisation charts have been covered in Chapter 9 on planning and in Chapter 12 on staffing. You will notice that including the main tasks of those involved has enhanced the chart illustrated in Fig. 12.1 on page 161. An organisation chart enhanced with task lists is a useful tool for providing everyone with a more accurate idea of roles and responsibilities at a glance. There should be no ambiguity as to who is responsible for what. In addition to the organisation chart, every person should have a job description listing their duties.

Job rotation is an important organisational task, particularly where paid or volunteer staff are required to man remote locations. Change from one role to another during a shift can alleviate boredom and reduce feelings of inequity.

Control

Checklists are useful control mechanisms. They can be used to check cleanliness, monitor the temperature of food, check for safety or security risks, and to ensure that procedures are followed for setting up and shutting down. A completed checklist is also intrinsically satisfying for the person carrying out tasks, especially if their job has no visible output. Most events are high risk, making control measures absolutely essential for risk and hazard minimisation. Tours of the venue (both front and back of house) to check that everything is safe are invaluable. Frayed carpets, loose wiring and chairs stacked in fire exits can all be dealt with using simple control tools, such as checklists.

People management

In terms of people management, the three skills shown in the model in Fig. 13.1 include informing, leading and reinforcing. Briefings, energising strategies and celebratory activities can achieve closure on short-term targets and are necessary for keeping staff interested and motivated.

People management is one of the most significant challenges for the event manager. Due to the short-term nature of events, the frontline staff do not have the commitment of employees embarking on careers with traditional organisations. A volunteer or casual employee who finds the work boring, the location unappealing, the weather unpleasant or the food unsatisfactory may simply not return the following day. Indeed, he or she may not return from a meal break! The ability to keep people informed, to inspire and motivate them through positive leadership, and to reinforce the attainment of specific results, is the key to successful people management in this fast-paced environment.

Inform

Briefings before and after shifts provide the opportunity to advise staff on the order of proceedings and to clarify issues of concern. If a single important piece of information is left out, and several hundred spectators ask the same question about it, it is frustrating for everyone involved and a mistake most event managers make only once in their career. If staff understand why they are performing what appear to be unnecessary tasks, such as checking accreditation or photocopying results, they are far more likely to understand how they fit into the big picture. Well-informed staff members (including all uniformed staff who are always the target for questions from customers, regardless of their role at the event) also respond well to positive feedback from guests and spectators.

Lead

Most event staff expect to have some fun at an event and most look forward to joining in the atmosphere. Positive actions on the part of management (including good verbal and non-verbal communication and the initiation of a range of activities to energise the team) can help to create positive staff morale. Event managers who are burnt out before an event begins are unlikely to provide inspired leadership or to solve problems with tact and diplomacy. Time and stress management are vital for everyone involved. As role models, event leaders demonstrate to their staff how to provide quality service to customers. Depending on the level of formality of the event, the service provided will vary in subtle ways. Staff look to management for these cues.

Finally, it is important that each staff member have accurate expectations of his or her role, especially the more mundane tasks. (Sometimes, jobs will be oversold and underdelivered, or undersold and overdelivered.) This provides the opportunity for the event manager to encourage the staff member to go beyond initial expectations by introducing motivational strategies such as job rotation, viewing the performance, meeting the stars and athletes, or assisting the public. Accurate expectations of the less exciting parts of the job, combined with a positive team spirit, are the outcomes of good leadership.

Reinforce

Positive reinforcement of key messages can enhance safety and service, two essential responsibilities of the whole event team. The range of ways in which core messages can be reinforced are outlined in Table 13.1 on the following page. Event staff are well known for their capacity to celebrate success at every stage of a project, so recognition strategies for individuals and groups, including parties and prizes, are essential in this industry where people work under tremendous pressure to pull off an event.

In summary, event leadership is about:
- planning for short-term assignments
- organising and simplifying work processes
- developing checklists and other control processes.

Table 13.1

Communication strategies.

Verbal	Visual	Written	Behavioural
Briefings	Photographs	Training material	Videos
Meetings	Displays	Memos	Working practices
Radio conversations	Models	Letters	Role modelling
One-to-one discussion	Demonstrations	E-mail	Non-verbal
Instruction	Printed slogans	Handbooks	communication
Telephone	Posters	Staff newsletters	
conversations	Videos	Reports	
Training	Internet	Information bulletins	
Word-of-mouth		Checklists	
messages			

Adapted from S. Cook, *Customer Care*, 1997.

One-on-one computer demonstrations are very useful for reinforcing core messages.

It is also about:

- briefing and communicating with the team
- motivating and energising on an hourly or daily basis
- reinforcing key messages and targets
- celebrating success.

The work of the event leader may extend to some or all of the following challenging contexts quite unlike those of the traditional business environment:

- one shift for one day
- single or multiple venues
- single or multiple session times
- a team separated by physical distance
- routine and dull jobs away from the action
- busy, pressured and high-stress roles in the midst of the action.

And the team itself may include all or any of the following:

- contractors
- volunteers
- temporary workers
- students
- committee members
- police and other stakeholders.

MANAGING TEMPORARY AND DIVERSE TEAMS

The characteristics of temporary groups differ dramatically from those of long-term groups. Long-term groups are able to focus on quality improvement initiatives, with quality teams contributing to ongoing improvements over a period of time. This is seldom the case for temporary teams. The differences are summarised in Table 13.2.

Table 13.2
Differences between long-term and short-term teams.

Long-term teams	Temporary teams
Commitment to organisation's mission	Commitment to task
Decisions by consensus	Leader solves problems and makes decisions
Group cohesion over time	Limited relationship building
Career development within organisation	No career/organisation orientation
Intrinsic satisfaction	Tangible rewards
Empowerment	Limited responsibility
Lifelong learning	Limited learning
Positive performance management	Positive reference

Not only is the event team temporary, it is also, as a rule, extremely diverse. The general approach to managing a diverse workforce is to assimilate everyone into a strong organisational culture. When individuals share common codes of behaviour and communication, and solve problems in routine ways, the positive benefit is consistency and this can be achieved in the normal organisational life cycle. However, this is hard to achieve in the dynamic event environment where there tends to be more on-the-spot decision-making and a wider acceptance of diverse standards of behaviour. With limited time, an event leader simply does not have the opportunity to assimilate the team into a strong organisational, or group, culture. Working with a diverse range of people with wide-ranging needs and interests is inevitable.

GROUP DEVELOPMENT

Studies by B. W. Tuckman as far back as 1965, and still applicable today, have shown that groups tend to go through five defined stages in their development:

1 **Forming** This is the period during which members grow used to one another and tentatively formulate goals and behaviours that are acceptable.
2 **Storming** In this stage there is generally some conflict over control and leadership, including informal leadership, known as sorting out 'the pecking order'.
3 **Norming** Once the hierarchy and the roles of all group members have been defined, the group tends to adopt a common set of behavioural expectations.
4 **Performing** During this productive stage, members focus on performance within the framework of the team.
5 **Adjourning** Faced with disbandment, successful teams share a sense of loss. In this stage, feelings of achievement are tempered by sadness that the group will be disbanding.

This analysis of group development is useful to those of us who are in the event business because the process of group formation does require special attention in this environment. Sometimes, the early stages of group development can be accelerated so that the performing, or productive, stage is reached quite quickly. This can be done effectively by using ice-breakers in team training sessions.

Where group members exhibit a wide range of individual differences, particularly in language or culture, the following strategies can help to develop effective communication between them:

1 Identify specific information needs of group members.

2 Use plain English.
3 Allocate buddies or develop sub-teams.
4 Use graphics to impart information.
5 Rotate roles.
6 Provide all members with opportunities to participate in the group.
7 Develop group rituals and a group identity.

Geert Hofstede (1980), well known for his work in cross-cultural communication, has identified the following value dimensions in communication.

The first value dimension he termed **power distance**. This indicates the extent to which a society accepts differences in power and authority. In some cultures, employees show a great deal of respect for authority, so Hofstede suggests that these employees have a high power distance. They would find it difficult to bring problems out into the open and discuss them with senior staff. The low power distance prevalent in other cultures encourages closer relationships at all levels, and questions and criticism from employees are more readily accepted. As you can imagine, if employees in an event team were to come from both high power and low power distance backgrounds, the first would be aghast at the audacity of the second when they brazenly pointed out problems and the low power distance employees would find it difficult to understand why the others did not speak up.

The second value dimension identified by Hofstede was individualism/collectivism. Some societies have a strong sense of family, and behavioural practices are based on loyalty to others. Such societies display higher conformity to group norms, and it follows that employees of these cultural backgrounds would feel comfortable in a group. In contrast, employees from highly individualistic societies would defend their own interests and show individual (as opposed to group) initiative.

These are just two cultural dimensions. There are many other variations in people's responses to situations, for example, their different attitudes towards punctuality.

Hofstede suggests that the main cross-cultural skills involve the capacity to:
1 communicate respect
2 be non-judgemental
3 accept the relativity of one's own knowledge and perceptions
4 display empathy
5 be flexible

In most event situations you are running on adrenalin from the start. There is never enough time. You have to deliberately stop yourself, focus on the person, look them in the eye and use their name. It is so easy to forget to do this when you have a hundred unsolved problems and the urge is to be short with them. Something as simple as using the person's name makes the difference between a good event leader and a mediocre one. The worst event leaders are so stressed they can't remember their own names!

EVENT STAFFING
MANAGER

6   take turns (allow everyone to take turns in a discussion)

7   tolerate ambiguity (accept different interpretations of what has been said).

IMPROVING COMMUNICATION

While the topic of event briefings has been covered briefly above, here are some additional guidelines for improved communication in the event team.

Establish the level of priority

It is important to establish the level of priority straight away. Emergency situations are of course the highest risk for any event and communication about an incident or potential incident should be given top priority.

Identify the receiver

By identifying the receiver, you will be able to match your message to the receiver's needs, thus demonstrating empathy. Your message will also reach the correct target.

Know your objective

Clarity in communication is often linked to the development of an action objective. If you know what you want to achieve, you will be able to express yourself more easily and clearly. Stating a problem and its ramifications is often only the first stage. By indicating what needs to be done, you can more easily achieve your objective and reach an agreed outcome.

Review the message in your head

In preparing to send a message, you should structure your communication effectively. It is also useful to review the receiver's likely response.

Communicate in the language of the other person

If you use examples and illustrations that the receiver will understand, your message will be more easily comprehended.

Clarify the message

If the receiver appears from their non-verbal behaviour not to understand your message, clarification is essential.

Do not react defensively to a critical response

Asking questions can help you to understand why your receiver has responded defensively and can diffuse the situation. By seeking feedback you can ensure that you have reached a common understanding.

TIME MANAGEMENT

To work effectively with event teams, which may be together for a very short period of time, an event manager needs to:

- plan effectively
- identify critical issues and tasks
- analyse and allocate tasks
- manage work priorities
- make quick but informed decisions
- build relationships quickly
- provide timely information
- remove barriers
- simplify processes
- solve problems immediately
- manage stress for self and others
- develop creative and flexible solutions
- constantly monitor performance
- reward the achievement of outcomes.

From this list, it is clear that outstanding time management skills (on a personal and a group level) are required in order to gain maximum benefit from the planning phases. An ability to develop instant rapport with new people is also essential when time is limited.

PLANNING AND MANAGING MEETINGS

Meetings are an important feature of the management of events, starting in the early planning phases and building to pre-event briefings and post-event evaluations. Meetings can be highly productive, or they can waste an incredible amount of time. In fact, a poorly focused, poorly managed meeting will simply confuse and frustrate everyone. One event management company introduced the idea of a standing meeting to curtail the length of their meetings.

Time-lines should be set and an agenda for discussion distributed beforehand with all relevant material so that everyone is prepared. During meetings a chairperson should manage the pace and outcomes of the meeting and someone should be designated to keep

● ● ● ● ● ● ● ● ● ● ● ● ● ● ●

SUMMARY

In this chapter we have discussed the time constraints in staging an event and the temporary nature of the event workforce, both of which have a major impact on event leadership. The event staff manager must be able to plan, organise and control tasks in such a way that all concerned are able to see their contribution to the aims and objectives of the event. In managing these temporary, and often diverse, teams, the event manager needs to accelerate group development processes, communicate effectively, lead constructively and develop recognition and reward programs.

● ● ● ● ● ● ● ● ● ● ● ● ● ● ●

notes for the record. The most important aspect of note-taking is the recording of actions and deadlines for those attending. Documentation from the meeting should be distributed and actions identified, prioritised and included in the planning process.

In addition to focusing on tasks at event meetings, focusing on people should be a priority. Meetings can be an excellent venue for relieving stress, building team spirit and motivating all involved.

Case study

I knew what I had to do. I had to stand at an access gate all day on my own and check staff passes. I was prepared for the boredom but I didn't bring my thermos or a portaloo. Can you believe it? I wasn't given a break for six hours! By then I was really looking forward to some relief. You would think that these managers would learn something about people's basic needs. In this situation I needed to keep warm and dry. A folding chair would have made all the difference. A drink and an opportunity to go to the toilet would have been welcome! In terms of the hierarchy of needs, I wasn't expecting self-actualisation but I was hoping to have my physical needs met by being given scheduled breaks and possibly having my job rotated. In fact by the time my shift was over for the day, my supervisor had long left the scene. It's good for some.

EVENT VOLUNTEER

- How could this person's needs be better catered for?
- Are there any strategies for helping to motivate this volunteer?
- What leadership approach would you take to managing your event team?
- Is a different approach needed for managing paid staff and volunteer staff? Explain.
- Explain one way in which you would energise your staff or celebrate success.

Activity

Select an event and develop a list of pros and cons of working in three different roles at the event. Describe the leadership challenges and your solutions for the management team of this event.

CHAPTER FOURTEEN

operations
and logistics

The Heineken Classic is one of Australia's best known international golf tournaments and is co-sanctioned by the Australasian and European PGA Tours. Since its inception, the event has attracted the world's top golfers, including Greg Norman, Nick Price, Fred Couples, Colin Montgomerie, Peter Senior, Frank Nobilo, John Daly, Robert Allenby, Ernie Els, Jose Maria Olazabal, Michael Campbell, Thomas Bjorn and Nick Faldo.

Television coverage of the Heineken Classic Perth, which includes picture postcards — 15 second information segments promoting Western Australian tourism destinations — is broadcast to more than 285 million viewers around the world.

http://www.eventscorp.com.au/calendar/index.html

An event such as the Heineken Classic has many operational demands. Firstly, a logistical plan would need to be developed to ensure that all competing golfers (and their entourage of managers, caddies, etc.) arrive as scheduled, that they are settled into the correct accommodation and that all their golfing equipment is accounted for and secure. Secondly, there would be the whole process of preparing the course, which the greenkeeper would start many months before the competition. This would also involve setting up spectator stands, scoreboards and crowd barriers closer to the actual time of the event (this could not be done overnight and adequate time would need to be allowed for this process). The setting-up process is often called bump-in. Finally, at the end of the competition, everything would need to be dismantled and stored, as

On completion of this chapter you will be able to:

- plan the logistics of an event, bringing all equipment and other resources on board at the right time
- plan bump-in and bump-out procedures
- develop policies and procedures for the smooth operation of an event
- develop performance standards to measure success against objectives
- clarify the roles of the various functional areas during the operation of an event
- motivate staff to effectively implement plans and follow through to event operation and bump-out.

Setting up crowd barriers is just one of the operational procedures for a major golf tournament.

Reproduced with permission
EventsCorp, Perth.

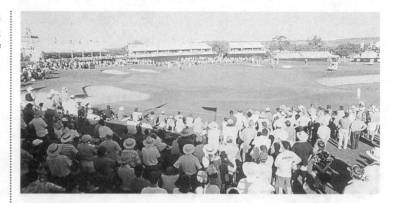

most items would be valuable assets, and the course restored to its original state for normal operation. This is referred to as bump-out. In between bump-in and bump-out, there is the event to run. (Naturally, with all events, the costing for the facility needs to include the period required for bump-in and bump-out.)

The focus of this chapter is the operation of an event, which is the culmination of many months, at least, of careful planning.

LOGISTICS

Simply put, logistics is about getting things organised, getting things (and people) in the right place and pulling everything down. Rock concerts and entertainment events featuring international artists present many logistical problems, particularly if the group is on a tour of several cities. Sometimes a complex array of musical equipment, some of which might have been airlifted into the country only days, or even hours, before the event, has to be set up. However, in most cases, the team supporting the artists would have identified specific requirements, sometimes down to the last detail, to be met locally. (These might even include requests for exotic foods and special dietary items.) Arranging accommodation has been known to be complicated by the inclusion of a weird range of pets, not commonly cared for in five star hotels, in the entourage.

The most amusing example of a logistical dilemma was that reported by the organisers of an equestrian cross-country event. A decision had to be made as to how to manage 'comfort breaks' for volunteers deployed over an enormous open venue. Should a buggie pick up the staff member and take them to the facilities? No, it was decided that a roving portaloo on the back of a small truck was the answer. Take the toilet to the staff member, not the staff member to

Operations staff busy at an athletics event.

the toilet! This avoided redeployment of replacement staff.

In most cases, however, logistics planning focuses on setting up and changing sets. Athletics events are particularly challenging as there are often several concurrent and consecutive events requiring different equipment. An event that involves catering also presents enormous demands when the product has to be served hot, often to hundreds of people in a very short time. One event co-ordinator describes an event where there was only one set of plates for each guest so that the plates had to be washed between the entrée and the main course. This involved a trip up and down lots of stairs and a very tiny washing-up area with a single cold tap, placing enormous pressure on the kitchen to plate the main course and serve it at the correct time. Cutlery (teaspoons in particular) is one of the biggest bugbears of the banquet department as a search for matching cutlery can delay a room set-up by an hour or more. Some chair covers take so long to stretch and position correctly that significant time can be lost carrying out this task (and significant labour costs incurred). The logistics manager needs to be one of the most efficient and organised people on the event team. With event operations, workflow planning becomes a fine art.

Adequate washing-up facilities are essential to the smooth running of an event. Water had to be transported for this event.

Bump-in

The process of bump-in involves setting up the structures and facilities required for the event. For some tasks, such as installing sound and lighting equipment, the services of specialist engineers are needed. Setting up can be a time-consuming process and a run-through must be built into planning. This is absolutely essential as it is imperative that all facilities and equipment work. Consider, for example, the event illustrated, which was attended by over 250 networked game players. The technical demands of this event, particularly the networking arrangements, defy description. Just for a start, each of the 250 computers required a network cable and at least two power sockets! By the end of an evening such as this it is not uncommon for plugs to have melted so that they cannot be removed from their sockets.

Networked game-playing event.

Bump-out

The process of bump-out involves pulling everything down. If this needs to happen immediately after the audience has left, sufficient staff will be required because, at this stage, everyone is generally exhausted, which itself presents a safety risk. If bump-out does not occur immediately, security staff will be needed to monitor the site until all materials and equipment have been removed. Some items are particularly expensive and if they are lost, stolen or damaged, this can have a dramatic effect on the bottom line of an otherwise successful event.

In most other industries, logistics involves managing the processes of manufacture, supply and distribution (including storage and transport) of the product to the ultimate consumer. The same general principles apply in event management, requiring an organised and structured alignment of key logistics functions. Procurement, transportation, storage, inventory management, customer service and database management are all examples of logistical aspects of event merchandise sales, such as T-shirts, caps, CDs and programs. In the same way, the supply of food and beverage to the event audience starts right back with the producer of the food and beverage product. For most events, food supply is unproblematic. However, in the case of a very large event, such as the Commonwealth Games, provision of sufficient stock of potatoes for fries may require importation of frozen fries, while ensuring an adequate supply of lettuce may require the sourcing of this out-of-season vegetable. For events that run over multiple days, food storage is also an issue, as is the logistics of fresh supplies needing to be delivered overnight, which has ramifications for staffing rosters and security.

POLICIES

Every event requires policies. These describe the general principles, or 'what is to be done'. For example, policies may be drawn up to prevent fraud, to limit misrepresentation, to manage the performance of staff and to promote the right image for the event. Having prepared the policies, the procedures for implementing the policies are then developed. For example, there may be a policy on customer complaints and a procedure to follow in the event of a complaint. There may be a policy on the recruitment and training of time-keepers and a procedure for reporting and recording performance times for athletes. The policy equates to 'what is to be done' and the procedure equates to 'how is it to be done'.

A uniform policy would say that event staff are to wear specific shirt colours, that they are supplied and laundered by the event company, and that staff who lose their uniforms have to pay for replacements. The policy might also list the personal items that staff are not allowed to wear and might recommend a certain type of footware. Uniform procedures would cover the steps involved in issuing uniforms to staff at the first training session, the steps involved in handing in and retrieving uniforms from the laundry using a ticket system, and the steps to take if a uniform were lost.

PROCEDURES

A procedure can take the form of a list of tasks or a checklist. Once procedures have been developed and integrated across the event functions, all the pieces begin to fit together. Sometimes, the timing of a procedure needs to be modified to meet the needs of another functional area. For example, if the grass surrounding the greens of a golf course were scheduled to be mowed the day before a golfing competition, it would not be possible to erect the crowd control fencing until this had been done. A procedure for entertaining sponsors for a full day is illustrated in Fig. 14.1 in the form of a run sheet.

Fig. 14.1

Daily run sheet — sponsor hospitality.

Start	Finish	Tasks
7.00 am		Security hand-over to Assistant Operations Manager.
7.00 am	7.30 am	Venue opened and checklists completed for safety, cleaning, layout and par stocks.
8.00 am	8.30 am	Staff check-in and briefing.
8.30 am		Staff commence first shift. Hospitality area opened for light meals/coffee/breakfast.
10.00 am	7.00 pm	Staff break area open.
11.00 am		Entertainment staff arrive. Acts as per daily schedule held by Operations Manager.
11.00 am	3.00 pm	Lunch service.
2.00 pm		Hand-over from Assistant to Operations Manager. Meal numbers for following day confirmed.
3.00 pm		Second shift commences, staff briefing. Catering staff meeting — Operations and Kitchen production.
3.30 pm		Deadline for lunch cash reconciliation.
4.00 pm	10.00 pm	Dinner service.
11.00 pm	12.00 mid	Set-up for following day service.
12.00 mid	1.00 am	Cleaning all areas, kitchen, dining area and facilities.
2.00 am		Security lock-up.

A procedure for checking the safety of a kitchen could be outlined in a checklist, as shown in Fig. 14.2. This procedure could also be shown as a flow chart or it could be based on a logical tour of the kitchen, with items re-ordered to match the kitchen set-up.

Fig. 14.2

Checklist for kitchen safety procedure.

Kitchen Safety Checklist

1 Food contact surfaces are clean and clear. ☐

2 Chopping boards for meat, chicken, vegetables are colour coded. ☐

3 Non-food surfaces clean and clear. ☐

4 Floors are clean and not slippery. ☐

5 Equipment is correctly cleaned and stored. ☐

6 Wiping cloths and cleaning equipment for different purposes
   correctly colour coded. ☐

7 Plumbing is functional. ☐

8 Refrigerator and freezer temperatures meet standards. ☐

9 Hand-washing facilities meet standards. ☐

10 Garbage disposal containers are labelled and covered. ☐

11 Storage areas are clean and clear. ☐

12 No evidence of insects or rodents. ☐

13 Lighting and ventilation is adequate. ☐

14 Gas supply is checked. ☐

15 All cooking equipment is functional. ☐

16 First aid box is fully equipped. ☐

PERFORMANCE STANDARDS

By establishing performance standards and inspection schedules, the operational success of an event can be more confidently assured. For example, in the case of a contract with a cleaning company, there will be clear expectations on both sides, the result generally being excellent customer service. In the case of the cleaning contractor, specific details about the level of service required would be outlined for the following:

- pre-event cleaning
- pre-event day cleaning
- during session cleaning

- turnover cleaning (between sessions)
- post-event cleaning
- removal of waste materials.

The criteria for performance standards may include efficiency (e.g. speed of set-up), accuracy (e.g. checklist 100 per cent), revenue (dollar sales per outlet) or courtesy (customer feedback).

FUNCTIONAL AREAS

While the division of responsibilities into different functional areas has already been discussed in previous chapters, it is useful to review the roles of these areas, known in most other businesses as 'departments'. Each of these functional areas develops their own policies, procedures and performance standards. Where there is more than one venue, a functional area, such as Medical, may be represented at each venue.

Procurement and Stores

This area is responsible for purchasing, storage and distribution of all products required for the event. Such items may include radios, computers, sound equipment and drapes, and are often hired from specialist suppliers.

If catering, for example, were contracted out to a subcontractor, the subcontractor would be responsible for food purchasing and storage, and the same would apply to other subcontractors. They, too, would be responsible for their product or equipment procurement and storage.

One of the main roles for this functional area during an event is the supply of event merchandise to the sales outlets.

Marketing

In the lead-up to an event, this functional area is responsible for the overall strategy for product, pricing and promotion. As the event draws near, image, sponsor liaison and sales promotion become priorities.

Ticketing

The ticketing area looks after ticketing in the lead-up to an event and during the event. In some cases this function is managed by the local Tourism Information Office; in other cases, tickets are sold by charitable organisations. For most profit-making events, the ticketing function is managed wholly by a major ticketing organisation.

Registration

Most sporting events, particularly those with large numbers of participants, need a functional area to manage the registration of participants in the race or the event. This involves completion of relevant forms by participants as well as the signatures of participants to acknowledge that participation is at their own risk.

Merchandising

The merchandising area is responsible for the sale of merchandise, ranging from caps and posters to CDs and videos. The range is frequently extensive and is sometimes advertised on the Internet.

Finance

As the event draws near, the main concern of this functional area is to maintain control processes, minimise expenditure and manage cash during the event.

Legal

In most cases, legal advice is sought before the event and it is only with very large events that a specific functional area is established to cover this role.

Technology

Networks linking different reporting systems can be developed to include those for sales of tickets and merchandise, registration of athletes and recording of results, and managing rosters and payroll.

Media

This functional area deals directly with the media, and during an event it needs to be constantly informed of progress. If a negative incident should occur, it is the media unit that writes the press releases and briefs the press. It also manages media interviews with the stars or athletes.

Community Relations

Generally speaking, this functional area is only represented when there is a significant community role, for example, at non-profit events.

Staffing

As the event approaches, the staffing area looks after training, uniforms, rosters and other schedules, and staff meal vouchers.

Services and Information

The provision of services and information to the event audience is obviously at its peak during the event, requiring staff to be extremely knowledgeable and resourceful.

All staff need to be able to provide event information

Cleaning and Waste Management

Very often this function rests with venue staff who undertake cleaning as a routine operation before, during and after an event. For larger events, such as street festivals, the local council may ask current contractors to expand their role for the period of the festival. For major sporting events, contract cleaners are often called in to manage this functional area.

Catering

In most cases, venue catering is outsourced to a catering company and there is generally a long-standing contract in place with that company. Sometimes, however, a decision needs to be made as to whether to employ one caterer to take on this role or several caterers, each offering different types of cuisine. Most event organisers leave this area to catering professionals.

Venue Operations

The management of the venue, in particular the operation of facilities and equipment, maintenance and the like, is the responsibility of the

Catering for both take-away and fine dining at event venues is mostly outsourced, so that this functional area is generally managed by contractors.

venue team. Health, safety and emergencies are the key areas of concern of this functional area.

Sports Operations

All aspects of a sporting competition, including results management and award ceremonies, are managed by sports operations.

Medical

The medical functional area provides first aid to both spectators and athletes. In some cases, this area is responsible for drug testing.

Security

Access to the event site by accredited personnel is managed by security, which also plays an important role in crowd management.

LEADERSHIP AND STAFF MOTIVATION

In addition to organising the tasks that need to be performed, an event organiser needs to focus on managing staff, volunteers and contractors during the operational phase of the event. Since there are few long-term job prospects for most of the front-line staff working at an event, there is a higher than average chance that they might not return the next day, or that they might disappear during a break or simply walk off the job. Some of the reasons they might give include:

- My skills are being wasted.
- I am not suited to this job.
- I feel as if I am being used and abused.
- I feel as if my time is being wasted.

This is one of the most important functional areas. If there is more than one event venue, medical facilities need to be available at all of them.

- My help is not appreciated.
- There is a lack of support.
- I don't understand how I fit in.
- The work is boring.
- I don't have all the information I need.
- I don't have the equipment I need to do the job.
- The procedures are not clear.
- I feel unwelcome and ignored.
- I don't like it.
- I got a better offer.
- I didn't expect to be doing this.
- Getting here was too difficult.

Unhappy staff say things such as:

'My supervisor arrived two hours late and I was kept waiting after getting up at 5 am.'

'Why can't we be given more information so that we can answer questions?'

'Somebody has to keep their head and be patient.'

So you can see why good leadership and an ability to motivate staff are crucial to the smooth running of an event. Some experienced event managers have made the following remarks and suggestions about staff management during the pressured moments of an event:

'Success is linked to goals, large ones and small ones. Be prepared to make the goals explicit and share achievement of these goals with your staff. This will motivate everyone.'

'Give the team an identity. Establish team roles and build cohesiveness. Games and fun are essential.'

'One of the most difficult things is assigning jobs. All staff want to be able to see the show.'

'A plan is a good thing, but be prepared to deviate from it.'

'Nothing can prepare you for it. Being faced with huge numbers of people descending on you, filling a venue within minutes, is incredible. Nothing can prepare you for the time-consuming nature of it. There are so many conflicting demands. You have to keep focused.'

'There is no quicker way to destroy team morale than for the manager to complain about the situation.'

'Facial messages are really important. You can ruin someone's day with the wrong expression.'

'Take the time to use the person's name and give clear and concise directions.'

'Once they are committed and settled, they will do anything. If you manage well, your team will walk over hot coals for you.'

'Information is provided to team leaders to pass on. They need to recognise the value of getting the information to the staff at the briefing, otherwise their radio will run hot all day answering the same question.'

'Sometimes it is difficult. You have a well-meaning staff member who comes to you with a suggestion. You are in the middle of doing a thousand critical things and they want your attention. You have to make time to talk to them later and explain why you can't listen right away. And you can't afford to forget to go back! If you don't they will feel undervalued.'

'Remember to be fair with recognition — you don't want to create a nasty competitive spirit in your team, especially in relation to give-aways.'

'Most of the organising committee were burnt out before the event began. Look after your physical health. It is like running a marathon. Prepare for it. Your tolerance for stress needs to be high.'

'Crack a few jokes when the going gets tough; initiate a dynamic and energetic team spirit.'

'Think about appreciation strategies beforehand — you have to plan celebrations for reaching milestones. This takes time and you won't have the time during the event.'

'People working at events expect to enjoy themselves; if they don't, the customers won't.'

Case study

You are organising a race for 20,000 runners. The biggest logistical problem you will face will be at the end of the race. At this time,

● ● ● ● ● ● ● ● ● ● ● ● ● ● ●
SUMMARY
This chapter has looked in more detail at logistics, including the often problematic bump-in and bump-out phases of an event. The task of identifying resources and equipment needed, bringing them on site and setting up in the required time takes careful planning. The emphasis in this chapter has therefore been on organisation and co-ordination to ensure that all functional areas work together smoothly and co-operatively through all phases of the event. The development of policies and procedures can assist in the fulfilment of this goal by outlining the interrelationship between functional areas and will also help to ensure that the event performance standards and objectives are successfully achieved.
● ● ● ● ● ● ● ● ● ● ● ● ● ● ●

runners crossing the finish line are exhausted and don't want to run or walk another step. Media wanting to take photographs and interview front runners compounds this problem. Enthusiastic supporters wishing to congratulate those who finish only adds to it. All runners need to get across the line without hold-ups, otherwise their times will be affected.

You need to make plans to ensure that all runners cross the line, that they are advised of their times, and that they receive free sponsor products, retrieve their belongings and attend the prize-giving ceremony. Some participants and spectators will not wait for the final ceremony and will wish to take the transport provided back to the race starting point and go home.

Develop detailed operational plans for the end of the race, using estimates of finish times and crowd flow patterns for participants and spectators.

Activities

Draw up an operational timetable for a wedding. This should include hire of outfits, table linen, candlesticks and chair covers. It should also include organisation of the cake, hire cars, floral arrangements and entertainment. The focus of this activity is the logistics of getting everything and everyone into place at the right time for the reception party.

Develop a mid-event appreciation strategy and a plan for a post-event party in order to celebrate the success of the event with your staff.

CHAPTER FIFTEEN

safety and
security

The woman from Sydney's northern beaches was found clinically dead shortly after Limp Bizkit was forced to stop during its first song because of a crowd crush.

A witness said they carried the woman into a St John Ambulance area by the stage.

The witness said, 'It was like a war scene in the tent. There were 25 kids on their back. Drips were being connected to them. It looked like a mass resuscitation was going on. It was absolute pandemonium.'

SUN HERALD, 28 JANUARY 2001

On completion of this chapter you will be able to:

- **identify situations in which police or security staff are required**
- **comply with laws, regulations and standards relating to occupational health and safety**
- **develop procedures to meet safety standards**
- **train staff to prevent risks to health and safety**
- **use systems that limit safety risks**
- **establish a system of communication for reporting incidents and emergencies.**

During this event, twelve people were taken to hospital and up to 600 treated, mainly for heat exhaustion. Prior to the event, the band had requested a T-style barricade through the centre of the audience to provide security access to the mosh pit, but the organisers had refused, saying that this measure was untested.

In the management of this type of event, careful analysis of crowd behaviour and the methods proposed for controlling crowds is required. Crowd management encompasses the steps taken to organise and manage crowds, while crowd control is the term used for dealing with crowds that are out of control. Security staff and security organisations play a major role in crowd control, particularly in events of this nature. First aid is also a necessity.

On the same day as the event described above, 220,000 people celebrated Australia Day with only a few minor incidents, none relating to crowd management. The behaviour of event visitors thus has an important role to play in the level of potential risk at a particular event and should form part of the analysis that begins with the risk management plan discussed in Chapter 8 and follows through to the contingency plans for safety and security discussed in detail in Chapter 16.

A well-behaved crowd at the Federation Day parade in January 2001.

Safety of the event audience, staff and subcontractors should be of paramount concern for every event manager, since all events carry safety risks which may result in anything from accidents to the evacuation of a venue. In this and the following chapter, we will look more closely at risks associated with the safety of the audience and staff and the security procedures used to manage such risks. In addition, we will look at the potential for injury being caused by fixed or temporary structures, which may in turn be subjected to damage.

Another issue for consideration for most events is that of queuing. Queuing can be managed very well or very badly. The delays getting into events such as Grand Final matches are sometimes so bad that the event manager has to direct staff to stop taking tickets and simply open the gates. Clearly this can lead to problems inside the venue if non-ticketed people manage to find their way in. On the other hand, if the Grand Final has commenced, and perhaps a goal scored while the spectators remain outside, there would be little else that could be done. However, if there were a number of people without tickets outside the venue, this would not be a viable option.

Orderly management of spectators leaving the venue is just as important, with clear directions and signage necessary to guide them to public transport. Sometimes revellers enjoy themselves so much at the event that they have to be marched out by security staff.

In this chapter we will deal with general security issues, occupational health and safety, first aid and effective communication of incidents. The topics of crowd control and emergency evacuation will be covered in more detail in the next chapter.

SECURITY

Security is generally required for premises, equipment, cash and other valuables, but the predominant role of most event security staff is to ensure that the correct people have access to specific areas and to act responsibly in case of accident or emergency. Accreditation badges (generally a tag hanging around the neck, showing the areas to which staff, media and spectators have access) allow security staff to monitor access. Ejection of people who are behaving inappropriately, sometimes in co-operation with police personnel, is occasionally necessary.

There are several considerations in the organisation of security for an event. Firstly, it is necessary to calculate the number of trained staff required for the security role. If the venue covers a large area, vehicles and equipment may also be required. (Four-wheeled buggies are usually used to deploy staff to outlying areas.) And finally, the level of threat will determine whether firearms are needed.

In all cases, security staff should be appropriately licensed and the security company should carry the appropriate insurance.

Ready for duty at an event.

Police Service

The Police Service often provides some of the required security services, generally at no cost to community events. However, with the growth of the event industry and the increased demands on police for spectator control, charges are now being levied by some Police Services for every officer attending a profit-making event. For major sporting events, about four police officers are provided free and the remainder are hired by the event organiser. The number of police required is negotiated by the police and the event manager, the number depending on any history of incidents and the availability of alcohol.

Mounted police often attend large street festivals and processions.

Security organisations

Laws exist in relation to security organisations and security personnel. The industry is well regulated and an event company must ensure that the appropriate licences are secured. A master licence is held by the security company, and there are various classes of licence for officers, depending on training and experience. All security officers are required to undergo a criminal record check.

The roles of security officers include:

- acting as a bodyguard, bouncer or crowd controller
- patrolling or protecting premises
- installing and maintaining security equipment
- providing advice on security equipment and procedures
- training staff in security procedures.

Security organisations must hold appropriate general liability insurance cover. General liability insurance cover is, in fact, a requirement of almost all contracts between event organisers and subcontractors. Subcontractors, including security companies, also need to cover their staff for work-related health and safety incidents.

OCCUPATIONAL HEALTH AND SAFETY

Occupational health and safety legislation aims to prevent accidents and injury in the work environment and is of particular relevance to the event organiser. The duties of employers, people in control of workplaces and suppliers of equipment and services are all described in the relevant state or territory legislation. The following extract, reproduced with the permission of WorkSafe Western Australia, gives a broad overview of these responsibilities.

Duties of Employers

Employers must ensure employees are not exposed to hazards at work. The Act also lists a number of specific duties for employers. All these depend on what is practicable for the workplace.

Employers must:

1 *provide and maintain workplaces, plant and systems of work that do not expose employees to hazards (This refers to the whole working environment, premises, machinery and methods of work, and also to lighting, ventilation, dust, heat, noise, fumes, and other factors such as stress, fatigue and violence in the workplace.)*

2 *provide information, instruction, training and supervision so employees can perform their work*

3 *consult and co-operate with safety and health representatives, if any, and other employees at the workplace, on occupational safety and health matters*

4 *provide adequate protective clothing and equipment free of charge where hazards cannot be avoided*

5 *ensure safe use, cleaning, maintenance, transportation and disposal of substances and plant in the workplace.*

Employers must ensure that persons not directly employed by them, such as contractors and subcontractors, are not exposed to hazards in the workplace.

Duties of People in Control of Workplaces

*People in control of a workplace must ensure it is safe, and **anyone** can safely enter or leave it.*

Owners, lessors and others who control any part of a workplace are bound by this duty. This includes people with a contract or lease which gives them responsibility for maintenance or repair of a workplace, including the means of access to and egress from the workplace. However, people are only responsible for matters under their control.

Duties of Manufacturers, Importers, Suppliers, Designers, etc.

People who design, manufacture, import or supply plant for use in workplaces have a duty to ensure that the article is designed, manufactured and marketed so that people installing, maintaining or using it properly are not exposed to hazards.

Plant must be tested and information supplied about its safe use and its hazards.

Manufacturers, importers or suppliers of workplace substances, such as chemicals, must provide toxicological and other information about safe handling, storage and disposal. This information should be given in a material safety data sheet (MSDS), and on the container label. MSDSs should be provided when the substance is supplied or whenever requested.

*People who design or construct buildings or structures have a duty to ensure that people constructing or **using the building** or structure are not exposed to hazards.*

All employers must take out workers compensation insurance. This covers all staff for work-related accident or injury, including their medical expenses, payment for time off work and rehabilitation. Volunteers are not covered by this insurance because they are not, by definition, 'paid workers', but they are covered under general liability insurance. Workers compensation insurance generally covers the employee in transit to and from their workplace, provided that they travel directly to and from their place of work. The most important element of this legislation is the **responsibility placed on supervisors and managers** for ensuring that employees have a **safe place of work** and **safe systems of work**.

Policies and procedures in relation to safety are essential, and these procedures need to be part of all employee training. In the sections below we will discuss the safe handling of items and the safe performance of certain activities that otherwise may be a threat to the safety of workers in the event environment.

Safe lifting techniques

Lifting techniques are generally part of training for anyone involved in lifting, carrying or moving heavy objects, such as sporting equipment or display stands. Two useful training aids for this purpose are illustrated in Fig. 15.1 and Table 15.1.

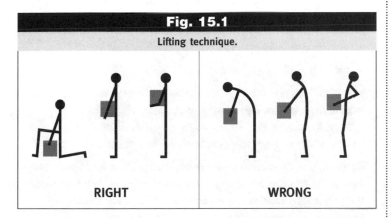

Fig. 15.1
Lifting technique.

RIGHT | **WRONG**

The correct way to lift a heavy object is to squat close to the load, keeping your back straight. Do not stoop over the load to get a grip and pick it up. Test the weight of the object before attempting to lift it. Lift using your knees and legs (not your back) as leverage. Keep your back straight, not bent forwards or backwards. Do not twist or turn your body while carrying the object or putting it down.

Table 15.1
How to prevent injuries caused by lifting and moving heavy objects.

Avoid	Common Causes of Injury	Common Solutions
Lifting and moving	Lifting boxes from the floor	Do not store items on the floor.
	Carrying boxes or equipment	Use proper lifting techniques. Get help or use a lifting aid. Use a cart. Avoid over-reaching, twisting or lifting over head.
	Pushing carts	Maintain casters in clean, operating condition. Match the casters to the floor type.

The WorkSafe Western Australia Commission's 2000 Manual Handling Code of Practice (Appendix G) provides the following guidance for the handling of heavy objects.

2.1 Heavy

The risk of injury increases as the weight of the load increases.

Evaluating the risk of weight of the object needs to take into account:

- how long the load is handled

- how often the load is handled.

As a guide, the risk of back injury increases when loads over 4.5 kg are handled from a seated position or when loads over 16 kg are handled from positions other than seated. As weight increases, the percentage of healthy adults who can safely lift, lower or carry decreases.

Generally, no single person should be required to lift, lower or carry loads over 55 kg. **This limit would only apply, however, when the load is within the person's capabilities and no other risk factors are present** (e.g. no bending or twisting is required to pick up the load; the load is compact and easy to grasp; it is held close to the trunk and not carried frequently or for long distances).

On occasions, objects over 55 kg may be moved but not lifted, e.g. rolling a 200 litre drum.

In conclusion, they suggest that a definitive, absolute safe lifting weight is not possible to determine and that a commonsense approach is required for assessing manual handling tasks. Weight should be considered, along with all other factors in the context of the task, including actions or postures, other load characteristics, the work environment and human characteristics.

Safety steps for electrical equipment

Electrical equipment is a significant hazard in the event environment, particularly in wet weather. All safety steps must be taken to prevent accidents involving electrical equipment, including routine tagging and inspection of equipment. Many venues are extremely rigorous in their demands for documentation which demonstrates correct licensing and inspection.

The following extract on Residual Current Devices (RCDs), from *Safetyline Magazine*, No. 23, July 1994, reproduced with permission of WorkSafe Western Australia, is still very relevant to safe use of electrical equipment, even though published some years ago.

Electrical hazards may exist where workers assume RCD safety cut-out switches make electrocution impossible. **Some workers may be taking risks with electricity under the false impression that RCDs (Residual Current Devices) make it impossible for them to be electrocuted.**

It is important that full safety procedures, such as lockout and tagging, are still followed when working with electricity. RCDs are an addition to safety measures, NOT a substitute for them. RCDs should be regularly tested and maintained.

RCDs would prevent the majority of electrocutions where electrical current has been earthed through the human body, but even with the use of RCDs, electrocution can still occur if contact is made between active and neutral wires.

Even if electrocution does not occur, the shock received before RCD cut-off operates may be severe enough to cause injury — for example, from the power tool coming into contact with the body, or in a fall.

Residual Current Devices (RCDs) are relay switches that measure current going through the active wire into a device, such as a power tool, and leaving it through the neutral wire. When current becomes diverted by being earthed (through a worker holding the tool, for instance) the RCD reacts to the electrical imbalance and cuts off the electricity within .03 of a second.

RCDs, also known as earth leakage circuit breakers, are mandatory in all workplaces using portable or hand-held power tools and extension leads.

The Occupational Safety and Health Regulations 1996 require RCDs to be installed as permanent switchboard fixtures or as portable devices.

Safe use of machinery

Regulations for safeguarding machinery in the workplace are provided in the Australian Standard, **AS 4024.1-1996 Safeguarding of machinery — General principles**.

This Standard identifies the hazards and risks arising from the use of industrial machinery and describes methods for the elimination or minimisation of them, as well as for the safeguarding of machinery and the use of safe work practices. It also describes and illustrates a number of safety principles and provides guidelines by which it is possible to assess which measure or method it is practicable to adopt in particular circumstances.

This Standard is intended for those who design, manufacture, supply, install, use, maintain or modify machinery, machinery guarding or safety devices, and identifies the existence of Standards for a number of particular classes of machine. It is also designed to be used by those concerned with information, instruction and training in safe work practices.

Safe handling of hazardous substances

Because different chemicals have different safe use requirements, it is important for staff to know as much about hazardous substances used in the workplace as possible. Material Safety Data Sheets should be used to provide the following advice on these substances to staff members:

- ingredients of a product
- health effects and first-aid instructions
- precautions for use
- safe handling and storage information
- emergency procedures.

Safety signs

Safety signs are particularly important in the event workplace since staff are generally only at the venue for a very short period. This does not allow much time for reinforcement of safety issues, however these can be stressed during briefing sessions. Posters and safety signs, such as those reproduced below, can be used to reinforce key messages, helping to prevent many accidents.

These cylinders contain a hazardous substance, requiring clear instructions for safe handling and storage.

First aid

In most cases, first aid is provided by organisations such as St John Ambulance, although venue and event staff should also be trained in first aid procedures. Some of these procedures will be specific to the event in question. For example, at road races, common first aid emergencies occur, including exhaustion, collapse, dehydration, road burns, and bone and muscle injuries, and procedures should be in place for dealing with them. In addition, participants in races such as these sometimes do not wish to accept help and staff would need to be trained in the correct procedure for dealing with such an occurrence.

INCIDENT REPORTING

For any event there are standard reporting relationships on all operational issues. On the whole, these reporting relationships concur with the organisation chart. However, there are many instances where communication is less formal and less structured, no less in the case of the event working environment where 'mayhem' or 'controlled chaos' may best describe it.

Despite some tolerance of rather haphazard communication before and during the event, **any communication relating to an incident or emergency needs to be very clear**. It must also **follow a short and specific chain of command**. The chain of command, or organisation chart, for an emergency is seldom the same as the organisation chart for the event as a whole. Emergency reporting tends to go through very few levels, and all staff must be trained in emergency reporting. Many stakeholders may be involved — general staff, security staff, first aid personnel, police, emergency services — but absolute clarity is needed as to who makes key decisions and how they are to be contacted. These lines of reporting and responsibility will be reviewed in the next chapter.

A railway security officer in radio contact with Operations.

Communication methods

Most event teams use radios as they are the most effective tool for maintaining communication. Different channels are used for different purposes, and it is essential that the correct radio procedures be followed. In Fig. 15.2 (see over) radio links to the Event Operations Centre are illustrated, with 'Control' serving as the link to the decision-makers. For example, in response to a request to remove a hazard, Control would ensure that the Site team responded to the call. If a spill were reported, Control would report to Cleaning, requesting that the spill be cleaned up. The Operations Centre also has links to emergency services that can be called if required.

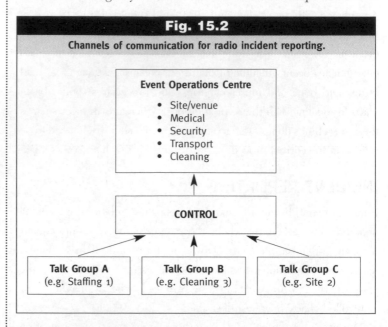

Fig. 15.2

Channels of communication for radio incident reporting.

At some events, mobile telephones are used, but the drawback of this method of communication is that the information transmitted can be overheard. Networks can also become overloaded if spectators are using their mobile phones, particularly during intermission and at the end of a match or concert.

Meetings between event staff, including security staff and emergency services, are necessary to plan and monitor security and safety, as difficulties can occur if the communications technology of the various services is not compatible. It is crucial that this issue be anticipated and that contingency plans be put in place to deal effectively with any communication problems.

Case study 1

The Gold Mining Company is a nightclub venue that is popular during the months of May, June and July for its Friday night dance events. The staff working at this venue are all casuals and turnover is high. During a conversation, two of the staff, Jason and Malik, find out that they have both been mugged on their way home from work in the early hours of the morning, but on different Friday nights. In both cases, the perpetrators waited in a nearby alley and threatened them with knives. Jason lost his wallet and $400 and Malik broke his ankle when trying to run away. Candice, another employee, has been harassed by patrons and was once burned deliberately with a cigarette by a particularly drunk and obnoxious customer. Management gave her some cash to get medical attention.

Discuss the occupational health and safety issues of the staff concerned. What are the responsibilities of the management in each of these cases?

Case study 2

The 2003 exhibition of *Designer Jewellery — Artists of the South Pacific* is being held in the foyer of a large city hotel. The State Premier will open the exhibition and several dignitaries from visiting countries will be in attendance. Some of these countries are currently experiencing political turmoil so there will be security risks associated with the guests, as well as with the items on display. Threats and protests could also disrupt the opening.

Discuss the following issues:
- Who will be responsible for security (probably more than one body).
- What are some of the potential security problems?
- What are the occupational health and safety issues?
- What steps can be taken to prevent a security incident?
- What plans should be in place should an incident occur?

Activity
Identify some of the security issues at the following events and prepare plans to prevent or deal with these issues:
- *dance party with mosh pit*
- *street festival*
- *private party for a celebrity*
- *product launch*
- *road race.*

Links
http://www.chubb.com.au/index.asp (cash logistics; security personnel)
http://www.workcover.gov.au
http://www1.safetyline.wa.gov.au/default.htm (WorkSafe Western Australia)

● ● ● ● ● ● ● ● ● ● ● ● ● ● ● ●
SUMMARY
The health, safety and security of staff and the event audience are very important concerns of the event management team. In this chapter we have discussed many measures for ensuring this is achieved, including the safe handling of heavy objects and hazardous substances and the safe use of electrical equipment and machinery. Safety and security are risks that need to be dealt with by assessing the risk, managing the risk and developing contingency plans for dealing with the risk. Not only must people be protected but also assets, and security personnel and the police are there to assist the event manager in managing these risks. Most importantly, an effective system of communication for reporting incidents will prevent the escalation of a situation and help staff to deal promptly with any emergency.
● ● ● ● ● ● ● ● ● ● ● ● ● ● ● ●

http://oshweb.me.tut.fi/index.html (international site for occupational health and safety)

http://www.worksafe.gov.au/nohsc/othersites/index.htm (OH&S sites)

http://www.detir.qld.gov.au/hs/legisl/whsact/act95v1.pdf (Workplace Health and Safety Act Queensland)

http://www1.safetyline.wa.gov.au/pagebin/manhhazd0029.htm (Manual Handling Code of Practice)

http://www.christie.ab.ca/safelist/ (Internet safety resources)

http://www.standardsaustralia.gov.au

CHAPTER SIXTEEN

crowd
management and evacuation

Paramedics from all across the city rushed to the scene, then battled to get through the crowds to attend to the injured. In some cases, police had to baton-charge a path through hordes of hysterical people in order for doctors and rescue workers to get into the stadium. An already appalling situation appears to have been worsened by security guards who fired tear gas at a stampeding crowd outside the stadium. People ran everywhere, dozens falling down and being crushed to death and many more severely injured.

THE CITIZEN, JOHANNESBURG, 12 APRIL 2001

On completion of this chapter you will be able to:
• identify the types of events and situations that might give rise to crowd management problems
• develop crowd management and crowd control systems and procedures
• identify the types of occurrences that may require evacuation
• develop procedures for evacuation.

As this article illustrates, contingency plans need to be in place in case of emergencies at an event and, clearly, easy access for emergency services is one of the first aspects that needs to be considered. Evacuation and crowd management are others. In this chapter we will deal with all three.

The initial task of the event manager is to develop a crowd management plan.

THE CROWD MANAGEMENT PLAN

The following are the key things to consider when developing this plan:
• the number of people at the venue (the event audience, staff and contractors)
• the likely behaviour of spectators (especially for events with a history of crowd behaviour problems)

- the timing of the event, including session times and peak periods
- the layout of the venue and/or other facilities
- the security services to be provided or contracted
- the legal requirements and general guidelines.

The last of these requires adherence to occupational health and safety legislation and the laws relating to fire egress (exits), as well as to a number of guidelines provided by Standards Australia, if applicable to the event, such as:

- **AS2187.4 Pyrotechnics — Outdoors** specifies the precautions to be carried out in storage, handling and use of pyrotechnics for outdoor displays.
- **AS2560.2.3 Lighting for Outdoor Football** deals with the level of lighting required for training, competition and spectator viewing for all football codes.
- **AS1680 Interior Lighting — Safe Movement** sets out the minimum requirements for electric lighting systems within publicly accessible areas of buildings in order to provide visual conditions that facilitate the safe movement of people in the normal use of the buildings.
- **AS/NZS2293.3 Emergency Evacuation Lighting for Buildings** provides building, maintenance and inspection guidelines for emergency evacuation lighting.

All of the above Standards, and many more that are relevant to building permanent and temporary structures, are available on the websites listed at the end of this chapter.

The crowd management plan covers readily available information, such as the dimensions of the venue or site, but it also goes further to encompass the probable number of spectators at particular times of the event and their flow through the site. Clearly the peaks are the most problematic from a crowd management perspective and the plan needs to address this and other challenges by covering the following:

- Estimate the level of attendance for specific days and times.
- Estimate the number of people using public corridors, specific entrances, specific aisles and seating at particular times.
- Estimate the number of ushers and service and security personnel needed for crowd management.

- Establish the requirements for crowd control measures, such as barriers.
- Identify the areas that need to remain restricted.
- Develop accreditation plans for restricted access by specific staff.
- Identify particular hazards (for example, scaffolding, temporary structures).
- Identify routes by which emergency services personnel will enter and leave the site.
- Establish the means of communication for all staff working on the site.
- Establish a chain of command for incident reporting.
- Check safety equipment (for example, the number of fire extinguishers and that inspections have been carried out according to legal requirements).
- Identify the safety needs of specific groups of people, such as people with disabilities, children and players/performers.
- Identify first aid requirements and provision.
- Develop an emergency response plan (ERP).
- Develop an evacuation plan and initiate training and drills for the staff concerned.

As we know, there are many different types of event venue, each having specific features and some being safer than others. They range from outdoor environments, such as streets and parks, to aquatic centres, indoor facilities and purpose-built venues. The last of these is generally the safest since crowd management and evacuation would generally have been considered at the time these structures were built, and rehearsed again and again by the venue team. However, a crowd management and evacuation plan would still need to be developed for each event held at the venue, as factors such as crowd numbers and movement would generally be different.

MAJOR RISKS

The major incidents that need to be considered in relation to crowd management and evacuation include:

- fire, smoke
- bomb threat, terrorism, threats to VIPs
- flood, earthquake or other natural disasters
- heat, failure of air-conditioning or lighting
- gas leaks or biological hazards

- crowd crush, overcrowding, congestion
- riots, protests
- vehicle accidents
- collapsing fences or other structures.

The density of this event audience illustrates the importance of appropriate crowd control measures.

For each of the above, the response of the public to the emergency should be evaluated so that the emergency team has procedures in place for preventing panic. Reassuring messages on the public address system is one way of reducing panic and ensuring orderly evacuation.

CROWD MANAGEMENT

Once a range of risks has been identified, in particular risks such as congestion, overcrowding and crowd crush, the circumstances that may lead to bad or destructive behaviour in these contexts needs to be analysed. The risks then need to be prioritised and plans put in place to avoid them (known as **preventative** measures) or to deal with them should they occur (known as **contingency** measures). An example of a preventative measure for reducing congestion at turnstiles is to employ staff to assist spectators and to monitor the area. Impatient crowds, however, might simply jump over the turnstile or knock it down. There would thus need to be a contingency plan in place for dealing with this situation. Property damage by spectators would also need to be covered and procedures would be required for ejecting the offending spectators. At worst, the police may charge them. (Streakers who disrupt play during sports matches spring to mind in this instance.) The more serious risk, however, are non-ticketed spectators who gain illegal entry.

Soccer Disasters

1971   Glasgow, Scotland. Sixty-six people were crushed to death in what became known as the Ibrox disaster when Glasgow Rangers and Celtic fans clashed after a late goal.

1982   Moscow, Russia. Police herded a group of fans into one section of the stadium during a European Cup match between Spartak Moscow and Haarlem. They were crushed by fans returning to the ground after a late goal. Official reports say that 60 people died but the actual number was reportedly closer to 340.

1985   Brussels, Belgium. Drunken British Liverpool fans attacked rival Italian Juventus supporters during a European Champions Cup at the Heysel Stadium. Thirty-nine people were crushed or trampled to death after a concrete wall collapsed. More than 400 were injured.

1986   Guatemala City. At least 82 people died and about 150 were injured by stampeding fans prior to a 1998 World Cup qualifying match between Guatemala and Costa Rica.

1989   Hillsborough, Sheffield. Ninety-six fans died, many by crushing and asphyxiation. Over 300 people were injured during an FA Cup semi-final.

1991   Orkney, South Africa. At least 40 people were killed when fans panicked after brawls broke out.

1996   Guatemala. Ninety people were killed and 150 injured in a crush during a World Cup qualifier.

2000   Harare, Zimbabwe. Violence broke out during a World Cup qualifier between South Africa and Zimbabwe after a late goal. Thirteen people were trampled to death when riot police fired tear gas.

2001   Johannesburg, South Africa. Forty-three people were crushed to death and many hundreds were injured when excited fans tried to get into a capacity stadium. Some died outside and others died inside, crushed against barricades at the side of the field.

2001   Accra, Ghana. A stampede triggered by police anti-riot tactics at a soccer match left over 120 people dead. Police responded to the disruption by firing tear gas into the stands. Thousands of fans then fled the gas attack by rushing to a pedestrian tunnel. A horrible crush resulted, according to reports from the scene.

The following strategies (adapted from the website at the end of this chapter) may help to prevent deaths and injuries suffered by fans at rock concerts and other large events:

- Review the behaviour of crowds attending similar past events.
- Review crowd responses to specific bands and performers at past rock concerts.
- Conduct an evaluation of all structures available for mosh pit management.
- Obtain engineering and specialist advice.
- Isolate the mosh pit from the general audience.
- Limit mosh pit capacity and density.
- Provide easy exits from the mosh pit area.
- Ban alcohol and cigarettes from the mosh pit.
- Station special first-aid assistance near the mosh pit.
- Ban stage diving, body surfing/swimming.
- Provide specially trained private security and 'peer security'.
- Provide special ventilation and drinking fountains for moshers.
- Pad the floor and all hard surfaces, including barriers and railings.
- Ban certain types of clothes and accessories worn by moshers in the pit.
- Introduce mosh pit safety announcements in advance of the show and during shows.
- Seek assistance from the performers in managing or preventing moshing.

EMERGENCY PLANNING

Emergency planning is Standards based. The following is a summary of the guidelines that are provided in **DR00180 Emergency control organization and procedures for buildings (Standards Australia)**.

A committee called the Emergency Planning Committee (EPC) should be convened to:

- establish the emergency response plan (ERP)
- ensure that appropriate people are assigned to specific roles, such as Chief Warden, and that their responsibilities in the Emergency Control Organisation (ECO) are clarified
- arrange training for all members of the ECO team
- arrange for evacuation drills
- review procedures

- ensure that ECO staff are indemnified against civil liability in situations where they act in good faith in the course of their emergency control duties.

When developing the emergency response plan, specialist advice is recommended. Most security organisations offer this type of consultancy support. When developing the emergency procedures, the following should be taken into account:
- peak numbers of people in the venue
- assembly and evacuation routes, and signage
- people with disabilities
- lifts and escalators (assume that these are not used, except by fire authorities)
- people check (making sure everyone has left)
- marshalling points (especially for very large venues)
- safeguarding of cash and valuables
- communication systems (emergency warning and emergency intercom system — AS2220.1 and AS2220.2) as well as public address systems
- emergency equipment
- control and co-ordination point/s (location/s) for emergency response by the Chief Warden and liaison with emergency services
- co-ordination with other agencies such as council and emergency services.

The Emergency Control Organisation is the team responsible for responding to the emergency. This team includes the following personnel:
- Chief Warden
- Deputy Chief Warden
- Communications Officer
- Floor/Area Wardens
- Wardens.

During an emergency, instructions given by ECO wardens should override those given by any other person in the organisation structure.

The structure of the ECO, together with identifying features, is illustrated in Fig. 16.1 (see over).

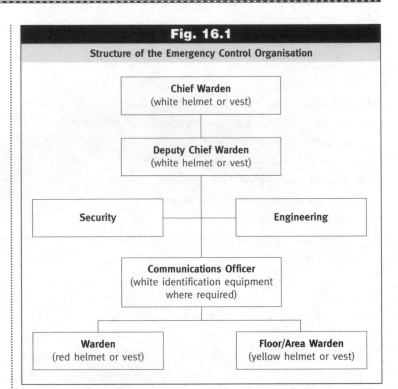

Fig. 16.1

Structure of the Emergency Control Organisation

- **Chief Warden** (white helmet or vest)
- **Deputy Chief Warden** (white helmet or vest)
- **Security** — **Engineering**
- **Communications Officer** (white identification equipment where required)
- **Warden** (red helmet or vest) — **Floor/Area Warden** (yellow helmet or vest)

Selection and training of emergency personnel should follow the comprehensive Standards guidelines provided in the relevant Standards document. It is essential that you read the full text of the Standards as this chapter provides only an overview of the Standards, roles and procedures.

In general terms, the people selected for roles in the ECO should be in attendance during the hours of operation, should show leadership qualities and sound judgement under pressure, and should be able to communicate clearly. The first of these attributes is the most problematic in the event business. For leased premises, the venue team is generally limited in number and few work for the full duration of an event. The question of availability during an event, especially one with multiple sessions, is a key consideration for the committee. There is no point in having a well-trained ECO that is not in attendance!

Below are the chief roles of each person in the ECO team.

Chief Warden

The duties of the Chief Warden include ascertaining the nature and location of the emergency and determining the appropriate action;

ensuring that emergency services and floor wardens are advised; initiating evacuation; and briefing emergency personnel on their arrival.

Deputy Chief Warden

The Deputy will take on the roles of the Chief Warden if unavailable or assist as required.

Communications Officer

The duties of the Communications Officer include ascertaining the nature and location of the emergency; confirming that the emergency service/s have been notified; and notifying, transmitting and recording instructions and progress.

Floor/Area Wardens

Implementing the emergency procedures for their area; checking the floor/area; and co-ordinating and communicating with the Chief Warden are all roles of Floor/Area Wardens.

Wardens

Checking, searching, giving instructions during an evacuation and reporting to the Floor/Area Warden are the tasks undertaken by the Wardens.

For all officers in the ECO, ensuring that emergency services have been notified is part of the job.

Full details of the roles and tasks of these officers are available on the Standards websites at the end of this chapter, as well as a number of videos on this type of planning and training. Specialist assistance in this area is recommended, as well as the use of Emergency Warning and Intercommunication Systems (EWIS).

IMPLEMENTING EMERGENCY PROCEDURES

In order to effectively implement emergency procedures, the following steps should be taken:

- Review implementation issues and integrate them with all other event operational plans.
- Ensure broad awareness of the procedures through wide dissemination of information and consultation with all concerned.
- Use signage and well-designed communication materials in a

simple format to provide information.

- Train all staff.
- Test the procedures by conducting evacuation exercises.
- Review procedures to check effectiveness.

Fire procedures

There are four major steps that ideally should be initiated concurrently:

1 Ensure the safety of everyone within the vicinity of the fire.
2 Call the fire brigade in any circumstance in which there is suspicion of fire.
3 Conduct evacuation.
4 Fight the fire with appropriate equipment or retreat and close all doors.

Note that there is no need for anyone to give permission for a call to the fire brigade. This call can be initiated by anyone.

Evacuation procedures

The evacuation procedure for most venues follows the same process: the Chief Warden uses the tone BEEP ... BEEP ... BEEP for alert and WHOOP ... WHOOP ... WHOOP for evacuation on the public address system.

The warden intercommunication phone (WIP) is used to advise the Chief Warden of danger in specific areas. All staff should be trained in their specific roles in this situation.

In the event of an evacuation it is important for staff to:

- remain calm
- be observant
- listen to and follow instructions
- provide information and instructions to staff and spectators when advised to do so
- maintain radio protocol (do not block channels)
- follow all safety precautions (such as not using lifts in case of fire).

The emergency response plan is reliant on the warden system and the chain of command. Early warning means fast intervention.

Bomb threat procedures

As with fire and evacuation procedures, there is a recommended procedure for dealing with bomb threats. Details are available from the Australian Bomb Data Centre which publishes a handbook, giving standard guidelines, that can be kept near all telephones. These include:

- evaluation (deciding whether or not to take action, and whether to search, with or without evacuation)
- notification (police should be advised)
- search (the aim is identification of the suspicious object, which should not be touched or moved).

In Fig. 16.2 is a checklist, which should also be kept near the telephone, outlining the questions to ask and information to secure about the caller.

Fig. 16.2
Bomb threat checklist.

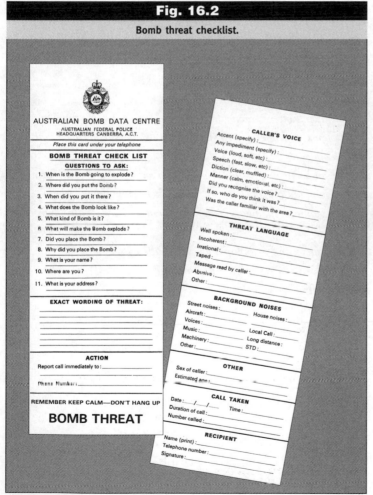

Reproduced with permission Australian Bomb Data Centre.

SUMMARY

In this chapter we have dealt with one of the most problematic issues for event managers: crowd control. Unfortunately, there are many examples of events at which people have lost their lives through fire or riot, and there are many examples of near-misses. For every event, emergency response plans for crowd control and evacuation in case of fire or other major risk must be developed. These plans must comply with the relevant legislation and Standards and be properly implemented. All possible preventative measures need to be put in place prior to the event. Staff training and contingency planning are other key aspects of the emergency response plan.

Case study

You are going to hire a venue for a fashion parade. The venue you have in mind is an old theatre that lends itself well to the event, with excellent sight lines for the audience. However, the décor and lighting planned by your Artistic Director for your fashion parade may compromise safety. Drapes over the ceiling area will obscure the normal lighting and prevent the fire sensors and sprinklers from working correctly. And there are a number of props that may hinder access into and out of the venue. On the other hand, the audience expected is quite small. Answer the following questions:

- What are some of the safety risks associated with this event?
- Who is responsible for the safety of the venue and the audience?
- With whom should you discuss the risks associated with your event concept?
- How could the risks be reduced?
- What sorts of contingency plans could be developed?
- What should the evacuation plan include?

Activities

1 Visit *http://www.crowdsafe.com* and list five major crowd control problems that have led to significant numbers of casualties at rock concerts.
2 Visit an event venue and evaluate the emergency plan in terms of:
    - *the venue's physical features and likely emergency risks*
    - *the venue map, emergency equipment and access for emergency services*
    - *entrances and exits for the event audience*
    - *the clarity of roles for staff involved*
    - *reporting relationships*
    - *communication technologies*
    - *record keeping*
    - *other legal compliance or adherence to Standards.*

Links

http://www.crowdsafe.com/mosh.html (strategies for ensuring crowd safety)

http://www.afp.gov.au/abdc/ (Australian Bomb Data Centre)

http://www.standards.org.au/ (Standards Australia)

http://www.standards.co.nz/ (Standards New Zealand)

CHAPTER SEVENTEEN

monitoring, control and

evaluation

The 1996 event, despite poor weather, proved an outstanding success by attracting a field of 1,256 entrants. This represented an increase of 75% over the 1995 field and indicated that a local 'fun walk' was capable of attracting at least twice as many people as the average 'fun run'. By 1999 the number of local entrants had increased to 74% of the total field. The fact that 26% of entrants were from outside the Macarthur region indicated that the event could have a positive impact on non-health fields such as local tourism and the local hospitality industry.

It is significant that over 80% of the field selected the 6 km distance and that entrant details showed considerable involvement by family and neighbourhood groups, as well as teams from schools, clubs and workplaces. These results indicate success in targeting participation rather than competitiveness and reinforce the findings of an entrant survey which revealed that, while most entered for the exercise, a significant 30% saw the event primarily as a family outing.

CAMPBELLTOWN CITY COUNCIL HEALTH PROMOTION UNIT

This is an outstanding example of event evaluation in that it demonstrates the council's achievement of its objectives, which were to raise awareness of walking as a viable form of exercise and to provide a motivational goal for commitment to regular exercise as an integral part of a healthy lifestyle. However, in addition to the findings that supported the health-related objectives, it was found that over a quarter of the participants were from outside Macarthur, resulting in a positive economic impact from tourism on

On completion of this chapter you will be able to:

- **develop and implement preventative and feedback control systems**
- **plan an evaluation strategy**
- **use research approaches to identify the composition of an event audience**
- **use research approaches to evaluate the success of an event from the customer, staff and management viewpoints**
- **write an event evaluation report.**

the region. Thirty per cent of participants saw the walk as a family outing, demonstrating a positive social impact as well.

In this chapter we will look at two aspects of event management: control and evaluation. Control systems are essential in ensuring that procedures are followed (for cash handling and recording entrants, for example) and that performance measures are achieved. Evaluation is the process of measuring the success of an event against its objectives. The data from performance measures is used in this analysis. Taking the example of the fun walk above, control systems would ensure that all participants were registered, while evaluation would involve an analysis of the questions on the registration form and feedback after the event. If a significant number of local residents joined the walk without registering, this would indicate a lack of control measures, and would naturally have an impact on the evaluation findings.

MONITORING AND CONTROL SYSTEMS

The challenge for the event manager is to delegate and monitor effectively and not to micromanage (become too involved with detail). While attention to detail is positive, this should be left to the event manager's team. A successful event manager needs to be aware that during the peak time of an event non-standard situations and incidents will require his or her time, which means that all routine procedures and control systems need to be in place before the event. Such control systems ensure that information filtering to the top of the event organisation will prompt management to make decisions to intervene only if things are not going according to plan.

Take, for example, the simple situation of T-shirts and caps being sold through an outlet at an event. How would an event manager know if the cash passed over the counter were reaching the till? Or if all the merchandise were reaching the outlet? A simple procedure for recording the number of boxes of stock issued and an hourly check of stock and cash levels would immediately show any shortfall.

Preventative controls and feedback controls

There are two types of controls: preventative and feedback. A preventative control is established early in the planning process. For example, checking the quality of incoming food for a banquet is a preventative control measure, as is monitoring food temperatures to avoid food poisoning. Signed requisition forms are another preventative measure designed to curtail unauthorised spending and budget blow-outs. A checklist for setting up sporting equipment before an international gymnastics event is another example of a preventative control measure. This would need to be designed to ensure that set-up would meet international specifications: if measurements were inaccurate, injury could be caused to an athlete or an athlete disqualified. In Fig. 17.1 we have included an example of a site inspection checklist.

Fig. 17.1

Site inspection checklist.

Venue Checklist

Plans to scale (all venue dimensions)	✓
Disability access	✓
Capacity for seating and standing	✓
Sight lines for event audience (no pillars, obstructions)	✓
Capacity for storage	✓
Appropriate number of toilets, suitable locations	✓
Suitability of food and beverage preparation and service areas	✓
Accessibility for delivery and installation of equipment, food, etc.	✓
Correct number of tables, chairs, plates, glasses, etc.	✓
Emergency evacuation plan	✓
Safety of venue (fire equipment, access and egress)	✓
Preferred contractors (e.g. security, catering)	✓
Fixed and hire equipment requirements	✓
Electrical supply	✓
Water supply (especially for temporary kitchens)	✓

Venue limitations

_____

Outstanding issues/actions

_____

Feedback controls are put in place to assist with decisions during an event. For example, feedback would be required to decide on the point at which event merchandise should be discounted to avoid having stock left over. If you discount too early, you lose revenue. If you discount too late, you find yourself with stock that has no sale value. Incident reporting is another form of feedback control: if a series of similar incidents have occurred, preventative measures will need be implemented. As an example, the reporting of a number of slips and falls in the kitchen over a period of days would require the implementation of a preventative measure which might be thorough overnight cleaning, sandpapering the floor and painting it with a non-stick surface, or providing mats to cover the slippery areas.

In most industries, information from point-of-sale and stock control systems are the feedback used for measuring and managing sales and profit levels over a particular period. However, in the event industry, decisions about price and other product features are made before the event, with sales occurring over a very short time period, allowing little opportunity to respond to financial information during an event. This is why it is so important to collect and store information on aspects of an event, such as merchandise sales, for use as a precedent for the next event of a similar nature.

OPERATIONAL MONITORING AND CONTROL

There are a number of issues in relation to operational procedures that need to be addressed before the event begins. These include the necessity for delegation of responsibility and flexibility in carrying out procedures, the effect of control systems on customers and the importance of financial controls.

Implementation of priority or high risk procedures

If the procedure is one that involves high risk, it must be fixed, detailed and well documented. There can be no deviation from this type of procedure. It must be part of training and readily available to those who need to use it. The procedure for emergency evacuation is a good example. Posters and signs must be erected to assist staff to remember their training on evacuation, and controls must be put in place for checking on emergency systems, such as exits, fire fighting equipment, announcement and crowd management equipment (for example, loud hailers), and access for emergency vehicles.

Delegation of decision-making

A flat organisational structure is essential for the successful operation of an event, so some parts of the event manager's role must be delegated. At most events, the pace is so fast that it is crucial that staff be in a position to make decisions on the spot. This is particularly important for volunteers (many of whom are well qualified in other roles) who generally need to know that they have a part to play in the problem-solving process. Only decisions on such important matters as evacuation need to be referred to the more senior staff on duty. Event staff need to be trained to make decisions when minor incidents occur, and each of these incidents needs to be recorded in a log book for analysis at the end of the shift or at the end of the day. Checks and monitors will ensure that delegation is managed well, that quality service is provided and that costs are contained.

Flexibility in operational procedures

Flexibility is required in many aspects of event management, most particularly in the operational phase, so it is important that the desired outcomes are fully understood by all staff. Staff, too, need to be able to think on their feet and make quick decisions about changing non-critical procedures where circumstances demand it. This is in fact one of the most desirable attributes of event operations staff.

Assuring customer satisfaction

In some cases, control systems can serve to frustrate customers and, at times, customers will endeavour to circumvent the system by trying, for example, to:

- enter areas without accreditation
- purchase alcohol for underage drinkers
- change their seating to a better area
- break the rules for rides (about height, attire or use of safety equipment, for example)
- cut across crowd control barriers
- stand or sit in the aisles.

In each of these cases, a decision needs to be made by event staff as to what to do. If a customer is refusing to wear safety equipment for a ride, for example, customer safety considerations should come before customer satisfaction. On the other hand, if you were confronted by customers frustrated by having to walk an extra distance as a result of crowd control barriers, when there are clearly no crowds, you may decide to move the barrier to allow them through.

Controlling finance

Financial control can be assured by:

- using a requisition system for purchases/expenditure that limits those authorised to spend over a certain dollar limit
- ensuring that all expenditure is accounted for and documented
- checking goods against requisition and order forms
- checking stock levels
- using financial systems that maintain up-to-date information on income and expenditure
- using financial systems to forecast cash flow
- ensuring that everyone understands the budget and current financial position.

Control of point-of-sale systems, or registers, can be achieved by:

- checking and securing cash floats
- checking that cash received is accurately recorded and/or processed through the point-of-sale system/register
- checking that point-of-sale terminal/register print-outs have been balanced against cash takings (after removing cash float)
- checking that cash and documents have been securely transported and stored
- checking that banking documentation has been retained and balanced against statements issued by the bank.

The following suggestions for monitoring and controlling event operations have been provided by experienced event organisers:

- CHECK everything, over and over.
- Write everything down, including promises made by your contractors and requests made by your client.
- Develop checklists for everything possible.
- Check the venue before you move in and note any existing damage.
- Never leave the venue until the last staff member has finished.
- Check the venue before leaving — some things may be left on (gas) or left behind (including people).
- Pay attention to detail at every stage.
- Schedule carefully as the audience has little patience with long-winded speeches, for example.
- Maintain a contingency fund for unexpected expenses.
- Involve the sponsor at every stage.

- Get approvals for use of logos before printing.
- Don't take safety knowledge for granted; repeat often.
- Train staff to be observant.
- CHECK everything, over and over.

EVALUATION

Evaluation is an area which is frequently neglected following an event. This is unfortunate as there are many benefits to be gained from a critique of the event. From a quality viewpoint, it allows those involved to learn from their experience and to improve operations. For those not involved, it provides a body of information for future planning of events. If you can't learn from your own experience, at least you can learn from someone else's.

Evaluation needs to be planned before the event, the event objectives generally guiding the evaluation process. In Chapter 9 on planning, the concept of developing event aims and objectives was introduced, and in Chapter 5 on marketing, the importance of understanding the target audience was discussed, together with the consumer's decision-making process. Now we will highlight the benefits of evaluation by reproducing below a comparison between the figures for the 1997 and 2000 shows of the Melbourne Comedy Festival, along with the objectives of the Festival. Clearly the Festival is meeting its objectives. Annual research into the demographics and behaviour of the fans has been a contributing factor to this outcome, allowing the event organisers to plan for the following event and to improve the figures every year. The results of the 2000 market research are also reproduced below.

Melbourne Comedy Festival

In 2000 the Festival attracted an audience of 350,000 and the Festival program listed a record 190 individual shows which staged over 2,000 performances making it one of the three largest comedy festivals in the world together with Montreal and Edinburgh. One of the outcomes of the 2000 Melbourne Comedy Festival was 20 hours of fantastically entertaining television broadcast to an estimated audience of 11 million.

Melbourne Comedy Festival CONTINUED

1997

56 shows/events

268 performances

$533,000 box office

65,500 attendance

420 participating artists

2000

190 shows/events

over 2000 performances

$3.4 million box office

349,000 attendance

1860 participating artists

1235 support staff

Background

The Melbourne International Comedy Festival began in 1987. It was very much a grass roots organisation, springing from the abundance of comic talent in Australia (particularly Melbourne), the public demand for access to Australian and international comedy at its finest, and the local comedy community's desire to shine a spotlight on what we have here and celebrate it. The pubs, clubs, cabarets and back bars of this city are an extraordinarily fertile breeding ground for funny people. Even the Melbourne Town Hall, once the no-mess fortress of the ruling class City Fathers, has embraced the role of Melbourne Comedy Festival and becomes an overflowing Comedy Central every April. Melburnians love comedy and comedians from all over the world love Melbourne, because our city generously nurtures and appreciates their work. The Melbourne International Comedy Festival is a celebration of this dynamic.

What are the Comedy Festival's Objectives?

The Art of Comedy

To promote and encourage the knowledge, understanding, appreciation and enjoyment of the musical, visual, performing, literary and comedic arts through an annual Comedy Festival.

Culture

To promote the importance of comedy as an artistic element in the cultural fabric of Melbourne, Victoria and Australia, and to ensure the legitimate place of members of the Comedy industry in the artistic community.

Profile

To maintain and further develop the Melbourne International Comedy Festival's national and international profile.

Community Participation

To organise a Comedy Festival that is accessible and encourages the general public to participate as audience members, performers or employees.

Tourism

To generate tourism to Melbourne by building on the competitive strength of Melbourne as the arts capital of Australia.

Advocacy

To be a public voice for, and to serve the interests of, the Comedy Community by operating year round as a representative and advocate of the Australian Comedy Industry.

Education

To contribute to the development of new talent in the field of comedy writing and performance, and to conduct educational activities in the musical, visual, performing and literary comedic arts.

Who goes to the Comedy Festival?

2000 Market Research Results

Young and Mostly Single

The Comedy Festival's audience is young and mostly single with 75% of respondents aged between 18–39 years of age; 51% describe themselves as single; and 41% married or in de facto relationships. The split between male and

Melbourne Comedy Festival CONTINUED

female is 30% and 69% respectively.

Very Social

Almost all respondents claimed to eat out at restaurants and cafes and visit bars (96%), most at least once a week (74%). Almost all claim to catch a film (93%) at least once a month (75%) and most others also go to live theatre/opera/ballet (65%) and live bands (58%).

Just over half the respondents have seen other live comedy performances in the last six months (52%) with most seeing between one and three performances (75%).

Most people attended a show with their friends (63%) and/or partner (46%).

No Kids

84% of respondents have no children under the age of 18 living at home.

Well-educated

Respondents are well educated — 90% have successfully completed Year 12, 33% have gone on to complete a university degree and a further 26% have completed a post-graduate degree.

Employment Status and Profession

61% of respondents work full time, 16% work part time and 13% study full time. Of these people, 44% work in managerial/professional positions with 10% in advertising and or marketing, 12% in medical positions and 7% in finance.

Physically Active

Sporting activities regularly participated in include walking (61%), swimming (27%), gym (25%), and cycling (17%). Attending sporting events is also popular, with AFL (40%) and the Australian Open (25%) the most popular of other events and festivals attended in the last 12 months.

Comedy Festival Fans

In 2000 there were no negative ratings of the Comedy Festival recorded with most patrons (61%) rating the Festival as excellent. The three leading,

unprompted descriptions of the Festival were: fun/lots of fun (23%), funny/very funny/hysterical/humorous (23%) and diverse/a feast/varied/wide-ranging/eclectic (20%).

Loyal Comedy Festival Fans

Around two in three respondents have attended the Comedy Festival in previous years (63%) with most having attended two to four Festivals (71%). The popularity of the Festival is further substantiated by most who planned to attend more than one show (83%).

21% of attendees are aware of the Festival through the official program, 26% through the newspapers and 30% via word of mouth.

Well-read

Most respondents regularly read the Age (70%), followed by the Herald Sun (28%) and local papers (28%).

Very Computer Literate

Most respondents have a personal computer (70%), a modem (52%) enabling access to their email address (77%) and the internet (59%). Most also own a mobile phone (65%) and a CD Rom (56%).

Regular Internet Surfers

The majority of Comedy Festival patrons surf the net (85%). Respondents over 35 years were least likely to surf the net (75%) compared to younger respondents (95% — 18–24 years; 90% — 25–34 years of age.)

Television Viewing

In the last seven days prior to competing the research questionnaire, a high proportion of respondents had watched the ABC rather than the commercial channels (33%); 24% watched channel 10 (36% of whom were aged between 18–24); 23% channel 9; 21% channel 7; and 6% SBS.

Reproduced with permission of Melbourne Comedy Festival. Research conducted by Quantum Market Research and funded by Tourism Victoria.

Evaluation methods

When planning evaluation, it is very important to work out what information you require. For example, participants entering a cycling race may be asked for their age and address, which would allow an analysis in terms of their general demographics. What a pity if they were not asked if they had participated before, how they had heard about the event and when they had made the decision to take part. This information would greatly assist the organisers of the next event.

The type of information described above can be obtained from surveys conducted before, during and after an event by completion of forms or through personal interviews. Alternatively, a small focus group of participants can provide valuable information through group discussion.

The following are examples of questions that may be included in a customer survey for an informal post-evaluation report. However, to obtain a more reliable report, the survey would need to be designed and analysed by a market research company.

- How did you find out about this event?
- Why did you decide to come to the event?
- When did you decide to come to the event?
- Did you come to the event with other people?
- Who was the main decision-maker?
- How did this event meet your expectations?
- Was the transport/parking adequate?
- Did you get value for money?
- Was the food and beverage adequate?
- Were the seating, sound and vision adequate?
- Would you attend this event again?
- Why would you recommend/not recommend the event to others?
- How could the event be improved?

In the case of an exhibition, the questions would be something like:
- Why did you come to this exhibition?
- Do you have the authority to purchase at this exhibition?
- Did you place any orders at this exhibition?
- Do you plan to place any orders as a direct result of the exhibition?
- Did you come to this exhibition last year?
- When did you decide to come to the exhibition?
- Have you travelled interstate to visit the exhibition?
- What were the best features of the exhibition?

• How could the exhibition be improved?

Staff debriefings

Meetings of event staff and stakeholders can generate valuable information for the evaluation report. Some of the questions addressed in this type of meeting include:
• What went well and why?
• What went badly and why?
• How could operations be improved?
• Were there any significant risk factors that we did not anticipate?
• Was there a pattern to any of the incidents reported?
• Are there any outstanding legal issues, such as injuries or accidents?
• Are there any implications for staff recruitment and training?
• How would you describe the organisation and management of the event — in the planning and the operational phases?
• What can we learn from this event?

Financial records

Audited financial records, together with a number of planning and other documents, are an essential component of post-event analysis and reporting. These include:
• audited financial statements
• budgets
• revenue, banking and account details
• point-of-sale reconciliation
• payroll records
• the risk management plan
• incident reports
• minutes of meetings
• insurance policies
• contracts with other agencies and organisations, such as hire companies and cleaning companies
• asset register
• promotional materials
• operational plans
• policies and procedures
• training materials
• database of attendees/participants if possible
• record of results of competitions

- event evaluation and statistics (including attendance)
- event or sponsor report.

It is one thing to know that you have managed a successful event but quite another to prove it. The event manager needs more than informal feedback from the after-event party. A summary report evaluating the event against specific aims and objectives is an absolute necessity.

THE BROADER IMPACT OF EVENTS

Events can have an economic, political, physical and social impact on the community (Hall, 1998, McDonnell et al., 1999). The economic impact of an event can be both direct (spending by international visitors) or indirect (the flow-on effect that occurs when related businesses benefit from the expenditure of event visitors). For example, farmers, wholesale suppliers of flowers and food production companies would benefit from increased sales and this in turn would prompt further expenditure on their part as demand for their products increased. Economists and tourism analysts have shown that events such as the Goodwill Games and the Sydney Gay and Lesbian Mardi Gras have an impact on the Australian economy. Tourism, in fact, plays a significant role in the economy. Spending by international visitors accounted for 11.2 per cent of total exports in 1997–98. In the same year, Tourism Gross Domestic Product (GDP) amounted to $25.2 billion, a direct contribution of 4.5 per cent to the total GDP, and tourism directly employed 513,000 people, representing 6 per cent of total employment (ABS Catalogue No. 5249.0). Events such as festivals, meetings, conventions and exhibitions that increase the level of international tourist visitation have a positive economic benefit by increasing export earnings.

Political benefits clearly accrue when events raise the profile of a town, city or country. When a region enjoys a surge in tourism, increased economic benefits and the associated reduction in unemployment lead to support for politicians at both local and state levels. Of course the reverse occurs when an event has a negative impact on the community.

Events often increase community spirit, bringing social benefits as well. For example, the many multicultural events held in Australia expand our cultural perspective, while on the other hand rave parties where drug abuse is prevalent can have a negative impact.

The physical impact of events is evident in the construction of new infrastructure, such as roads, railways and sporting venues. However events can have a negative environmental impact by causing damage or creating offensive noise. The best example of an event with an extremely positive environmental impact on the community is Clean Up Australia Day, which now operates in countries throughout the world.

Case study

The Australian University Games brought together tertiary students from all over Australia to compete in sixteen team and individual sports at venues across Perth.

Many of Australia's finest international competitors in track and field, swimming, rugby union and soccer are past participants of the Australian University Games.

The Games were conducted over five days in an atmosphere of friendly competition, with a strong focus on social activity and interaction.

Universities compete in regional lead-up competitions to qualify for the Australian University Games — 53 universities were represented by more than 3,500 participants. The Australian University Games generated $10.3 million in revenue for Western Australia.

More information can be obtained from http://www.eventscorp. com.au/history/index.html

Develop a range of objectives for this event and a corresponding strategy for evaluating the success of the event.

Activity
Investigate a control system to be put in place at an event and evaluate its effectiveness (or lack of it). This system may relate to:
- *registration of participants*
- *cash handling*
- *safety*
- *food hygiene*
- *purchasing and control*
- *staff accreditation.*

SUMMARY

This chapter has looked at two neglected aspects of event management: control and evaluation. Control systems are necessary to ensure that plans are carried out, yet often the event deadlines draw near too soon for these systems to be developed. Preventative controls are established during the early planning phase of an event, while feedback controls help with decisions during the event. If control systems meet best practice standards, they will reduce risk and ensure that there will be ample evidence if a court action should occur. Evaluation is required to ensure that an event meets the aims and objectives identified in the planning strategy. The capacity to show that these objectives (for example, financial, safety, customer satisfaction) have been met is one way of guaranteeing that the event management team is selected for future events.

CHAPTER EIGHTEEN

careers
in a changing environment

Cultural tourism is based on the culture of a destination — the lifestyle, heritage, arts, industries and leisure pursuits of the local population. Australia is increasingly being recognised as a distinctive, diverse, vibrant and sophisticated tourist destination which has much to interest visitors beyond its world-renowned natural attractions.

Many tourists are keen to learn about and experience the culture of the places they visit — from planned attendance at cultural events to meeting local people. More and more domestic and international visitors are looking for cultural experiences as a major component of their holidays. Cultural tourism encourages us to showcase those qualities and experiences that make us distinctly Australian and to demonstrate to the world our excellence in internationally recognised art forms. The cultural and tourism industries, and the wider Australian economy, can benefit from the development and pursuit of the dual themes of cultural identity and excellence.

http://www.isr.gov.au/scripts/search/sthome_search.idq

C ultural festivals include arts festivals, popular and classical music festivals, film festivals, and dance and craft festivals. In addition to cultural events, Australia hosts numerous sporting events, some with international profiles, such as the Australian Masters Golf Tournament. The meetings, incentives, conference and exhibition industry (MICE) also contributes to the total number of events held in Australia, as do all product launches and large-scale private parties.

On completion of this chapter you will be able to:

- discuss economic, social and other changes that will have an impact on the field of event management
- discuss the attributes of a successful event manager
- evaluate a range of career choices in the area of event management
- discuss the similarities and differences between event management and project management in other industries.

The Tourism Forecasting Council estimates that the number of international visitors to Australia will grow from nearly 5 million in 2000 to 10.2 million in 2010. With this projected growth rate, the level of interest in Australian festivals and events will undoubtedly grow. In addition to the level of international interest, there is the long-standing support for festivals and events by local residents and domestic tourists. This continues to be the mainstay for event organisers: Australia Day celebrations and Anzac Day parades are being attended by increasing numbers of people, while the level of interest in the Corroboree Walks in support of Aboriginal reconciliation also illustrate this trend.

This chapter is about employment prospects and specialisations for those planning a career in the event industry which, as you can see from the above, is a growth area. It also covers the current issues of concern for event organisers since up-to-date knowledge of the industry is essential for everyone involved in it.

Crowd management and crowd control are the most problematic areas. Attending or participating in an event is a risky leisure pursuit and event organisers have ethical obligations to ensure that the latest knowledge and the latest technology are applied to ensuring the safety of staff, the audience and the participants. Knowledge of audience psychology, as we have seen, can help to more accurately predict crowd behaviour and some of the problems that might occur.

An event manager thus needs to be an expert in psychology, crowd behaviour, consumer decision-making, financial management, human resource management, marketing, safety and logistics. Legal knowledge is also helpful, as is a solid understanding of risk issues.

Nonetheless, the event business provides an adrenalin rush for all those involved. As happy and excited faces stream out of the venue, the memories of all those planning problems — and your tiredness — soon fade. While the event manager's role is hardly that of party host and more about long hours and hard work, it is still fun.

JOB OPPORTUNITIES

Apart from the position of Event Manager for which you would require education, training and experience in other roles, there are many other jobs available in the industry. As someone wishing to enter the event industry, you could consider positions in one of the functional areas described in Chapter 14, such as venue operations, catering, technology or registration. These positions include:

- Operations and Logistics Manager
- Entertainment Manager
- Sports Competition Manager
- Risk Manager
- Tourism Event Co-ordinator
- Security Co-ordinator
- Venue Manager
- Catering and Waste Manager
- Pyrotechnics Consultant
- Administration Co-ordinator
- Sponsorship Manager
- Lighting/Sound Engineer
- Technology Support Officer — Meetings
- Technology Support Officer — Exhibitions
- Event Designer
- Registration Manager
- Equipment Rental Sales Manager

There are many jobs for catering staff in the events industry.

The following job descriptions (lists of tasks) provide some insight into just a few of the above-mentioned positions.

Event Manager

As the overall organiser of an event, the manager performs a large number of roles. Below are some of the duties you may find in a

Dear Lynn

Dona and myself work for Spotless Catering (SSL O'Brian) in Melbourne. We also work at the Melbourne Cricket Ground (MCG) and at Optus Oval, and for major events such as the Golf Classic, the Royal Melbourne Show and the Flower and Garden Show.

During the Grand Prix, Dona and I worked together to create a happy environment so that the customers were always satisfied. We love working with people because we believe we both have great communication skills. We always have a smile on our face. Dona and I are very happy people, and if a customer has a problem we solve it straightaway. We're easy to get along with, which makes it easier for everyone.

We enjoyed the four days working at the Grand Prix and we both wished that it would never end. Meeting new people every day was great. We left work tired but always with a smile.

Dona and I both love performing in front of people and entertaining our friends. (Oh, by the way, watch the Centenary of Federation Parade next week to see me. I'll be representing Trams of Melbourne.)

So, it's been easy for us to work in the hospitality industry.

Hope to see you when you're next in Melbourne.

Noelle

job description for Event Manager.

Tasks

1 Develop an event concept, purpose and objectives.
2 Establish a committee and/or event planning team if not already in place.
3 Review the feasibility of the event to maximise strengths and opportunities.
4 Conduct a risk management analysis to miminise weaknesses and risks.
5 Develop a marketing plan for the event.
6 Develop budget, break-even and cash flow analyses.
7 Prepare detailed event plans and obtain the support of the stakeholders, as well all required approvals.
8 Organise specific theme and staging effects.

9 Recruit and select staff, train and lead staff effectively.

10 Develop detailed plans for event safety and security, including emergencies.

11 Develop policies and procedures for event logistics and daily operation.

12 Develop monitoring and control systems, as well as evaluation procedures.

13 Write a post-event evaluation report to be presented to sponsors/stakeholders.

Venue Manager

The Venue Manager is generally a permanent employee who is familiar with all aspects of the venue and provides a service to anyone who books the venue. It is essential that the roles of the Venue Manager and the Event Manager are clear as these two individuals are often employed by different organisations. For example, a venue will have preferred security contractors and/or cleaning contractors and this can sometimes lead to conflict with the event organising committee if it, too, has preferred suppliers of these services.

Tasks

1 Develop a site diagram, site dimensions and specifications.

2 Negotiate contracts and deposits/fees.

3 Negotiate organisational structure and staffing with the event organiser (e.g. responsibility for cleaning and/or security).

4 Discuss site needs for performers.

5 Discuss site needs for the event audience/spectators.

6 Review the feasibility of plans for logistics and operations.

7 Provide support for bump-in (set-up), including signs and crowd management facilities.

8 Ensure development and implementation of safety and security plans.

9 Monitor the site for health, safety and cleanliness.

10 Work with the event team to ensure that the emergency evacuation plan is in place and that roles are clear.

11 Check entrances, exits and equipment (e.g. public address system, warden communication system).

12 Assist with bump-out at the end of the event.

13 Check all assets and monitor security during bump-out.

14 Manage payment of fees.

Exhibition Registration Manager

The registration of people visiting an exhibition is a key role, and in many cases exhibition organisers do their best to register participants beforehand for two reasons: it saves time on entry to the exhibition and it allows for the registration of participants who intend to visit but do not make it on the day. When completing the registration form, the person indicates their area of interest in the exhibition and this allows exhibitors to target this person for advertising. The database of visitors to an exhibition is a most valuable asset. Therefore, technical hitches must be avoided at all cost as they can cause delays and, at worst, loss of data. (One exhibition manager reported that the loss of his data resulted from a 'spike' in electrical supplies.)

Tasks

1 Meet with the committee/organiser to establish registration requirements, in particular the system for registration and the data to be captured.
2 Develop a registration plan, including selection of software or specialist subcontractor, and a schedule for the complete process.
3 Develop an operational plan and diagram for the registration area and review feasibility with the venue concerned, with particular emphasis on network cabling and back-up electrical supply.
4 Recruit, select and train staff for registration duties.
5 Assist with planning of advance mail-out advertising, including information on pre-registration.
6 Organise name tags, magnetic cards or other materials for registration.
7 Set up registration area.
8 Allocate duties to staff and schedule tasks to suit level of demand.
9 Manage operational issues, questions, problems and complaints.
10 Monitor and manage queues.
11 Close registration and provide required reports to exhibition managers.

The positions available in the event business are many and varied. Quite often people find themselves working on events having come from other fields such as sport administration, entertainment, television production and even nursing. This last example is indicative of how a medical background can be highly relevant to other roles such as first aid training and occupational health and safety training, leading ultimately to a role in risk management. Extracts from a number of recently advertised positions are given below.

EVENTS MANAGER

We are a city of over 38,000 people with surrounding towns and villages adding a further 20,000 people. The city provides a vibrant cultural atmosphere with visual, performing and literary arts joining the expanding food and wine industry. Council is seeking a highly motivated person with excellent customer service skills to manage our hospitality, entertainment, events and venues management area.

EVENT CO-ORDINATOR

The Council is about to start implementing an array of exciting events for the community, such as open-air cinema nights, bush symphony series, sport awards and food and wine festivals, to name but a few. To co-ordinate this program we are seeking a highly motivated and enthusiastic event specialist with a proven track record in overseeing major celebrations and community events.

ENTERTAINMENT DIRECTOR

Guest relations professional with flair, creativity and initiative is required to take on a new and exciting opportunity. The position will involve creating and managing entertainment, as well as social activities for our guests, and assisting the sales team in liaising with journalists and photographers. If you have energy to burn and love to be on stage please apply.

CONFERENCE AND TRAINING PROGRAM MANAGER

The role involves the extensive research of topical issues and development of strategic and forward-thinking programs for senior business executives. This stimulating, creative and dynamic role has fast-track promotional prospects and overseas opportunities.

FUNCTIONS SALES MANAGER

This is a pivotal role responsible for dealing with enquiries regarding the planning, booking and execution of conferences and functions. Working within the sales team, the role will maximise the revenue of the conference/function facilities, ensuring excellence in customer service and therefore repeat and referral business.

BUYER

We are back for another exciting tour and you are invited to join our multi-talented crew. Reporting to the Technical and Site Operations Manager, the successful candidate will be responsible for purchasing, co-ordinating, reception and despatch of goods on site, and scheduling of courier and runner in each city. Responsibilities will include updating the bank of suppliers in each city; set-up and tear-down of technical department; managing petty cash; and inventory of all tour assets. Must be available for full-time travel in the Asia Pacific region.

COMMUNICATION EXECUTIVE

We are looking for a special person with strong communication skills to manage the content, production and presentation of all event communication material, whether written, published or electronically presented. You will be required to manage a comprehensive media program.

CATERING AND CONVENTIONS EXECUTIVE

You will co-ordinate catering and convention activities, ensuring that our guests receive the very best in hospitality when attending their function. Experience in a similar role is essential.

SPONSORSHIP EXECUTIVE

In conjunction with our external consultants, you will be involved in the development of proposals and identification of prospective sponsors. You will be responsible for developing and delivering all sponsorship benefits to a large sponsor base.

TRAINING MANAGER

Working with our Human Resources Manager and all functional area managers, the training professional will be involved in conducting a training needs analysis for volunteer staff, preparing training materials and arranging for print production before training commences.
You will be responsible for delivering core components of the training and will thus need a proven record as a trainer/facilitator. You must be able to demonstrate your success in developing and delivering customer service training. Tourism,

hospitality or event experience would be a bonus.

EVENT SUPERVISORS

This role involves overseeing the service provided by ushers and event staff. This involves managing a team for a minimum of three shifts over four days. Previous experience with two-way radio, large crowds and volunteers would be useful. You must have excellent communication and team leadership skills. These are paid positions.

CATERING MANAGER

This position involves the selection and management of the event contract caterer. It is thus a co-ordinating as opposed to a

hands-on role. You will work closely with the caterer on menu planning and costing, on service standards and food hygiene plans. Qualifications at certificate level and relevant experience in similar environments, such as hotels or sports venues, is essential.

PROMOTIONS CO-ORDINATOR

Our bar and nightclub requires an enthusiastic, creative and energetic person to create and promote theme nights, special events and all aspects of the bar, restaurant and nightclub with a capacity to cater for over 600 people. The position entails organising promotions from concept

design to execution. A marketing or event management background would be ideal.

BANQUET SALES CO-ORDINATOR — CONFERENCES

Boasting one of the city's biggest conferencing facilities, the hotel currently has an opening for a Banquet Sales Co-ordinator. Sales and project management experience in a similar role would be an advantage.

RISK MANAGER

Responding to a senior executive, the appointee will be responsible for the ongoing assessment of risk exposures, controls and responses and overseeing compliance. A major focus

will be the enhancement of risk management systems, policies and strategies and the analysis and reporting of risks.

SPONSORSHIP AND EVENTS MANAGER

We are a non-profit organisation. Your role would involve managing the delivery of all fund-raising activities, developing and maintaining relations with corporate sponsors, planning and budgeting, as well as management of operational committees. You must have the ability to communicate with the 'top-end of town' and need to demonstrate your experience in business development.

KEEPING UP TO DATE

Anyone planning a career in events must stay up to date with trends. Fashions change rapidly and one cannot afford to come up with stale or outdated ideas. It is thus essential to stay up to the minute with trends in entertainment and the arts. The website for Bizbash provided at the end of this chapter is just one site that will stir your imagination. The website also lists a number of event fiascos from which some good lessons can be learned, such as remembering to turn off the sprinkler system before the guests assemble on the lawn! The activity suggested at the end of this chapter involving the development of a portfolio relevant to the event industry is also designed to stimulate your creativity.

However, in addition to creative ideas, it is also essential to stay up to date with economic trends. Regular visits to tourism websites, particularly to the corporate planning areas, will keep you informed of the latest in strategic planning for events. Collecting this information will ensure that you are both informed and creative — an ideal combination for the rapidly changing event environment.

Case study

Having read a number of job descriptions for event roles in this chapter, develop a letter of application and résumé for two of these jobs at any event discussed in this book. Note that each time you apply for a position you need to modify your résumé to stress your relevant knowledge and experience. For example, one résumé might stress your knowledge of marketing principles and the other might illuminate your understanding of operational issues. If your experience is limited, you can fabricate some relevant experience for the purpose of this exercise.

Activity

Develop a scrapbook of newspaper and magazine articles that are relevant to the event industry so that you can remain up to date with current trends and issues.

Links

http://www.bizbash.com/ (imaginative ideas for events)
http://www.isr.gov.au/sport_tourism/index/html
http://www.isr.gov.au/sport_tourism/publications/factsheets/
   culturaltourism.doc

SUMMARY

This final chapter has looked at a range of social, economic and other changes that have had, and will continue to have, an impact on the field of event management in the future. Staying up to date with fashion, entertainment, tourism trends and the like is essential. A number of employment choices are available for those considering a career in the event industry, and a number of these positions have been described in this chapter. Most importantly, the management skills developed by event managers are relevant to many other occupations in which risk is high, deadlines are tight, people management skills are a priority and there is only one opportunity to get it right.

appendix 1 Supplementary internet links

TOURISM

Australian Tourist Commission
http://www.atc.net.au/

Canberra Tourism
http://www.canberratourism.com.au/welcome.html

Northern Territory Tourism Commission
http://www.nttc.com.au/

South Australian Tourism Commission
http://www.southaustralia.com/

Tourism New South Wales
http://www.tourism.nsw.gov.au/

Tourism New Zealand (market research)
http://www.tourisminfo.govt.nz/

Tourism New Zealand (travel)
http://www.purenz.com/indexnz.cfm

Tourism Queensland
http://www.queensland-holidays.com.au/pfm/index.htm

Tourism Tasmania
http://www.discovertasmania.com.au/

Tourism Victoria
http://www.tourismvictoria.com.au/

Western Australia Tourism Commission
http://www.westernaustralia.net/

World Tourism Organisation
http://www.world-tourism.org/

TOURISM TRAINING

NT Tourism Training Board
http://www.ntttb.org.au/

Tourism Training ACT & Region
Email: ttact@interact.net.au

Tourism Training Australia
http://www.tourismtraining.com.au/

Tourism Training NSW
http://www.ttnsw.com/

Tourism Training QLD
http://www.ttq.org.au/

Tourism Training SA
http://www.ttsa.com.au/

Tourism Training TAS
Email: tourtraintas@bigpond.com.au

Tourism Training VIC
http://www.ttvic.com.au/

WA Hospitality & Tourism Training Council
http://www.wahtitc.com.au/

STATISTICS AND FORECASTS

Australian Bureau of Statistics
http://www.abs.gov.au/websitedbs/d3310114.nsf/Homepage

Bureau of Tourism Research
http://www.btr.gov.au/

Commonwealth Department of Sport and Tourism http://www.tourism.gov.au/

Festivals Australia
http://www.dcita.gov.au/graphics_welcome.html

World Tourism Organisation
http://www.world-tourism.org/

World Travel and Tourism Council
http://www.wttc.org/

GOVERNMENT

Australian Commonwealth Government Information and Services
http://www.fed.gov.au/

Austrade http://www.austrade.gov.au

Australian Local Government
http://www.algin.net.au

City of Sydney
http://www.cityofsydney.nsw.gov.au

New South Wales Government
http://www.nsw.gov.au

Northern Territory Government
http://www.nt.gov.au

Queensland Government
http://www.qld.gov.au

South Australian Government
http://www.sa.gov.au

Tasmanian Government
http://www.dpac.tas.gov.au

Victorian Government
http://www.vic.gov.au

Western Australian Government
http://www.wa.gov.au

MEETINGS AND EVENTS ASSOCIATIONS

Australian Amusement, Leisure and Recreation Association
http://www.aalara.com.au/

Australian Incentive Association
http://www.aia.com.au/

Australian Tourism Export Council
http://www.atec.net.au/

Exhibitions & Events Association of Australia http://www.eeaa.org.au/

International Congress and Convention Association http://www.icca.nl/

International Festivals & Events Association http://www.ifea.com/

International Special Events Society
http://ises.com

International Association Exhibition Management
http://www.iaem.org/default.asp

Media, Entertainment & Arts Alliance
http://www.alliance.org.au/

Meetings Industry Association of Australia
http://www.aia.com.au/

Meetings, Incentives, Conferences and Exhibitions http://www.mice.net.au

Pacific Asia Travel Association
http://www.pata.org/

Venue Management Association
http://www.vma.org.au/

CONVENTION BUREAUS

Cairns and Region Visitors Bureau
http://www.tnq.org.au/crcb/

Canberra Convention Bureau
http://www.canberraconvention.com.au/

Conventions New Zealand
http://www.conventionsnz.co.nz/conventions/index.asp

Melbourne Convention and Visitors Bureau http://www.mcmb.net.au/

Perth Convention Bureau
http://www.pcb.com.au/

Sydney Conventions and Visitors Bureau
http://www.scvb.com.au/index_s.html

INTERNATIONAL EVENTS

Clean Up the World
http://www.cleanuptheworld.org/m

Dakar Rally http://www.dakar.com./

Edinburgh Festival http://www.eif.co.uk/

Fairs and Festivals of India
http://travel.indiamart.com/fairs-festivals/

FIFA http://www.fifa.com/index_E.html

International Events http://www.frontrow.com/international.shtml

Le Tour de France http://www.letour.fr/

Oscars http://www.oscar.com/

St Patricks Day Events
http://www.emigrant.ie/patrick/events.
htm

Search International Events
http://www.whatsgoingon.com/event/
intl/

Superbowl http://www.superbowl.com/

Tall Ships Races http://www.cutty-
sark.com/tallshipraces/

Toronto Film Festival
http://www.e.bell.ca/filmfest/2000/index
.asp

Tourism Thailand
http://www.tourismthailand.org/festival/
index.htm

Webnet World Conference
http://www.aace.org/conf/webnet/

Wimbledon
http://www.wimbledon.org/valid2000.
htm

AUSTRALIAN EVENTS

Arafura Games
http://www.nt.gov.au/arafura/2001/

Australia Day Council (National)
http://www.nadc.com.au/index.php

Australian Motorcycle Grand Prix
http://www.grandprix.com.au/bikes/

Australian Open http://www.ausopen.org/

Australian Science Festival
http://www.sciencefestival.com.au/
indexf.htm

Big Boys Toys
http://www.krbigboystoys.com.au/

Big Day Out
http://www.bigdayout.com/the_show.ph
tml?flash_please=1

Blessing of the Fleet
http://www.blessingfleet.asn.au/

Camel Racing
http://www.camelraces.asn.au/

Canberra Floriade
http://www.floriadeaustralia.com/

City to Surf Sydney
http://www.coolrunning.com.au/races/
citysurf.shtml

Classic Car Rally
http://www.classicrally.com.au/

Clean Up Australia
http://www.cleanup.com.au/

Comedy Festival
http://www.comedyfestival.com.au/

Gay & Lesbian Mardi Gras
http://www.mardigras.com.au/
flashintro.asp

Goodwill Games
http://www.goodwillgames.com/2001/
2001_index.html

Grand Prix
http://www.grandprix.com.au/cars/

Henley-on-Todd Regatta
http://www.henleyontodd.com.au/

Hobart Fringe Festival
http://hobartfringe.com/

Hobart Summer Festival
http://203.16.7.7/festival2001/

Hunter Valley events
http://www.atn.com.au/nsw/syd/
event-e.htm

International Horse Trials
http://www.adelaidehorsetrials.com.au/
TheEvent/

Juvenile Diabetes events
http://www.jdfa.org.au/

Le Mans
http://www.lemansadelaide.com.au/

Melbourne Comedy Festival
http://home.vicnet.net.au/~comfest/

Melbourne Cup
http://www.acn.net.au/articles/1998/10/
melbcup.htm

Melbourne Flower Show
http://www.melbflowershow.com.au/

Melbourne Food and Wine Festival
http://www.melbfoodwinefest.com.au/
index.html

Melbourne Moomba Festival
http://www.melbournemoombafestival.
com.au/

Mercedes Fashion Week
http://www.afw.com.au/html/flash_
intro.asp

Mt Isa Rodeo
http://www.isarodeo.com.au/

National Days of Commemoration
http://www.awm.gov.au/atwar/commem
orative_days.htm

National Folk Festival
http://www.folkfestival.asn.au/

Perth Festival
http://www.perthfestival.com.au/

Reef Festival http://www.reefestival.
org.au/timetable.phtml?id=9

Royal Easter Show
http://www.royalshow.com.au/

St Kilda Film Festival
http://www.stkildafilmfest.com.au/

Scarecrow Festival
http://www.maleny.net.au/scarecrow

Summernats
http://www.summernats.com.au/
Summernats%20Info.htm

Sunrace (Solar)
http://www.sunrace.netlink.com.au/
home.htm

Surf Lifesaving Championships
http://www.slsa.asn.au/Web/Slsa/
Slsaweb.Nsf/Sectionpage/Australian+
Championships

Sydney Events Listing
http://www.sydney-events.com/sydney/

Sydney Writers Festival
http://www.swf.org.au/about/

The Big Swim
http://www.thebigswim.org.au/

Womadelaide
http://www.womadelaide.ozemail.com.a
u/welcome.html

Woodford Folk Festival
http://woodfordfolkfestival.com/
festival/index.html

World Solar Challenge
http://www.wsc.org.au/

NEW ZEALAND EVENTS

New Zealand Events http://www.nz-
events.co.nz/index.html

NZ Festival
http://www.nzfestival.telecom.co.nz/

Pure NZ
http://www.purenz.com/shocked.cfm

Rally NZ http://www.rallynz.org.nz/

Royal Easter Show
http://www.royaleastershow.co.nz/

Volvo Ocean Race http://www.volvo
oceanrace.org/homepage.html

Winter Festival
http://www.winterfestival.co.nz/
welcome.asp

OTHER EVENT SITES

Eventclicks http://www.eventclicks.com/

Events Unlimited
http://eventsunlimited.com.au

Special Events Ideas
http://www.bizbash.com/

Special Events Magazine on-line
http://www.specialevents.com.au

Visual Event Management
http://www.vem.com.au/

appendix 2 Event proposal

EVENT DESCRIPTION
- Event name
- Event type
- Location, suburb and council
- Date(s)
- Duration/timing
- Event overview and purpose/concept
- Aims and objectives

EVENT MANAGEMENT
- Management responsibility
- Major stakeholders and agencies
- Physical requirements
  - Venue
  - Route for street events
  - Event map
  - Event layout (indoor)
- Audience
- Impact
  - Social
  - Environmental
  - Economic

APPROVALS AND CONSULTATION
- State and federal government
- Council
- Roads and Traffic Authority/Department of Transport
- Liquor Licensing
- Police
- Building
- Insurance
- Health
- Environmental
- Entertainment
- Music licensing
- Security

MARKETING
- Competitive analysis
- Market analysis and planning
  - Customer segmentation
  - Meeting audience needs
  - Consumer decision-making
  - Price and ticket program
- Advertising and promotion
  - Messages
  - Media
  - Budget
- Public relations
  - Press releases
  - Media briefing
- Marketing evaluation

FINANCIAL CONTROL
- Capital and funding requirements
- Fees (police, council, transport, music, etc.)
- Costs (including insurance)
- Control systems (e.g. cash handling)
- Taxation
- Profit and loss statement
- Cash flow analysis

RISK MANAGEMENT
- Identification of risks and hazards
- Assessment of risks and hazards
- Management of risks and hazards
- Incident reporting

EVENT STAGING
- Theme
- Décor
  - Layout
  - Entertainment
  - Special effects, lighting
  - Sound
- Services
  - Electricity
  - Water
  - Transport (including air travel, access to venue)
  - Traffic management
  - Street closure
  - Impact on local traffic
  - Notification of affected businesses, etc.
  - Diversions
  - Marshalling
  - Support vehicles
  - Parking
  - Disability access
- Catering
  - Providers
  - Facilities
  - Food safety plans
- Waste and environmental management
  - Toilets
  - Waste management, recycling
  - Noise
  - Water pollution
- Cleaning

STAFFING
- Selection and recruitment
- Rosters
- Training
- Briefing
- Recognition strategies
- Industrial relations
- Recruitment of volunteers

SAFETY AND SECURITY
- Safety of the event audience
- Safety and security of the performers, VIPs, etc.
- Health and safety of the staff
- Security for premises, equipment, cash, etc.
- Communications
  - Meetings
  - Reporting relationships
  - Emergency reporting relationships
  - Communication methods (radio)
- Emergency access and emergency management
- First aid

OPERATIONAL PLANS
- Policies, e.g. complaints, crowd control
- Procedures and checklists
- Performance standards (link to objectives)
- Contingency plans
  - Weather
  - Electrical supply, lighting
  - Fire
  - Accident
  - Crowd crush
  - Delay or cancellation
  - Bomb threat or other security incident
- Logistics
  - Bump-in/set-up
  - Structures and facilities
  - Lighting
  - Sound
  - Bump-out/move out

EVALUATION
- Post-event evaluation
  - Objectives
  - Measures
  - Analysis
  - Report

bibliography

Allen, J., Harris, R., Jago, L. & Veal, A. (eds). *Events Beyond 2000: Setting the Agenda*. Australian Centre for Event Management, Sydney, July 2000.

Australian Bureau of Statistics. 'Attendance at Selected Cultural Venues, March 1995'. Cat. No. 4114.0. ABS, Canberra, 1995.

Australian Bureau of Statistics. 'Australian National Accounts: Tourism Satellite Account 1997–98'. Cat. No. 5249.0. ABS, Canberra.

Axtell, R. *The Do's and Taboos of Hosting International Visitors*. John Wiley and Sons, New York, 1990.

Bureau of Tourism Research. 'International Visitors Survey 1997'. BTR, Canberra, 1998.

Catherwood, D. W. and Kirk, R. L. *The Complete Guide to Special Event Management*. John Wiley and Sons, New York, 1992.

Cook, S. *Customer Care*. Kogan Page, London, 1997.

Cordato, Anthony. *Australian Travel and Tourism Law*. 3rd edn. Butterworths, Sydney, 1999.

Denvy, D. *Organising Special Events and Conferences*. Pineapple Press, Sarasota, Florida, 1990.

Getz, D. *Event Management and Event Tourism*. Cognizant Communication Corporation, New York, 1997.

Goldblatt, J. J. *Special Events: Best Practices in Modern Event Management*. John Wiley and Sons, New York, 1997.

Hall, C. *Hallmark Tourist Events: Management and Planning*. Belhaven Press, London, 1992.

Handy, Charles. *Understanding Organizations*. 4th edn. Penguin Books, London, 1993.

Hofstede, Geert. *Culture's Consequences: International Differences in Work Related Values*. Sage, Beverly Hills, 1980.

Joel, Asher. *Australian Protocol and Procedures*. 2nd edn. Angus and Robertson, Sydney, 1998.

Karpin Task Force. 'Enterprising Nation. Report on the Industry Task Force on Leadership and Management Skills'. AGPS, Canberra, 1995.

McCaffree, M. and Innis, P. *Protocol: The Complete Handbook of Diplomatic, Official and Social Usage*.

Prentice Hall, New York, 1977.

McDonnell, I., Allen, J. & O'Toole, W. *Festival & Special Event Management*. John Wiley and Sons, Brisbane, 1999.

McGill, M., Slocum, J. and Lei, D. 'Management Practices in Learning Organizations'. *Organizational Dynamics*, 42, Summer 1992.

Malouf, Lena. *Behind the Scenes at Special Events*. Wiley, Brisbane, 1998.

National Volunteers Orientation Kit. Volunteering NSW, Sydney.

Office of Multicultural Affairs. *Best Practice in Managing a Culturally Diverse Workplace*. Australian Government Printing Service, Canberra, 1994.

Reader's Digest Book of the Road. Reader's Digest (Australia), Sydney, 1999.

Richardson, John. *Travel and Tourism in Australia: The Economic Perspective*. Hospitality Press, Melbourne, 1995.

Robbins, S. and Coulter, M. *Management*. 5th edn. Prentice Hall, New Jersey, 1996.

Robbins, Stephen P. *Organizational Behaviour*. 8th international edn. Prentice Hall, New Jersey, 1998.

Standards Australia Publications. Head Office, 286 Sussex Street, Sydney. http://www.standards.com.au

'TOURISM — A Ticket to the 21st Century: National Action Plan for a Competitive Australia'. Office of National Tourism, Commonwealth of Australia, 1998.

Tuckman, B. W. 'Developmental Sequence in Small Groups', *Psychological Bulletin*, 63, 1965, pp. 384-99.

Vecchio, R., Hearn, G. and Southey, G. *Organizational Behaviour*. Harcourt Brace, Sydney, 1996.

Watt, David. *Leisure and Tourism Events Management and Organization Manual*. Longman, London, 1992.

Weaver, David and Opperman, Martin. *Tourism Management*. John Wiley and Sons, Brisbane, 2000.

Workcover News, Issue 16. Workcover NSW, Sydney.

index

accommodation 155
address, styles of 131
advertising 69

balance sheet 94
bomb threat 23-31
branding 69
break-even point 91
budget 81
bump-in 196
bump-out 196
business registration 43

cash flow analysis 92
catering 25, 154
code of ethics 13
communication 190
computer assisted drawing
  (CAD) 117
concept 15-27
  analysis of 22
  development of 15
  logistics of 26
consumer decision-making 58
contracts 50
control systems 234
copyright, music 44
crowd management 221-32

demographics 33
dress, formal 132

emergency planning 226
emergency procedures 229
environment 156
ERP (emergency response
  plan) 107-9, 226
event
  aims 113
  audience 20
  code of ethics 13
  concept 26
  definition 3

evaluation 239-44
feasibility 28-40
logistics 26, 194-6
marketing 53-61
marketing mix 61
mission 112
monitoring 233-8
objectives 115
planning 111-26
proposal 116, 258
purpose 112
security 48, 209-10
site 141
size 4
staging 140-58
team 12
theme 18, 144
type 7

financial control systems 94-5
fire 230
flag flying, rules 138
functional areas 200-2

gantt charts 119
group development 188-9

hallmark events 5

image 69
incident reporting 105-7
insurance 47

job descriptions 163
job opportunities 248

leadership 181-92, 203
legislation 41
lighting 147
line of sight 144
liquor licensing 45
local acts, regulations 42

major events 5

Maleny Scarecrow Festival 17
marketing 53-61
  mix 62
  process of 55
  product 55-6
meetings 191
meetings and exhibitions 8
mega events 4
minor events 6

noise 46

occupational health and safety
  174, 211-16
official bodies 49
Olympic Games 4, 7, 29-37
order of precedence 128
organisation charts 159-63

performance standards 199
policies 197
price 59
procedures 198
profit and loss statement 93
promotion 60, 61, 67-74
protocol 127-38
  cultural 133
  religious 133
  speakers 132
  sporting ceremonies 136
public relations 75
publicity 71-4

recognition 175-6
  strategies 175
  volunteers 176
rehearsals 150
risk management 37, 98-102,
  223
  process of 103-7
  standards for 109
run sheet 121

safe food handling 46
seating plans 132
sound 147
sponsorship 62-5
staff 159-76
  briefing 174
  motivation 203
  recognition 175
  recruitment and selection
    169
  rosters 170
  training 170
staging terms 152
stakeholders 21, 49
Standards (Australian and NZ)
  109
styles of address 131
SWOT analysis 38-9

ticketing 59
time management 191
titles 129
Trade Practices 45

venue, selection of 19
VERP (venue emergency
  response plan) 107
vision 147
volunteers
  management 176
  recognition 175

workers compensation 49